D1552991

Human Rights in the West Bank and Gaza

Syracuse Studies on Peace and Conflict Resolution
Harriet Hyman Alonso, Charles Chatfield, and Louis Kriesberg
Series Editors

HUMAN RIGHTS
in the
WEST BANK and GAZA
Legacy and Politics

ILAN PELEG

Syracuse University Press

The paper used in this publication meets the minimum requirements of American
National Standard for Information Sciences—Permanence of Paper for Printed
Library Materials, ANSI Z39.48-1984.∞™

Library of Congress Cataloging-in-Publication Data

Peleg, Ilan, 1944–
    Human rights in the West Bank and Gaza: Legacy and Politics /
Ilan Peleg.—1st ed.
        p. cm. — (Syracuse studies on peace and conflict resolution)
    Includes bibliographical references and index.
    ISBN 0-8156-2682-7 (cloth : alk. paper).
    1. Human rights—West Bank. 2. Human rights—Gaza Strip.
    3. Palestinian Arabs—Civil rights—West Bank. 4. Palestinian
Arabs—Civil rights—Gaza Strip. I. Title. II. Series.
JC599.W47P45   1995
323'.095695'3—dc20   95-7834

Manufactured in the United States of America

To the blessed memory of
Dr. Elza Ashkenazy (1910–1986)
and
Dr. Yitzhak Ashkenazy (1904–1969)

Ilan Peleg is the Charles A. Dana Professor of Government and Law at Lafayette College. He is the author of *Begin's Foreign Policy, 1977–1983: Israel's Move to the Right,* coeditor of *The Emergence of Binational Israel: The Second Republic in the Making* (with O. Seliktar), and editor of *Patterns of Censorship Around the World,* as well as numerous scholarly articles.

Contents

Map

Preface

THIS study deals with one of the most controversial conflicts of our time—that between Israeli Jews and Palestinian Arabs. It focuses on the status of human rights in the West Bank and the Gaza Strip until the early 1990s and evaluates the likely condition of human rights within the context of a variety of possible solutions to the conflict. This is an attempt to analyze the Israeli-Palestinian dilemma from a human rights perspective and to offer solutions within a human rights context.

The topic of human rights in the environment of an intense interethnic conflict guarantees that this book will be controversial: some readers will find all of it objectionable, others will find parts of it objectionable, and a very few will agree with all of its conclusions. Yet, if the volume causes most readers to concentrate on human rights as an essential dimension not only of the present but also of the future, as it relates to a solution to this international conflict, the book will have achieved its major goal. Nevertheless, it would be useful to tackle some possible objections explicitly and at the outset.

The study of human rights in the West Bank and the Gaza Strip could be—and, I predict, will be—criticized from a variety of angles. Some individuals will argue that the relationships between Arabs and Jews in the territories are, essentially, a matter of national conflict, not of human rights. According to this thesis, we are dealing with a violent clash between two peoples, a clash that ought to be regulated by the international legal standards developed specifically for governing warlike situations, and not by humanitarian provisions designed to protect individuals. Put differently, this position identifies Israel's occupation of the territories as mainly a political condition, not a legal one. It emphasizes the collective interests, rather than individual rights, as describing the nature of the conflict and as the key for its resolution.

This line of critique could come equally from the right or from the left, from those supporting or those opposing Israel's prolonged occupation of the territories, from those who believe that Israel must eventually annex the territories or those who are convinced that Israel ought to exchange the territories for peace. Supporters of the occupation argue that examining Israel's behavior in the territories in light of international human rights standards, which this volume proposes, is fundamentally unfair: Israel is an occupying power in the territories and cannot possibly meet stringent human rights standards, especially in the face of the popular uprising that has been a continuous fact of life in the territories since December 1987.

On the other hand, opponents of the occupation could very well maintain that the focus on human rights, rather than on the occupation, would shift world attention from what they interpret as the fundamental problem at the present time—the occupation— to a peripheral one—the treatment of individuals by the Israeli authorities. A focus on human rights might even imply that had Israel faithfully fulfilled all of its humanitarian obligations in the territories, the continuation of the occupation could become legally acceptable and the efforts to find a political solution to the conflict less urgent.

After 1967 and until the beginning of the Palestinian uprising, the "peace camp" in Israel concentrated mainly on the conditions that might lead to the end of the occupation and on the development of political relationships with moderate Palestinians. Some may have felt that improving the overall political picture had higher priority than human rights, and that focusing on human rights might give the impression that the "peace camp" had accepted the permanent incorporation of the West Bank and Gaza.

These arguments deserve a serious reply at the outset of this study, not for the sake of polemics but to clarify the context of the analysis. In the first place, it ought to be noted that since the beginning of the Intifada, there has been a dramatic increase in the attention to the status of human rights in the territories. This situation makes the concentration on them more important than ever before.

Second, it must be emphasized that a focus on human rights (within the analytical framework proposed in chapter 1) does not detract from the necessity of solving the question of the territories' political status. On the contrary, by arguing (as I do in chapter 1) that Israel's policies in the territories ought to be evaluated by both the law governing armed conflict and belligerent occupation (e.g., the Fourth Geneva Convention of 1949) and the much newer law governing human rights in the contemporary world, the volume assumes that the Israeli-Palestinian dilemma could be resolved only by accounting for both political factors (those relating to international relations) and human rights (those relating mostly to individual rights). Human rights issues in the territories are contained within the Israeli-Palestinian national conflict. In chapter 5 there is a discussion dealing with alternative political solutions for the Israeli-Palestinian conflict and their potential impact on the human rights of the peoples involved: the link between the political side of the coin and the human rights side of the coin is organic and inevitable.

In general, the distinction between the political arena and the domain of human rights is overdrawn. Although Israel's treatment of the Palestinians in areas such as administrative detention, house demolition, and deportations (see chapter 3) is often presented as human rights violations, negative comments on these practices are usually made within the political context of the conflict. People who focus on what they perceive as Israel's violations of Palestinian human rights are invariably committed to the notion that Israel's occupation is in and of itself a violation of the Palestinian right of self-determination, a fundamental political and, some would say, human right. Thus, the focus on human rights strengthens the focus on the political aspects rather than detracting from them. Similarly, those who tend to defend Israel's behavior on the West Bank and Gaza by arguing that the Israeli government conforms to the international standards of human rights to the highest degree possible, tend to adhere to the political argument that Israel is not an occupier in the territories but a liberator or, at least, a claimant with a valid case for sovereign rights. Here again, political arguments and positions on human rights are intimately linked.

The argument that Israel ought not to be judged by the international standards pertaining to human rights, but by its behavior in accordance with the laws of war alone—for instance, by the provisions of the Fourth Geneva Convention—also deserves a reply.

First, whether one likes it or not, Israel's behavior in the territories is already being judged by human rights criteria. In view of this reality, the matter deserves a close, comprehensive, and scholarly treatment. Second, the Israeli government itself, particularly under Likud, refused to define Israel as an occupier in the territories and, accordingly, did not accept the applicability in toto of the Fourth Geneva Convention to these areas. Third, it could be argued that the prolonged occupation of the territory—regardless of the sovereignty question—puts on Israel the onus of behaving in accordance with the acceptable standards of human rights in the contemporary world. Ironically, the position that Israel's long-term control over the territories is legitimate and that it ought not to be viewed as a temporary occupation imposes on Israel more severe demands insofar as human rights are concerned.

This volume deals with a politically sensitive topic. Almost every statement made on human rights in the territories is likely to be construed as favoring one political position or another. Yet, in view of the events of the last few years, the issue of human rights in the West Bank and the Gaza Strip demands thorough consideration and analysis. The issue touches on values fundamental to both the contemporary international community and the core of the Jewish tradition, values on which the state of Israel was founded.

In this study, a genuine effort will be made to offer as balanced an analysis as possible of the status of human rights in the territories. It is well known that objectivity in the social sciences is elusive and never completely achievable, but it is the sacred obligation of the scholar to try to achieve it. It is with this commitment that this study is launched.

Numerous individuals have assisted me in bringing this study to conclusion. Yossi Amitai, Benjamin Beit-Hallahmi, Eva Hadar, and Susan Hattis Rolef sent me, on occasion, useful material from Israel. A few of my students worked with me through the years on various aspects of human rights in the territories: under my direction Julie Lefkowits wrote an honors thesis on the topic, Jeff McCafferty spent the summer of 1988 (and beyond) collecting data on the subject, and Brian Walsh read the text several times and offered numerous grammatical (and on occasion substantive) corrections.

Three individuals—Suriya Chindawongse, Dan Simon, and

Henry Steiner—have read the manuscript in its entirety and offered many useful comments. Obviously, the responsibility for the
final product or any parts of it is not theirs, but mine alone. Nevertheless, I would like to express my gratitude for their generous
help.

My secretary, Ruth Panovec, struggled heroically and efficiently, as usual, with the numerous versions of the manuscript.
She was ably assisted by Rose Miller. And my family proved once
again a source of invaluable support for my work.

Easton, Pennsylvania   Ilan Peleg
March 1994

Abbreviations

ACRI	Association for Civil Rights in Israel
DER	Defense (Emergency) Regulations
Geneva IV	Fourth Geneva Convention Relative to the Protection of Civilian Persons in the Time of War (1949)
HCJ	The Israeli High Court of Justice
ICPR	International Covenant on Civil and Political Rights
ICRC	International Committee of the Red Cross
IDF	Israeli Defense Forces
MAG	Military Advocate General
MEW	Middle East Watch
M.K.	Member of the Knesset
NRP	National Religious Party
PLO	Palestine Liberation Organization
Shin Bet	General Security Service (Israel)
UDHR	Universal Declaration of Human Rights

Human Rights in the West Bank and Gaza

1
ඌඌ

The Political and Legal Environment

BEFORE one can analyze, or even describe, the status of human and civil rights in the territories, it is essential to understand the political and legal environment existing in the territories occupied by Israel since 1967. The political conditions in the areas under discussion determine the legal framework under which they are governed, ruled, or administered; this legal framework determines the attitudes and actions of the government in the territories toward human and civil rights. Politics and law in the territories are intimately interwoven, a reality that has an immediate impact on the conditions of human rights today and, as will be argued, in the future.

In the interest of unambiguous communication and analytical approach, an important terminological clarification must precede our discussion. The areas occupied by Israel in 1967 are referred to by a variety of names. Nearly all of these carry a considerable bias toward the political position of one group or another. For most of the world, the territories are known as the West Bank and the Gaza Strip, and many analysts routinely use these terms.[1] The Israeli government began referring to the territories, especially after 1977, as "Judea, Samaria and the Gaza district"; some analysts endorsed this terminology, arguing that it refers to "a well defined geographical region."[2] Both names carry ideological baggage, and so does the familiar concept of "the occupied territories," which is being used by all Arab governments, numerous international organizations, and even many Israelis.[3] Some commentators, in an effort to avoid the ideological problems, refer to the areas simply as "the territories."

1

Moreover, despite popular conception to the contrary, the legal status of the various territories conquered by Israel in 1967 is not identical. The West Bank is ruled by a military government, as is the Gaza Strip; but whereas the former was previously under Jordan's control—the Hashemite Kingdom even claimed full sovereign rights over it and formally annexed it—Gaza was occupied and administered as a military zone by Egypt. East Jerusalem was a part of the West Bank until 1967, when it was formally annexed by Israel. In the Golan Heights, previously under Syrian control, Israel has applied its laws and administration, a step of somewhat lesser legal impact than a full-fledged annexation.

In brief, the different regions not only have different names, each with far-reaching political connotations, but also have distinct legal statuses. To deal with the status of human rights in these areas as dispassionately and as analytically as possible, when the discussion refers to all of them, the term "the territories" will be used. When the situation in a particular region is discussed, the various names in circulation will be used interchangeably so as to neutralize, as much as possible, any potential bias. On occasion, however, there may be a particular reason for preferring one name to another. Thus, while discussing the application of Israeli regulations to the territories previously under Jordan's control, it will be useful to refer to them as "Judea and Samaria," the names used in the official Israeli language. While describing Arab and other opposition to various Israeli practices in the territories, it will be useful to term them the "West Bank and Gaza" or even "the occupied territories," in accordance with the analyst's frame of reference and linguistic preferences. Although a study of human rights in the territories can never be even remotely depoliticized, the most neutral terms available ought to be used in an effort to deal with the issue at hand in a dispassionate manner.

Human Rights in a New Environment

As this preliminary terminological discussion indicates, the territories in question have been the center of an intense political struggle since their occupation by the Israeli Defense Forces (IDF) in June 1967. This political struggle seemed to have changed dramatically in September 1978 when Egypt, the most powerful Arab state, signed the Camp David Accords with Israel (and the United States as observer). In effect, Egypt declared that it would not be involved in future wars between Israel and its Arab neighbors, a commitment strengthened significantly with the signing of a full-fledged Egyptian-Israeli peace treaty in March 1979, followed by Israel's withdrawal from the Sinai.

Despite hopes, Egypt's withdrawal from active participation in the Arab-Israeli conflict did not bring about an end to the dispute. It merely brought about a transformation in the nature of the conflict. After 1978, the conflict between Israel and the Arab states receded; the Arab states lost their military option, and a full-fledged war initiated by them became less and less likely. In fact, no total war between the IDF and an Arab army has been fought since October 1973. The Lebanese confrontation of 1982 was essentially an Israeli-Palestinian clash, accompanied by a partial collision between units of the IDF and the Syrian army. Also, the Iraqi attack on Israeli cities during the Gulf War never developed into an Israeli-Iraqi war.

Furthermore, since 1978 there has been a significant decline in the number of attacks on Israel from the territory of any Arab state (except Lebanon). Equally important, from a political perspective, has been the increasing willingness of the majority of the Arab states to accept Israel as a political reality in the region.

Surprisingly, since the Lebanon war even the intensity of the confrontation between Israel and the Palestine Liberation Organization (PLO) has declined. The 1982 collision led to a clear military (although not a political) victory for the Israelis. Israel's invasion of Lebanon resulted in the loss of the PLO territorial base, a base necessary for an effective military challenge of Israel. In the period preceding the Palestinian uprising of December 1987, the Israeli-PLO conflict, especially in its military manifestations, ceased to be the central element determining the intensity and character of the Palestinian-Israeli confrontation.

Yet, as the interstate conflict between Israel and its Arab neighbors subsided and as the effectiveness of the PLO military challenge to Israel's power declined, a new form of confrontation emerged: a Palestinian-Israeli intercommunal confrontation. The intercommunal clash, hidden and unrecognized for a long time, suddenly burst to the forefront in December 1987, ushering in Israel's winter of discontent or the Intifada, as it is called by the rebelling Palestinian population.

The new phase of the Arab-Israeli conflict, to some extent a surprising return to the situation of the 1930s, had tremendous implications in the area of human rights. In fact, although the stage of interstate conflict was dominated by notions of balance of power, deterrence, force structure, and the like, and although the stage of terrorism was dominated by another set of concepts, the new stage, that of intercommunal strife, could best be discussed in terms of civil rights and human rights.

The shift in focus from the interstate to the intercommunal stage, from international conflict and terrorism to human rights, is unmistakable and profound in its long-term impact. The center of attention has shifted to the treatment of the Palestinians in the territories. Changes in the character of the conflict necessitate the employment of a new conceptual framework for its analysis. This study tries to offer such a framework.

Reflecting this transformation in public attention to the conflict, since the beginning of the Intifada a large number of reports on the human rights situation in the territories have been published in Israel, by Palestinians living in the West Bank or in Gaza, and, most important, by organizations outside the region. Of particular significance are the following studies of the human rights situation in the territories:

1. The reports by the U.S. Department of State on human rights conditions in the territories, which were published as part of the annual State Department compilation under the title *Country Reports on Human Rights.*[4]

2. A 335-page report released in December 1988 (under the title *Punishing a Nation*), by the Ramallah-based Palestinian human rights group Al Haq/Law in the Service of Man.[5]

3. A 95-page report issued (also in December 1988) by the New York-based Lawyers Committee for Human Rights under the title *An Examination of the Detention of Human Rights Workers and Lawyers from the West Bank and Gaza and Conditions of Detention at Ketziot.*[6]

4. A revised book by the Palestinian lawyer Raja Shehadeh, *Occupier's Law: Israel and the West Bank,* published in early 1989, updating an original manuscript of 1985 with an epilogue devoted to developments since the beginning of the uprising.[7]

5. A 230-page report issued jointly by the Committee to Protect Journalists (New York) and the London-based organization Article 19, under the title *Journalism under Occupation: Israel's Regulation of the Palestinian Press* (October 1988).[8]

6. A report issued by two Knesset members of the Civil Rights

Movement, Yossi Sarid and Dedi Zucker, under the title "A Year of Intifada" and published by the Israeli periodical *New Outlook* in January 1989.[9]

7. A very long series of reports, appearing in both English and Hebrew, issued by the Israeli human rights organization B'Tselem, which was established as a direct result of the Intifada. These reports will be continuously referred to in the body of this work.

These reports differ in length and in depth of description and analysis, in their approach to the topic, and in their focus. The Sarid-Zucker report is three pages long, and some others are substantial books; some reports are political, and others take a painstaking, legal approach to the issue at hand; some reports deal with a fairly specific human right (e.g., freedom of expression or detention), and others are much more comprehensive, dealing with the overall human rights situation in the territories.

Nevertheless, all of the reports mentioned here, and others, paint a similar picture of what their authors perceive as widespread abuse of human rights and violation of the norms of international law. In support of this position, the Al Haq volume argues that the number of administrative detainees imprisoned without charge or trial increased by 4,000 percent in the first year of the Intifada. It maintains that the Intifada "has marked the first time that ongoing flagrant violations of human rights have been publicly proclaimed and pursued as policy at the highest levels of the Israeli government," a reference to Defense Minister Yitzhak Rabin's statement of January 1988, which declared a policy of "might, force and beatings" in response to the Palestinian uprising.

The Lawyers Committee report, dwelling on the conditions under which detention of Palestinians is administered, especially at the detention center of Ketziot, describes them as "crowded and inhumane." It ought to be mentioned that the Israeli Supreme Court urged an investigation into the conditions at Ketziot, a prison located in the harsh Negev Desert.

The report on the Palestinian press maintains that close to forty Palestinian journalists have been detained, mostly without charge or due process; it highlights the closure of Palestinian publications and news agencies. Although the report recognizes that Israel "tolerates" a Palestinian press, it maintains that Israel's censorship "extends beyond clear security concerns and often becomes political censorship" (p. 4).

The post-Intifada human rights reports of the U.S. Department of State have proved harsh in dealing with human rights violations in the territories. The 1988 report criticizes human rights practices in the territories, stating that Israeli troops caused "many avoidable deaths and injuries," using gunfire in situations that did not present mortal danger to the troops. The report also argues that there were cases in which Palestinian detainees "died under questionable circumstances" while in detention "or were clearly killed by the detaining officials." It maintains that 154 houses of Arabs were demolished or sealed for security reasons and that 36 Palestinians were deported from the territories in 1988, a dramatic increase in both cases.

The Sarid-Zucker report is in general agreement with the other reports, although it focuses more on the impact of the Intifada on the Israeli society. It maintains that the Intifada has "eroded the IDF's moral values" (p. 48), that acts of vigilantism have increased, that "the settlers do as they please in the West Bank and Gaza Strip" because "they see themselves as a garrison force" (p. 49), and that the imposition of collective punishments on the Palestinian population is now an "accepted procedure" (p. 49). The publications of B'Tselem tend to take a similar position, and document it with large amounts of data.

The overall degree of agreement among the writers of the various reports on the status of human rights in the territories is surprising. There is a generally held conviction among them that the Intifada swept away the claim that Israel's occupation was "liberal" and instead strengthened the notion that due process of law cannot be maintained while the occupation continues. At the same time, some authors (but by no means all) emphasize that although Israel proper (in its pre-1967 borders) is run as a functioning and even vibrant democracy, with a respectable human rights record, the territories are governed by harsh military means. This is, for example, the position taken by the U.S. Department of State in its annual human rights reports.

The Legal Status of the Territories: Human Rights Implications

The status of human rights in the territories and the extent to which various rights ought to be observed by the military government and its agents depend to a large extent on the political and legal status of these territories. There is a fierce disagreement regarding the status of the West Bank, Gaza, East Jerusalem, and the Golan Heights.

One of the most fundamental questions regarding the territories is whether they ought to be regarded as occupied. The status of the territories as "occupied" could determine the applicability of such agreements as the 1949 Fourth Geneva Convention Relative to the Protection of Civilian Persons in Time of War (hereafter: Geneva IV), and this determination would significantly affect the human rights obligations of the Israeli government in the territories.

Between 1949 and 1967, the West Bank (including East Jerusalem and the Old City) was under Jordanian control, and the Gaza Strip was under Egyptian rule. In 1950 Jordan formally annexed the West Bank, an action that was tacitly accepted by the rest of the world (including Israel) but formally recognized by Britain and Pakistan alone. At the same time, Egypt imposed military control over Gaza. During the 1967 war, Israel conquered both the West Bank and Gaza. Since the end of the Six-Day War, the formal Israeli position regarding the legal status of these territories has been ambiguous, and a serious political split regarding their status has emerged within Israel.

Two fundamentally opposing positions in regard to the territories have been formulated. Some political forces in Israel have perceived the territories as occupied lands to be exchanged (all or some) for peace with Israel's Arab neighbors, and possibly the Palestinian Arabs, in the framework of a negotiated settlement. The nationalist, right wing in Israel has perceived the territories as liberated lands, taken from usurpers (Jordan and Egypt) and destined to be annexed by the state of Israel. By adopting the first position, the Labor government (1967–77) preferred to leave open the question of the applicability of Geneva IV to the territories. Following the establishment of the Likud government (1977), the official Israeli position became less equivocal. In one of his first Knesset addresses, Israel's Premier Menachem Begin declared unambiguously that as far as international law was concerned, Israel's rule over the land of Israel was not that of an occupying power. Begin and others argued over the years that the West Bank and the Gaza Strip belong to Israel not only by the right of history and tradition, but also because Israel liberated these territories in a war of self-defense.[10] Thus, the application of the Geneva IV to the territories was unacceptable to the Likud on ideological grounds as well as legal ones.

The views of the Israeli right regarding the status of the territories proved problematical to the vast majority of analysts on a number of counts. As such, they were almost universally rejected by the international community. First, Jordan and Egypt ruled the territories for almost two decades prior to the Six-Day War and acquired some international status there; their removal from these territories by the IDF in an armed conflict led, in fact, to an Israeli occupation of the territories in question. Immediately following the takeover of the West Bank and the Gaza Strip, Israel formally established military rule in these territories under the supervision of its minister of defense. Not surprisingly, the international community has perceived the territories as occupied.

Second, the territories in question (both the West Bank and the Gaza Strip) were allotted to a would-be Palestinian-Arab state by the U.N. General Assembly in its famous Partition Resolution of November 29, 1947. As successor to the League of Nations, the United Nations had a supervisory status over the Palestine mandate. According to the Canadian legal expert Thomas Kuttner, the decision (Resolution 181) meant that "the reversionary right of sovereignty [in mandated Palestine] was vested in the inhabitants, Jew and Arab alike."[11] If Jordan and Egypt acted in 1948 as unlawful usurpers, grabbing the lands given to the Palestinians, the argument goes, Israel is now doing the same. The absence of a Jordanian right to the West Bank and an Egyptian right to Gaza does not in any way give sovereignty rights in these territories to Israel; in fact, arguments directed in the past against these Arab states could now be effectively directed against the current occupant of the territories, Israel. If Jordan indeed imposed its sovereignty illegally on the inhabitants of the West Bank—as the Israeli right maintains —ought not the international community now take action designed to restore this sovereignty to the Palestinian Arab inhabitants of the territories?

Third, the right wing's claims for national and religious rights in the territories in question—rights that to them sanction annexation—are not validly based on any acceptable legal document granting Israel the right to Eretz Israel in its entirety. The Balfour Declaration (1917) and the League of Nations' Palestine Mandate (1922), which incorporated the British commitment included in the Belfour Declaration, promised the establishment of a Jewish national home in Palestine, not necessarily but possibly in all of Palestine. The 1947 Partition Resolution was accepted by Israel's provisional government, thus committing Israel to the principle of partition. The West Bank and the Gaza Strip were to be included in the would-be Arab state. The principle of national self-determination for Arabs and Jews in Palestine was specifically accepted by the United Nations and by Israel (although, ironically, not by the Arabs) in 1947.

Fourth, the argument that the conquest of territories in self-defense confers the rights of sovereignty on the occupier also has proven problematical. It is certainly true that historically many victors have forced defeated powers to cede territories; numerous peace treaties have legitimized the transfer of occupied territory from the vanquished to the victor. Yet, this traditional method of land acquisition has hardly any bearing on the modern use of the term "self-defense." The legal provisions regarding self-defense today are quite clear: a state under armed attack is indeed entitled to stop, repel, and crush such attack, if necessary by conquering territories from which the attack is launched, organized, or staged. Yet, no territorial changes of a permanent nature are allowed under the doctrine of self-defense in contemporary international law. If there are to be such changes, they ought to be negotiated as part of a peace settlement between the warring parties.[12]

In recognition of the uniqueness and complexity of the sovereignty question, Gerson suggests that Israel be viewed as a "trustee-occupant" in the territories, a power whose duty is to temporarily manage the territories in accordance with the rules of international law (specifically those of belligerent occupation), including Geneva IV.[13] Israel's status will continue to be that of a trustee-occupant until a formal cessation of belligerency is obtained through peace negotiations. In essence, this was the position taken by the Israeli government following the 1967 war, but it was completely rejected by the government established after the 1977 elections.[14] Jordan's decision in 1988 to cut off all links to, and withdraw all claims on, the West Bank strengthens Gerson's perspective on the status of the territories. So does the Israeli-Palestinian agreement of September 13, 1993.

The Applicability of the Fourth Geneva Convention and the 1907 Hague Regulations

From a legal perspective one can distinguish three main positions regarding the status of the territories.[15] Each of these positions has implications in terms of the applicability of Geneva IV and other documents that include humanitarian provisions. First, Israel may be perceived as what Blum calls "the missing reversioner," a state that has a better claim to the territories than any other state.[16] If that is so, then the territories may not be regarded as occupied and Geneva IV may not apply. Those who take this position point out that ARTICLE 2 of Geneva IV requires—according to their interpretation—that an occupied territory in question have belonged, prior to its occupation, to "a High Contracting Party"; otherwise the convention does not apply.

A second approach to Israel's status in the territories is simply to see Israel as an occupier bound by the laws of belligerent occupation, including the Hague Regulations of 1907 and Geneva IV. Such a position, which has been acceptable to the vast majority of the world community, international organizations, and legal scholars,[17] does not necessarily imply that Israel came to occupy the territories in an illegal way or that Israel cannot make future claims to sovereignty status in the territories. It merely states that the territory is occupied; therefore, the international conventions regarding occupation are fully applicable.

Finally, Israel can be seen neither as a "liberator" (the first approach) nor as an "occupier" (the second approach), but as what Gerson calls a trustee-occupant. According to this innovative approach, the case of the territories is sui generis: Israel is a trustee holding areas in which the inhabitants have the rights of sovereignty until they establish self-government. According to this approach, Israel has to respect the provisions of the Hague Convention and Geneva IV as long as the occupation lasts. In general, the essential function of these conventions has always been to protect the rights of the population in an occupied territory regardless of the final decision on sovereignty in that territory. At the same time, they give the occupier the powers necessary to govern effectively.

Most analysts believe that Geneva IV and the Hague Regulations apply in situations where the question of sovereignty in the pre-occupation era is clear, and also in situations where it is unclear or debatable, as is the situation in both the West Bank and the Gaza Strip. The Hague Regulations of 1907 apply to occupied territories in a way that is even clearer than that of Geneva IV: they are considered part of customary law and apply to any occupation.[18]

Even if one views Jordan as a usurper, illegally grabbing and annexing the West Bank, by gaining control over this area Israel now finds itself bound by the norms of Geneva IV and the Hague Regulations. If Jordan's territorial rights in the West Bank are successfully challenged—as they indeed seem to have been—the rights of the Palestinian Arabs, particularly those inhabiting the West Bank, are strengthened and Israel's status in the territories may change from that of an "occupier" to that of a "trustee-occupant." In either case, Israel is equally bound by the provisions of Geneva IV, which defines, at least in part, the standards against which her treatment of an occupied population ought to be compared.

Geneva IV, to which Israel has been a signatory since July 1951, is quite specific about its applicability. Paragraph 1 of ARTICLE 2 states that "the present Convention shall apply to all cases of declared war or *any other armed conflict* which may arise between two or more of the High Contracting Parties." Paragraph 2 of ARTICLE 2 states that "The Convention shall also apply to *all cases of partial or total occupation* of the territory of a High Contracting Party."[19] Shamgar's position that "there is no rule of international law according to which the Fourth Geneva Convention applies to each and every armed conflict whatever the status of the parties"[20] seems to contradict the language of ARTICLE 2 of Geneva IV.

The official position of the Israeli government regarding the applicability of Geneva IV has changed substantially since the end of the 1967 war. Article 35 of Military Proclamation no. 3 of June 7, 1967, stated that IDF personnel must follow the terms of the 1949 Geneva Conventions. However, Military Order no. 144 of October 12, 1967, repealed this provision and signaled a policy change and the adoption of a more ambiguous position.[21] Since this change, there has been a movement toward a new stance: because the territories were not acquired through the ouster of a legitimate sovereign, as Geneva IV allegedly requires, the convention does not apply; the convention is relevant only to territories "of a High Contracting Party."[22]

This claim has not been accepted by the international community or by most scholarly authorities in international law; even the government of the United States, Israel's chief international supporter, has stated repeatedly (e.g., in its 1989 and 1990 State Department reports on human rights) that it "considers Israel's occupation to be governed by the Hague Regulations of 1907 and the 1949 Fourth Geneva Convention Relative to the Protection of Civilian Persons in Time of War."[23]

The arguments on behalf of the applicability of Geneva IV to the territories are straightforward. Even if one accepts the position that Paragraph 2 of ARTICLE 2 applies exclusively to the territories of states—namely, when the question of sovereignty is nondebatable—Paragraph 1 of ARTICLE 2 is quite unambiguous in its determination that the convention applies to *all cases of "armed conflict"* between "High Contracting Parties." The West Bank fell into Israel's hands as a result of an armed conflict with Jordan, and the Gaza Strip was conquered from Egypt as a result of an armed conflict between Israel and Egypt. All three countries—Egypt, Israel, and Jordan—are signatories to Geneva IV; the applicability of the convention is, thus, quite clear.

According to ARTICLE 2 of Geneva IV, the convention is applicable in either of two cases: (1) when an armed conflict between signatory states results in occupation; (2) when there is a partial or total occupation of the territory of a signatory to the convention. This is the meaning of the word "also"—"the Convention shall also apply . . ."—at the beginning of Paragraph 2 of ARTICLE 2. The occupation of the West Bank and the Gaza Strip clearly falls under case 1.

But the question of applicability requires that we look at Geneva IV not only technically, verbally, and microscopically but also contextually, broadly, and comprehensively. Esther Rosalind Cohen, in a book based on a doctoral dissertation submitted to the Hebrew University of Jerusalem, examines Geneva IV in such broad terms and concludes that the convention applies to the "Israeli-occupied territories" regardless of the question of sovereignty over these territories.[24] Boyd maintains that Geneva IV "was meant to be people-oriented, not territory-oriented,"[25] and Cohen notes that Geneva IV emphasizes the "inviolability of the rights of protected persons" rather than territorial issues. Above all, it is "concerned only with the human rights of the civilian population of occupied territories" and intentionally ignores the legal status of these territories.[26]

Gerhard von Glahn, an authority on international law as it relates to war, also agrees (as do the vast majority of experts in the field) that Geneva IV applies in full to the West Bank and Gaza Strip. He maintains that Israel, as the occupying power in the territories, is bound particularly by ARTICLES 1–12, 27, 29–34, 47, 49, 51–53, 59, 61–77, and 143 of Geneva. ARTICLE 6 states that the occupying power in a territory, to the extent that it "exercises the functions of government in such territory," is bound by the provisions of these specific articles.[27]

Some of the Geneva IV articles listed above (and reiterated by von Glahn as binding on the occupying power) have received special attention in the context of the human rights situation in the territories: ARTICLE 33 prohibits the application of collective penalties;[28] ARTICLE 49 prohibits "deportations of protected persons from occupied territory to the territory of the Occupying Power or to that of any other country . . . regardless of their motive," as well as the transfer of the Occupying Power's "own civilian population into the territory it occupies;"[29] ARTICLE 53 prohibits "any destruction by the Occupying Power of real or personal property belonging individually or collectively to private persons . . . except where such destruction is rendered absolutely necessary by military operations;"[30] and ARTICLE 76 states that "protected persons accused of offenses shall be detained in the occupied territory and if convicted shall serve their sentence therein."[31]

A few of the provisions of the Hague Regulations also have been perceived as having particular relevance for the subject of this study. ARTICLE 46 of the annex titled "Regulations Respecting the Laws and Customs of War on Land," which states that private property cannot be confiscated, and ARTICLE 50, which forbids collective punishment, are good examples.

In declaring that it does not see itself bound by Geneva IV, the Israeli government stated that it would nevertheless respect the humanitarian provisions of the convention. However, the government never specified which provisions are to be considered "humanitarian" (and therefore binding on its government in the territories). It seems that practically all the Geneva IV articles mentioned above deal with humanitarian aspects of the occupation: collective punishment of the population, expulsion of convicted and suspected persons, destruction of homes and confiscation of property, conditions of detention, and so on.

Some analysts have noted that despite the government's position that Geneva IV is not legally binding, its spokesmen often have justified official actions—such as press censorship, prohibition of political activity, administrative detention, and book banning—as legitimate in accordance with the provisions of that Convention. Thus, Defense Minister Yitzhak Rabin justified the closure of schools in the territories by stating that this action was compatible with the provisions of Geneva IV.[32]

A continuing fundamental problem with regard to the applicability of Geneva IV to the territories is that although Israel might be obliged by the convention internationally, because it signed and ratified the convention, its courts cannot apply Geneva IV domestically. Geneva IV and the other 1949 Geneva conventions are constitutive conventions that change and add to existing international law, not part and parcel of customary international law, which is universally applicable. A lawmaking international treaty cannot serve as the basis on which a plaintiff in the territories may seek legal assistance within the domestic judicial framework.[33] A state must explicitly adjust its internal legal system to its international obligations; in the absence of such adjustment, these obligations are domestically meaningless. It is the national legal system that determines the status and force of law established in a treaty within the domestic legal system, that is, whether national judges will apply the norms of a treaty in a specific case. Israel, like Britain, does not have automatic incorporation but, rather, legislative incorporation of international law: the national parliament, the Knesset, has to enact legislation implementing a treaty before the treaty becomes part of Israel's national law. The Knesset has not incorporated Geneva IV.

Professor Yoram Dinstein, an Israeli expert on international law, explained his position on the applicability of the convention: "Since a legislative incorporation of the Geneva Convention into the domestic Israeli law has not taken place, one cannot rely upon the convention in Israel (but with the agreement of both parties). Yet, one must remember that the Convention definitely commits Israel internationally. The fact that the High Court of Justice cannot express an opinion [as to whether an act violates Geneva IV] does not mean that the State is free of its international obligations."[34]

Israel's High Court of Justice has adopted the position that for Geneva IV to apply domestically and for the Court to enforce it in individual cases, the Knesset has to incorporate the convention into domestic law. For a number of years, the High Court of Justice refused to accept either Geneva IV or the Hague Regulations: as a result of an article by Professor Dinstein, the Court decided to accept the 1907 regulations as obligatory and emphasized their status as part of customary international law.[35] Although the Court has not allowed violations of Geneva IV, it has stated that it cannot enforce the convention.

Although it is consistent with Israel's legal tradition, the position of the Israeli High Court has not been well received in the international political and legal communities. It has allowed the government to violate its obligations under Geneva IV, including those related to the transfer of Israel's population to the territories, house demolition, and collective punishment. Professor Amnon Rubinstein, one of Israel's senior jurists and a minister in several Israeli governments, wrote that this situation "has a bizarre implication: in reality it created a condition according to which the Convention must apply in the territories, but the Government's refusal to allow adjudication according to the Convention leads to the Government's violation of the implicit commitment it took upon itself."[36]

Although Rubinstein agrees that in parliamentary regimes such as Britain's or Israel's, only the legislature can change domestic law, he states that "when we deal with a convention that *by its very nature does not apply to the jurisdictional area of the state* and is not supposed to interfere in the essence of the domestic law, and a convention which deals exclusively with *areas and relations outside the jurisdictional territory,* there is a doubt whether there is a need for this type of incorporation process."[37]

In view of the Court's refusal to apply it, Geneva IV has become less and less important in Israel. At the same time, it has become increasingly important in the eyes of the world as a measure of Israel's human rights record in the territories. Some scholars even believe that Geneva IV has become an integral part of customary law, in its own right and as a reiteration of most of the Hague Regulations dealing with the protection of civilian persons.[38] Dinstein proposed in the wake of the Intifada that the Knesset pass a law fully applying Geneva IV to the territories, as part and parcel of Israel's domestic code. According to Dinstein, such a law would make it possible for the High Court of Justice to review and criticize any action taken by the military government in the territories in light of Geneva IV.[39]

It seems that the applicability of Geneva IV to Israel's rule over the West Bank and Gaza Strip can be argued for either directly or indirectly. If Jordan is recognized as the pre-1967 sovereign in the West Bank, then Israel is straightforwardly the occupying power and bound by the provisions of Geneva IV. If the Palestinian Arabs are perceived as the true sovereign in the territories, Israel could be perceived (as proposed by Gerson) as a trustee-occupant, governing the territories temporarily and also bound by Geneva IV.

Geneva IV also applies, albeit indirectly, if the area is somehow perceived as politically "vacant," a territory in limbo, a land over which there is no clear-cut sovereignty. As a person-oriented, humanitarian document, Geneva IV applies to any territory occupied as a result of a military confrontation between signatories to it. Not surprisingly, for more than two decades there has been a virtual unanimity in the international community that Israel is bound by Geneva IV. Even Israel's closest friends have held this opinion.[40]

Hillel Sommer, an Israeli jurist, argued that Geneva IV applies in Israel because it was officially adopted and incorporated domestically through General Staff (Matkal) Order no. 33.0133. This order (July 20, 1982) specifically directs all Israeli soldiers to behave in accordance with the Geneva Conventions. According to Sommer, even though Geneva IV has not been incorporated by the Knesset, the military government and all its personnel are committed to it through Order no. 33.0133. He sees this situation as a solution to the contradiction between Israeli domestic law and Israel's international obligations in accordance with Geneva IV.[41]

The Applicability of International Human Rights Standards

Geneva IV imposes limitations and obligations on any occupier: although it was written and signed as a document regulating what was expected to be short-term military occupations, it is applicable to a prolonged belligerent occupation as well. Nevertheless, some international legal scholars feel that in a situation of prolonged occupation, Geneva IV is "insufficient to ensure adequate protection for the needs of the civilian population."[42] Further protection of the fundamental rights of the occupied population is required.

Cohen suggests that in governing an occupied territory, a belligerent occupant may be guided by the U.N. Universal Declaration of Human Rights (1948), as well as by the two international covenants of human rights approved by the U.N. General Assembly in 1966: the International Covenant on Economic, Social, and Cultural Rights and the International Covenant on Civil and Political Rights.[43] Dedi Zucker, a member of the Knesset and a leading proponent of human rights in the territories, takes a similar position in his comprehensive study of human rights in Israel's occupied territories.[44]

Insofar as the UDHR and, to a lesser extent, the two international covenants of human rights reflect the generally agreed-upon attitude of the international community toward human rights, it could be argued that they indeed apply to all territories: those under sovereign rule and those under occupation. These documents impose limitations on all governments. Technically speaking, the UDHR was intended as a nonbinding, aspirational document that is appropriately called a "declaration"; yet, many believe that by now "it has largely assumed the status of customary international law."[45] Fleischman states categorically that "although the degree to which the UDHR constitutes customary international law is not completely settled, it is nevertheless appropriate to apply [its] standards, since the rights they invoke are in any case internationally recognized rights."[46]

The Civil and Political Rights Covenant expands, elaborates, and interprets the UDHR. It strengthens the claim that the latter is part and parcel of customary law today. Israel is, of course, a signatory to the UDHR. As such, its activities—in and out of the territories—could legitimately be measured against the standards of the UDHR even though the latter is not a legally binding document. Although Israel is not a party to the International Covenant on Civil and Political Rights, which it signed in 1966 but declined to ratify, its signature indicates a willingness and intention to become a party and a commitment to the document's provisions. Therefore, Israel's activities could be assessed against the standards of this document as well. Although it is impossible to challenge the military government in an Israeli court on the basis of the UDHR (just as it is practically impossible to do so on the basis of Geneva IV), the provisions of the UDHR are relevant standards for evaluating the behavior of any government, especially a signatory to the UDHR.

The West Bank and the Gaza Strip, perhaps more than any other territory in the world today, are in a political and legal limbo, as they were in the pre-Oslo days. They are governed by a country that the overwhelming majority of their inhabitants view as an occupier. In this sense, these territories are militarily occupied and Geneva IV seems to apply to them perfectly. At the same time, after twenty-eight years of occupation (only recently limited by the provisions of Oslo) their inhabitants should enjoy all or at least most of the rights specified in the UDHR and in similar human rights documents. The undetermined, volatile status of the territories and the reality of a military government in a day-to-day control over them made Israel (especially in the pre-Oslo days) answerable to Geneva IV, the Hague Regulations, and other international agreements designed to protect civilians under belligerent occupation.[47] The duration, intensity, and depth of the pre-Oslo occupation made Israel increasingly answerable to the provisions of the UDHR and similar international documents.[48]

Although it is clear that, in principle, human rights in an occupied territory are more limited than in an area under the sovereignty of the governing state, elementary human rights ought to be kept even under occupation. The longer and the more permanent the occupation, the more extensive are the human rights obligations of the state controlling the occupied area. In a decision in the case *Christian Association for the Holy Places* v. *Minister of Defense,* the Israeli HCJ (337/71) stated that the longer the occupation, the greater the social need for new legislation in the territories. This position is stated in other judgments as well (e.g., 69/81 and 383/82). The same position could be taken toward the observation of human rights in the territories in general.

Drori proposes that when the occupation continues for an extended period of time, the military government is "entitled to act as government and legislative branch."[49] A balanced approach would require it to respect human rights to a greater degree than in a short occupation. Kuttner emphasizes that the function of the law of belligerent occupation is to protect the basic civil rights of the inhabitants of the occupied territories.[50] If that is so, a prolonged occupation requires even more intensive protection of these basic rights. In recognizing the need for a balanced approach, Dinstein states that "the needs of the occupier and the occupation should not negate the needs of the civilian population [in the occupied territory]."[51] Von Glahn also emphasizes the need to balance the "military necessity of the occupier against a humanitarian standard of conduct."[52]

In this volume, the approach will be to examine the human rights situation in the territories against the human rights standards included in Geneva IV and the UDHR. This position seems to be appropriate in view of Israel's dual role in the territories as a military occupier and as a government with numerous "civilian" functions.

The marriage of Geneva IV and the UDHR, of the law of war and the law of human rights, may not be a natural one; however, the abnormal situation in the territories requires it. Esther Cohen defined the functional need for interaction between the law of war and that of human rights: "There are situations governed by the law of armed conflicts in which the law of human rights can serve to limit the more brutal requirements of military necessity contained in the law of armed conflicts. Such a situation is that of *prolonged belligerent occupation after the cessation of general hostilities.*"[53]

In other words, although the law of war is overwhelmingly important in regulating armed conflict and short-term occupation, the much newer law of human rights has an important role to play in prolonged occupation. The humanitarian requirements increase as the occupation lengthens and becomes more permanent. It is ironic that the efforts of various Israeli governments, especially of the political right, to integrate the West Bank and Gaza Strip into Israel have enhanced Israel's human rights obligations toward the population in the territories.

Assessing Israel's Human Rights Performance

Israel's human rights performance in the territories will be assessed in this volume both on the basis of the standards included in major documents regulating the law of war (Geneva IV in particular) and in light of the main standards of the emerging law of human rights (UDHR in particular). Insofar as Geneva IV is concerned, special attention will be given to the following rights and freedoms of an occupied population, and duties of the occupying power:

1. The right of the population under occupation not to be the subject of collective punishment, namely, punishment resulting from an offense that the punished person has not personally committed.[54]

2. The right of protected persons not to be deported "from the occupied territory to the territory of the occupying power or to that of any other country" and the obligation of the occupying power not to transfer "its own civilian population into the territory it occupies."[55]

3. The prohibition (imposed on the military government) against destruction of property in the occupied territory, "except where such destruction is rendered absolutely necessary by military operations."[56]

4. The obligation of the occupying power in regard to the management of the justice system in the occupied territory, which includes the following demands:

a. The penal provisions enacted by it be published and "brought to the knowledge of the inhabitants in their own language."[57]

b. Accused persons who are prosecuted by the occupying power are to be promptly informed, in writing, in a language they understand, of the specific charges brought against them.[58]

c. Accused persons have the right to be assisted by a qualified lawyer, who shall be able to visit them freely and enjoy "the necessary facilities for preparing the defense."[59]

d. The right of appeal be guaranteed.[60]

e. Accused persons be detained in the occupied territory and, if convicted, serve their sentence therein, as well as their right to "enjoy conditions of food and hygiene . . . sufficient to keep them in good health," and conditions "which will be at least equal to those obtained in prisons in the occupying country."[61]

Insofar as the UDHR is concerned, the following rights and freedoms will be focused upon:

1. Freedom from arbitrary arrest, detention, or exile.[62]

2. The right to be presumed innocent until proven guilty, according to law, in a public trial.[63]

3. The right to travel in one's own country or to other countries and to return.[64]

4. Freedom from arbitrary deprivation of one's property.[65]

In measuring Israel's human rights performance in the territories, it is useful to rely upon some of the provisions of Geneva IV, some of the provisions of the UDHR, and some additional important elements included in the contemporary law of human rights. The latter additional elements are extracted from a human rights classification scheme developed by Charles Humana.[66] In addition to the rights and freedoms included in Geneva IV and the UDHR, Humana's comprehensive list includes some standards against which Israel's human rights performance should be evaluated:

1. Freedom to monitor human rights violations.[67]

2. Freedom from extrajudicial killings.[68]

3. Freedom from "indefinite detention without charge."[69]

4. The right to be protected against police searches of one's home without a warrant.[70]

5. The right to be protected against seizure of personal property.[71]

The Humana classification reflects a wider spectrum of fundamental human rights than does Geneva IV or the UDHR. If we want to evaluate Israel's human rights performance against the existing and the evolving human rights of the present, Humana's list—in addition to the lists developed on the basis of Geneva IV and the UDHR—could help us to do so systematically and comprehensively.

Human Rights and Politics

Obviously, the human rights measurement system proposed here is extremely demanding, a high order for most of the world's states. Israel's very real security concerns and genuine political dilemmas make it virtually impossible for her always to meet all of the human rights requirements enumerated above. Yet, to correctly assess the obstacles for peace inherent in the pre-Oslo and in the current situations, a thorough evaluation of human rights is needed. Furthermore, only a comprehensive analytical framework of the type suggested here could allow us to examine (in the last chapter of the book) the possible impact of a series of solutions to the Israeli-Palestinian conflict on the human rights of the people involved.

The next three chapters assess the status of human rights in the territories prior to Oslo, using the criteria established in this chapter. The status of human rights in the territories will often be examined by comparing the pre-Intifada era with the post-Intifada era. It is the objective of this study to evaluate whether, and to what extent, the human rights situation deteriorated between December 9, 1987, and the end of Likud's rule in Israel. The hypothesis that it has, ought to be evaluated against the empirical data rather than be accepted at face value.

Chapter 5 will be mostly analytical. It will identify a series of alternative political solutions[72] to the Israeli-Palestinian conflict and then assess the likely status of human rights if each of these alternative solutions is implemented. The Israeli-Palestinian dilemma has often been analyzed from a purely political or military perspective:[73] a similar, future-oriented analysis, in terms of human rights, has not been offered to date. The final chapter will attempt to close this gap.

2

The Settlement Policy and Its Consequences

THE human rights situation in the West Bank and Gaza Strip ought to be understood and analyzed within the context of Israeli settlement policy in the territories, especially the policy adopted by right-wing governments after 1977. Many human rights violations in the territories can be linked to the overall settlement program. The territorial issue has been the common denominator tying and integrating a variety of otherwise unconnected policies. The settlement policy has had significant implications for the status of human rights in the West Bank and Gaza.

In the beginning of this chapter, the political context of the settlement policy will be reviewed, focusing on both the ideological and the practical aspects of that policy since 1967. The focus will then shift to the land acquisition, use, and control policy in the territories, and then to the Israeli settlers in the territories. The individuals and groups that took up residence in the West Bank and Gaza after the Six-Day War continue to play an extremely important role within the matrix of Arab-Jewish relations. The role of the settlers ought to be evaluated within the more general framework of the demographic policy in the territories.

The Political Context of the Settlement Policy

The policies of the various Israeli governments toward the West Bank and Gaza have changed a number of times since 1967.

The changes have been significant not only insofar as the type and intensity of the effort to settle Jews in the territories but also in terms of the human rights of the local population.

The first place of Israel's settlement effort in the territories lasted from 1967 to 1975; carried out by the Labor-led governments of Levi Eshkol, Golda Meir, and Yitzhak Rabin, it generally followed the outlines of the Allon Plan.[1] Yigal Allon, one of Labor's prominent leaders, and a former general and a foreign minister in the Rabin government (1974–77), argued after the 1967 war that Israel must obtain defensible borders by taking advantage of the topographical features of the newly acquired territories. Allon believed that Israel could guarantee the political permanence of its borders by establishing settlements along them. He therefore proposed that Israel establish its security and political border on the Jordan River and annex a strip ten to fifteen kilometers wide in the Jordan Valley. Allon also supported the annexation of the uninhabited Judean desert and the western slopes of the Hebron mountains, and thought that for military and historical reasons, Israel ought to maintain control over the Etzion Bloc and the Latrun Salient. However, he emphasized that for political and demographic reasons most of the West Bank, including all major population centers save East Jerusalem, ought to be returned to Arab rule within the framework of a peace agreement.

Although the Allon Plan was never officially adopted, the Alignment (Labor) government followed it quite closely. By 1975 two chains of settlements had been established, one on the Jordan riverbed and the other on the eastern slopes of the Samarian mountains. All the settlements were small and agricultural, and the Arab population in the region of their establishment was extremely small. When the Rabin government fell in May 1977, two-thirds of all Jewish settlements in the West Bank were located along the Jordan River, an area perceived by almost all Israelis as crucial for the country's strategic defense. The remainder of the settlements were established in regions over which a national consensus existed: the Jerusalem area, Latrun, and the Etzion Bloc. Kiryat Arba (adjacent to Hebron) and two other settlements were the exception to the rule, which was "settlements for security." Although some commentators thought that the Israeli government used the security rationale as an excuse for settlement and annexation,[2] the government was formally committed to territorial compromise and adopted a settlement policy that made such a compromise possible (see map 1).

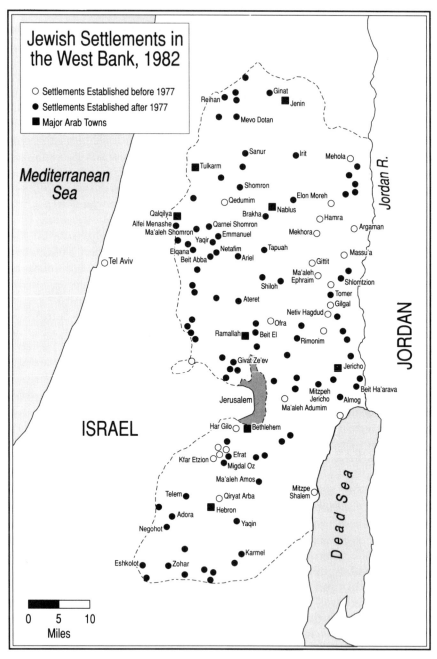

Source: Mark Tessler, *The History of the Israeli-Palestinian Conflict* (Bloomington: Indiana Univ. Press, 1994), 522. Reprinted by permission.

As a matter of principle, the Alignment was committed to the idea that Jewish settlements ought not to be placed inside or even near large Arab population centers. Although it is impossible to prove that the Alignment leaders foresaw the negative human rights implications of establishing Jewish settlements near Arab towns, their cautious settlement policy prevented, until 1977, the type of human rights problems that became commonplace when Likud assumed power. When the Alignment rule came to an end, there were only 24 Jewish settlements, inhabited by 3,200 persons, in the West Bank and Gaza.[3]

Toward the end of the Alignment rule, its restrained settlement policy began crumbling under the combined pressures of the opposition and the extraparliamentary (and often illegal) activity of a new organization, Gush Emunim (Bloc of the Faithful). The Gush, founded in February 1974, demanded the intensification of Jewish settlement activity in all parts of Eretz Israel. Taking advantage of the disunity and weakness of the Rabin government, it began to establish settlements without governmental authorization, not only in rural areas but also close to and even inside major Arab cities. The implications for the human rights of the local Arab population, although unforeseen at the time, proved far-reaching.

Following the electoral victory of Likud in 1977, the settling activity of the Gush received the ideological support of the new prime minister. Visiting the illegal Gush settlement of Elon Moreh immediately following the election, Prime Minister Menachem Begin publicly declared: "There will be many more Alonei Moreh!" For all intents and purposes, the settlement plan of Gush Emunim was adopted as the settlement policy of the Likud government. The Begin regime was committed to the idea of Greater Israel, as was Gush Emunim; therefore, it did not have any difficulty enthusiastically endorsing the Gush settlement activities. The government support for an aggressive settlement effort was not only ideological but also organizational and, above all, financial. The Gush, which began as a poor underground group during the Labor government, now received, under Likud, large governmental grants, attractive loans for housing, and enthusiastic political support.

The most controversial aspect of the Gush/Likud settlement activity was the location of the new settlements. Amana (Covenant), the settling organ of Gush Emunim, established no fewer than forty settlements during Begin's first term as prime minister (1977–81).

Most of these settlements were in Samaria's central massif, an area that was heavily populated by Arabs and, therefore, essential for any genuine political compromise. When the last Alignment government fell, there were only two Jewish settlements on the mountain ridge of Samaria and one near Hebron, Kiryat Arba. By 1984 there were 26 settlements on the mountain ridge and 12 on Mt. Hebron; the total number of settlements in the West Bank climbed from 34 in 1977 to 114 in 1984.[4]

Though the Likud settlement program in the central massif was not a spectacular demographic or economic success—mainly due to a severe shortage of ideologically motivated settlers—it significantly contributed to the deterioration of Arab-Jewish relations and to the development of severe human rights problems. The Arabs sensed that their very existence as a community in the territories was now, for the first time since 1967, threatened. Their anxiety led to violence and in turn to an increasingly repressive policy. The link between settlement activity and human rights violations was inevitable from the very beginning.

As a result of the limited popularity of the Gush settlements in the Samarian mountains, a third phase of settlement activity emerged during the early 1980s. The idea behind what might be called the suburban phase was to attract Israelis to the West Bank through economic incentives rather than ideological arguments. The Likud settlement strategists believed that by using the natural demand for land in central Israel, they would quickly be able to form a large pool of new settlers for the West Bank. Indeed, although in the last five years of Alignment's rule (1972–77) the annual growth of the number of settlers averaged 65 percent, during Likud's rule it almost doubled, averaging 121 percent for the period between 1977 and 1984. Whereas under Alignment, an average of 770 settlers per year moved into the territories, under Likud the number swelled to about 5,400 settlers.[5]

The *WZO Plan, 1983–86*, prepared by Likud member Matityahu Drobles, reflected the new settlement strategy. Insofar as this phase brought Arabs and Jews into even closer proximity than before, it did not improve the human rights dimension of the conflict.

In general, under the leadership of Menachem Begin and Yitzhak Shamir, Israel moved with giant steps toward a de facto annexation of the West Bank and the Gaza Strip, or at least toward the prevention of any nonannexationist solution to the Arab-Israeli conflict. A dramatic numerical increase in settlements and settlers had occurred,[6] the character of the settlements had changed from agricultural to semiurban and even fully urban; and, most important, a different type of settler dispersion model had been adopted. As the intensity of Jewish-Arab contacts on the West Bank and Gaza had grown significantly under Likud, an equivalent deterioration in the human rights situation in the territories had occurred. Although with the establishment of a National Unity government in 1984, a noticeable change in Israeli budgetary allocations to settlement areas occurred. With more equal distribution of funds to areas included in the Allon (Labor) and Drobles (Likud) plans, the momentum toward an Arab-Jewish intercommunal clash on the West Bank, to which the settlement program contributed immensely, seemed unstoppable.

From a purely legal perspective, Israel's settlement effort, particularly the one endorsed by Likud, has been perceived by many as highly problematical. No other single policy of the Israeli government has generated more opposition than the settling of Israelis in the territories.[7] Commentators have noted that transfers of population into occupied territory by the occupier are clearly in violation of ARTICLE 49, Paragraph 6, of the 1949 Fourth Geneva Convention, which reads: "The occupying power shall not deport or transfer parts of its own civilian population into the territory it occupies." The illegality of the settling effort has been almost universally accepted by analysts,[8] governments (including that of the United States),[9] and the U.N. General Assembly and Security Council.[10] Many saw the settlement activity as a prelude to annexation.[11]

Justifications of the settlement policy failed to convince the international community in view of the clear ban on such activity included not only in Geneva IV but also in the Hague Regulations (ARTICLE 85(49), as amended in 1977). As explained in chapter 1, the argument that Geneva IV did not fully apply to the territories, that Israel was not an "occupant" because Jordan had acquired the West Bank by aggression, that Israel took the areas in a war of self-defense, and that the settlements were legal because the territories were parts of the ancient Jewish patrimony were rejected by the vast majority of countries and by most legal scholars. Even the argument that Israel needed the settlements for national security, which is substantially stronger than the national rights arguments, did not change the perception that the settlements were fundamentally illegal. The Alignment settlement plan was more defensible than the Likud plan because it relied heavily on security considerations, which are accepted in international law as a legal basis for numerous acts of the occupant.[12] However, both Labor and Likud ran into serious political opposition from the international community.

Despite the High Court of Justice's willingness to be accessible to the residents of the territories, and thus potentially to affect the status of their human rights, it proved only marginally effective as a barrier to human rights violations resulting from the settlement effort. However, the Court has been more effective in the area of settlement than in other areas of activity, which indicates that Israel's legal system has not been completely unresponsive to human rights problems stemming from the occupation.

As early as 1969, Arab residents of the Rafah Salient appealed to the High Court of Justice (HCJ) to ban land confiscations for establishing Jewish settlements in the region. The Court responded by deciding that according to international law, the establishment of settlements on private land is conditional upon the existence of a definite *"military and security need."* In 1978 (in the Beit-El case) the HCJ ruled that for a settlement to be legal, it must be temporary. Although the Court accepted the IDF position that the Beit-El settlement was necessary for security and agreed to the settlement's continued existence, its rationale in the Beit-El case was important. In October 1979, the Court reiterated these principles in the famous Elon Moreh case, in which it prohibited the expropriation of private land for settlement. The HCJ saw Elon Moreh as a permanent settlement motivated by political reasons; therefore, it ordered the settlement dismantled.

Following the ruling on this case, the Begin government changed its tactics: while abstaining from further confiscation of private land for settlements, it focused on settling Israelis on lands it declared "state lands." The government lawyers discovered a forgotten Ottoman law according to which any uncultivated land "beyond shouting range" of the closest village or town was the sultan's property. Considering itself the sultan's heir, the government laid claim to these extensive "state lands." The channel to the HCJ for people claiming ownership of "state land" was subsequently blocked by the establishment of a military review board to consider such claims.

Land Acquisition, Use, and Control

Under the Alignment the overall settlement policy of the Israeli government was designed to assure that, within the context of an overall peace agreement, Israel would be able to effectively claim parts of the territories and eventually annex them. For that purpose, the Alignment government allowed and sometimes encouraged the establishment of Jewish settlements along the Jordan River and in the Etzion Bloc. On the other hand, Likud's settlement policy was designed to guarantee the total annexation of the West Bank and the Gaza Strip by Israel. Both political positions had a far-reaching impact on the government policy in regard to land acquisition, ownership, and use in the territories. In turn, this policy had a significant impact on the status of human rights in the West Bank and the Gaza Strip.

The initial land acquisition policy of the government was politically and legally cautious. In July 1967, the military government issued an order forbidding any land transaction without a written permit. When Defense Minister Moshe Dayan proposed in 1973 that private Israeli corporations and Israelis as individuals be allowed to purchase lands in the territories, he was turned down by a vote in the government.[13] The early land policy was clearly not to allow private interests into the territories' land market.

The Alignment government in the post-1967 era emphasized the purchasing of land for security and military purposes only. It maintained that this policy was in accordance with international legal norms, specifically ARTICLE 52 of the Hague Regulations (1907). Some military orders issued by the authorities in the territories proclaimed privately owned lands to be "vital for immediate military need." Although such lands theoretically remained under private ownership, the owners lost their rights of possession and use. Jewish settlements were built on such lands. The total area seized for "military use" under such provisions was estimated at 35,000–50,000 *dunams* (1 *dunam* = 0.25 acre).[14] This method of acquiring land was commonly used especially under Alignment rule (1967–77). Although it was argued that the establishment of civilian settlements on land taken for military purpose was inconsistent with the Hague Regulations, the Israeli High Court of Justice accepted the government's position that Jewish settlements on the West Bank were an essential part of Israel's defense.

Additional areas in the West Bank were closed on the grounds that they were "security zones" needed by the army for training, firing ranges, and similar functions. Some of those lands were later allocated to Jewish civilian settlements, the most notable case being that of Kiryat Arba, near Hebron. By 1988 these restricted military areas amounted to about 1.11 million *dunams* or, by some calculations, 53 percent of all the land seized by the Israeli government on the West Bank.[15] By early 1985, as many as twenty-three closure orders were in affect in the territories. Although most of this land was categorized as "state lands" and was used for training areas, roughly 80,000 *dunams* were closed within populated areas and allocated for Jewish settlements.[16]

Following the 1967 war, the Israeli government issued an order that property, including land, belonging to a person who had left the area was to be forfeited by the custodian of abandoned property. According to some estimates, the custodian has seized a total of 430,000 *dunams* since the 1967 war.[17] Most of this land (350,000 *dunams*) is stony and nonarable. Of the arable land, some was transferred to relatives of the absentees, some was leased to them, and some was leased to Jewish settlers. The latter category is the most problematical. Palestinians and others have argued that "the Custodian is handling 'abandoned' property as if he were an absolute owner and transferring it, usually through 49-year leases, to third parties to use to establish Jewish settlement."[18]

The declaration of West Bank areas as "state lands" has resulted in the largest transfer of lands to Israeli hands. The Likud government of Menachem Begin adopted this method as its main vehicle of land acquisition, and abandoned Alignment's more modest and cautious (and legally more defensible) technique of declaring lands crucial for security. Whereas Labor's legal approach emphasized the temporary nature of land acquisition, Likud's emphasized its permanent nature; whereas Alignment's activity resulted in limited transfer of lands, Likud's led to large-scale transfer.

In 1980 the custodian of abandoned property began to declare uncultivated, unregistered land "state land" on the basis of an Ottoman land law of 1855, which identified such land as *mawat* (dead land). The new approach was highly problematical: (a) the burden of proof regarding the ownership of the land was put not on the custodian seizing the land but on the Palestinian farmers from whom the land was taken; (b) the appeal of the custodian's decision was vested in a review board composed of officials of the military government, not in a local court or even the Israeli HCJ; (c) the definition of "state lands" was not the one used by the Jordanian government, in whose name the land was seized; (d) the declarations of lands as "state lands" were clearly made to transfer land, on a long-term basis, to Israeli civilian settlers—in this sense these declarations violated the provisions of Geneva IV in regard to population transfer.

Despite these difficulties, by the mid-1980s 2,150,000 *dunams*, or 40 percent of the area of the West Bank, were declared state lands by the military authorities, acting to fulfill the Likud policy. This area included government lands (527,000 *dunams* previously registered in the name of the Jordanian government and now transferred to Israel as the occupying power). The Likud's new legal approach to land acquisition resulted in the additional transfer of more than 1.5 million *dunams* of land to Israel.[19]

Benvenisti emphasizes that "until 1980 the Israeli government did not view uncultivated lands of the *mawat* and *miri* categories as government lands, since it continued Jordanian practice," as it had to do according to international law.[20] *Mawat* was considered dead land because it lay further from a village "than the human voice could be heard," in the words of the Ottoman Land Code. The Ottoman system and those which followed it, the British and the Jordanian, acknowledged that the land surrounding the village belonged to the villagers "as common pastures or for the future development of the village." *Miri* was land over which the sultan continued to have ultimate ownership but "whose use he has granted to the public under certain conditions." In 1953 the Jordanians removed all restrictions on the possessors of *miri* land. Similarly, they declared all *miri* lands within the municipal areas to be legally held by their owners.[21] The Likud policy broke with this long tradition, declaring *mawat, miri,* and *matruke* (land for public purposes) to be "state land."

The policy of declaring "state lands" in accordance with this broad definition reflected the determination of Likud leaders to intensify the Israeli settlement activities in the territories. The land policy was an organic outgrowth of the more general, annexationist policy. The much smaller areas of land transferred for Jewish settlement under the Alignment were perceived as insufficient to facilitate the large-scale settlement effort of the Likud.

The mode of land purchasing also changed under Likud. Under Alignment, land purchasing was done by the government for national goals supported by a solid public consensus. When the Likud came to power, the government lifted the ban on private land purchasing by Jews on the West Bank (September 1979). As expected, and as the government hoped, a rush of land speculation began. Land values went up, and some Arabs could not resist the temptation or the pressure to sell. The process was accompanied by massive forgeries and coercive acts.

These activities were documented in a series of articles published by the reputable Israeli daily, *Ha'aretz*, in September-October 1985. *Ha'aretz* wrote that the Likud government and the police minister did not want a broad inquiry into private land purchasing in the West Bank. The sacred goal was grabbing land by all means. Revelations regarding land purchasing on the West Bank could have harmed this goal. Thus, the Likud government was involved in covering up the schemes for land grabbing in the territories, thereby promoting its annexationist policies.

Benvenisti believes that the total area sold to Israeli public and private bodies amounted to 125,000 *dunams*, of which 25,000 were fraudulently acquired. He describes "a national scandal" in which plots with dubious titles were sold, Arabs were forced to sell their land by intimidation, and shady operations were carried out by both Jewish and Arab speculators. Because land acquisition was considered "a patriotic endeavor," speculators enjoyed the "close cooperation of the military government."[22]

Under the legal guise of declaring an area "state land," the Likud government initiated extensive Jewish settlement, a process that dramatically changed the political atmosphere in the occupied territories. The "state land" rationale was of questionable legality. It took advantage of the fact that the land situation on the West Bank was highly complex and unclear, and that two-thirds of the area had not yet gone through formal registration. Using this situation for political purposes, Israel's Land Authority issued a directive stating that if an area was not registered and cultivated, one could assume that it could be claimed as "state land." Thus, with a stroke of a pen the Likud government laid claim to 2.15 million *dunams* on the West Bank (May 1980), declaring it "state land."[23]

The land policy of the Begin government left the Palestinian population on the West Bank bewildered, radicalized, and anxious. Even the moderate elements in the territories lost faith in the government. Said one old Arab farmer, "I don't care who governs. They are all bad. First we had the Turks, then the British, and the

Jordanians, and now the Israelis. Everyone wanted our money and the Turks forced us to serve in their army. But we never had a government that wanted to take the land under our feet."[24]

The last few years prior to the Intifada saw a slowdown in Israeli land acquisition. By 1985 about 40 percent of the West Bank land had been registered for the use of Jews, close to the maximum that could have been registered through the various legal means. However, Shehadeh maintains that the land over which Israel actually had gained control approached 60 percent (he includes in his estimate military zones, parks, and land expropriated but not registered).[25] Benvenisti estimates that by 1986, on the eve of the Intifada, 41 percent of the West Bank was under direct Israeli possession (2,268,500 dunams) and an additional 11 percent (570,000 *dunams*) was under severe use restrictions, for a total of 52 percent.[26] Although the specific numbers differ, it is clear that the process was extensive.

The land use policy of the military government in the territories, as differentiated from the land acquisition policy, has also had a dramatic and negative effect on the Palestinian population. Some observers have found Likud's land use policy to be anti-Arab and extremely threatening to the local population. First, the shift from military interest in the Jordan valley to political interest in the entire West Bank created a natural anxiety in the Palestinian population centers. Second, Likud planners began restricting Arab construction outside Palestinian towns and villages, a process some called ghettoization; placed Jewish settlements so as to separate Arab towns and prevent continuous Palestinian regions; and attempted to encircle Arab-populated areas with Jewish settlements. This policy intensified following the beginning of the Intifada, as reported by the *Christian Science Monitor* (July 5, 1989) and other sources. It was perceived by the local inhabitants as provocative, especially because it was carried out within the publicly announced, grand annexationist schemes of Greater Israel. On the whole, the land use and control policy on the West Bank has been a well-integrated design that served the needs of the settlers and pressured the local population to surrender its economic interests and political will.

In general, the land use classification system on the West Bank has become politically controlled. The most important question regarding land use has become not what function the land is being used for but who controls the land, Israeli Jews or Palestinian

Arabs. Benvenisti has argued that the formal land classification has in fact become a cover-up for the actual use of it: "The classification 'rocky land, unsuitable for cultivation' means 'land which may be declared state land and transferred to Israeli use and ownership.' Declaration of a 'nature reserve' means taking it out of Arab hands and transferring it to the Nature Reserve Authority 'to prevent uncontrolled Arab development.' Designating an area as 'essential military territory' means opening it up for the construction of Israeli settlement."[27]

Shehadeh has pointed out that Palestinian lands not only have been expropriated but also have been subjected to severe use restrictions. Thus, some private lands cannot be used because of archaeological considerations, others have been barred from use due to zoning measures (or, more precisely, the withholding of building permits), and so on. The Palestinians and many others have felt that the complicated laws regulating land use have been selectively applied.[28]

The legal status of Israeli land acquisition, use, and control has become highly problematical. First, according to the international law of belligerent occupation (e.g., ARTICLE 43 of the Hague Convention of 1907), the occupying power has to maintain the legal process regarding land as it was when the occupation occurred. This requirement has not been met, especially not by the Likud governments. The policy of declaring huge parts of the West Bank as "state lands," and similar regulations affecting smaller parts of the West Bank (e.g., areas considered important for archaeological excavations), have dramatically changed the picture regarding land acquisition, use, and control in the territories. Also, many procedural matters regarding lands have been unilaterally revised, leaving the local courts, which enjoyed considerable power over land matters prior to 1967, to rule only on disagreements between Palestinians.

Second, according to many sources, including Israeli sources, the process of settlement on the West Bank has often been accompanied by illegal practices, among them the forgery of landowners' documents, pressure on individuals to sell their land, and deception. Although this part of the settlement story has not been fully documented to date, there is sufficient evidence to indicate large-scale illegality backed by powerful political interests.

ARTICLE 17 of the Universal Declaration of Human Rights seems to have been violated. It states that (1) everyone has the right to own property, and (2) no one shall be arbitrarily deprived of his property. More specifically, ARTICLE 23(g) of the Hague Regulations forbids the occupying country to "destroy or seize the enemy's property, unless such destruction or seizure is imperatively demanded by the necessities of war." The Likud settlement policy and land acquisition have not been demanded by the necessities of war; they have been driven by ideological considerations.

Third, the very essence of the settlement activity—the establishment of Jewish communities in the territories—has been problematical in the eyes of numerous commentators. ARTICLE 49 of Geneva IV clearly states, "The occupying power shall not deport or transfer parts of its own civilian population into the territory it occupies." Although the placement of soldiers and possibly even paramilitary units in occupied territories is authorized by the law of belligerent occupation, this is clearly not the case in regard to civilians or permanent civilian settlements.

The Settlers

The Israeli settlement effort in the territories and its human rights implications cannot be fully understood without attention to the Jewish settlers.[29] The settlers have become an important factor in determining the type and the extent of human rights violations in the territories.

The settlements established by the Alignment government in the period immediately following the Six-Day War were small, located away from Arab towns, and agricultural. The interaction between their inhabitants, individuals belonging mostly to Israel's labor movement, and the local Arab population was minimal. Although one may be able to raise questions concerning the legality of these settlements, they had little impact on the local population.

When the Likud under Begin came to power, the nature of the settlements as well as of the settlers changed, with unforeseen consequences for human rights. Even though the Likud was ideologically committed to the idea of retaining the West Bank, it had very little settlement experience, organization, or personnel; the Revisionists lacked the tools for practically affecting the annexation of the territories. This was the background for the emergence of the political alliance between Gush Emunim and the Begin government.

Despite their different philosophies and approaches (with Begin's emphasis on Israel's historical rights in the territories and the Gush tendency to employ a religious rationale), the Begin government and Gush Emunim shared the dream of Jewish control over Judea, Samaria, and Gaza, and they had something concrete to offer to each other. The alliance dramatically changed the character of the Israeli settlement in the West Bank and, with it, the nature of the relationships between Jews and Arabs in the occupied territories.

Begin needed the Gush in several different ways:

1. As a cadre of young, enthusiastic settlers, willing to go to the places that proved unattractive to other Israelis (the rough terrain and politically controversial territory of the Samarian mountains).

2. As a political instrument for pressuring an unfriendly government (Rabin's government until 1977), for settling in all parts of Eretz Israel, for supporting the Likud government in its annexationist policy, and for forming an ever-ready, powerful lobby that would prevent any future Israeli government from even entertaining the idea of a territorial compromise.

3. As the glue between the different parts of the new right in Israel: the old-time Revisionists and Herutniks;[30] the ultranationalist religious circles; and the activist, expansionist elements within the socialist camp.[31]

The Gush proved to be Begin's strongest ally. It was a catalyst for radicalization of the Israeli society, as it had been within the National Religious Party.

A number of factors propelled Gush Emunim into national and international prominence, giving it great influence over Israel's policy. First, the Gush reaped the fruit of religious revival of unprecedented proportions among religious and secular Israelis alike, a revival that could be psychologically explained by the 1967 trauma of national crisis and victory. A full-fledged theology emerged around the historical-spiritual meaning of the Six Day-War, and the adherents of that theology, who concentrated in Gush Emunim, believed that the 1967 crisis was nothing short of *Atchalta De'geula,* the beginning of the long-prophesied redemption.[32]

Second, Gush Emunim, even though a rather small organization, enjoyed the ideological support of numerous rabbis and others in Israel's religious establishment.[33] Thus, Yitzhak Nissim, chief Sephardic rabbi of Israel, said: "According to the Torah law no Jew, including the Israeli government, is allowed to return even one inch of the land of Eretz Israel."[34] Other noted rabbis made similar arguments, openly claiming that the question of the occupied territories was not political and military but religious and spiritual.

Third, and most important, the Gush enjoyed the sympathy of the entire Israeli right, headed by Menachem Begin (first as the leader of the opposition and then as Israel's prime minister). The support was essential for Gush Emunim's development and survival under an unfriendly government (1974–77) and for its flourishing following Likud's victory.

The Gush people first appeared in the occupied areas in 1968; during early days, they set the pattern of settlement for years to come. In April 1968, a few days before Passover, several dozen Jews headed by Rabbi Moshe Levinger asked General Uzi Narkiss of the IDF Central Command for permission to spend Passover night in Hebron, promising that they would leave the next day. Narkiss authorized the request, but on the next day the group remained in Hebron and declared itself "the first settlers renewing the Jewish community of Hebron."[35]

Gush Emunim was formally and publicly organized following the 1973 war, when increasing signs of serious diplomatic movement began to occur. It quickly became the focal point for radical, unauthorized settlement activity in the West Bank, activity designed to embarrass the Rabin government and undermine any movement toward peace. In this activity the Gush enjoyed the sympathy of its ideological allies in the Likud. Following Likud's 1977 election victory, the Gush settlement program became virtually identical to that of the government. Under Begin, the Gush served as a leading force in settlement,[36] moving into areas where others would not and serving as the spearhead of the opposition to any territorial compromise.[37] It quickly became the representative of most West Bank settlers and effectively controlled their institutions.

Gush Emunim's initiatives regarding the location, timing, and impact of settlements fit perfectly with Begin's political objectives. From the start, Gush intentionally selected settlement sites upon which there was no national consensus, and where the presence of Jews would make any Jewish-Arab compromise impossible. Their objective was to generate the greatest possible provocation of the local population. Gush Emunim settlements in central Samaria, near and even inside major Arab population centers (Hebron, Nablus, Rammalah), met those requirements.

The time of the settling act was carefully selected to undermine the delicate peace process following the 1973 war. In 1974, when the possibility of an Israeli withdrawal in the Jericho area (as a gesture to King Hussein) was discussed, complementing Israeli withdrawals on the Egyptian and Syrian fronts, the Gush demanded to settle in Jericho. In March 1979, during the week when the Knesset decided to endorse the peace treaty with Egypt, which required the dismantling of Israeli settlements on Egyptian soil, Gush Emunim, with the full assistance of the Begin government, established a new settlement, Shikmona, in the Rafah region.

The Likud government willingly cooperated with Gush Emunim's actions. In March 1983, the Begin government approved eight new settlements on the crest of the Samarian hills near the centers of the Arab populations. Viktor Shemtov, M.K., said that the purpose was to slam the door in the face of King Hussein and block any political compromise.[38] The eight settlements were Begin's reply to the Reagan plan and to the subsequent Hussein-Arafat negotiations.

The cooperation between the Begin government and Gush Emunim was not limited to settlement policy. Possibly a more important, though less visible, aspect of the cooperation was ideological. Rabbis close to the Gush often talked about the Arabs in terms similar to those used by Begin, Defense Minister Sharon, and Chief of Staff Eitan: the battle against the Arabs was considered an "obligatory war"; the Arabs were said to have no right to possess any part of the land, because they were like the seven Canaanite tribes; they must admit that the political sovereignty in the land belonged only to the Jewish people or leave the country —indeed, in the future they *would* have to leave.[39] These views were the root cause for major human rights violations: they gave them ideological justification.

Even though Gush Emunim and the Begin government started from different philosophical perspectives, they ended up at a similar place on the central question of the future of the West Bank and the status of its Arab inhabitants. Both (a) supported the eventual annexation of the West Bank while signaling their willingness to give up (though never in a final way) their demand for the East Bank; (b) believed that Arabs could enjoy personal rights as individuals but could not have political rights as a collective group in Eretz Israel; (c) accepted the means of settlement, coercion and land seizure, as legitimate for imposing Jewish rule over the West Bank and its inhabitants. The agreement on the practical means enabled Begin to use the Gush as a major instrument of political control in the occupied territories.

During Begin's tenure in office, Gush Emunim became a main instrument not only of settlement but also of coercion. By orders of Chief of Staff Eitan, the settlers were organized into units of the IDF Territorial Defense. All settlements in the territories were defined as border settlements, and their population was heavily armed by the IDF. Within a short time, these small bands of farmers-settlers turned into settlers-soldiers and were used to control the increasingly restless Palestinian population in Judea and Samaria.

An important phenomenon in the territories was the enthusiasm of some Gush members for using violence. Many cases of vigilantism by Gush settlers were reported. Avraham Achituv, the former director of Israel's General Security Services (Shin Bet, equivalent to the FBI), thought Gush Emunim settlements had become a "psychological hothouse for the growth of Jewish terror" on the West Bank.[40] He wrote that since the rise of the Likud, the settlers learned that their actions, even if illegal, "are made kosher because of the political homefront that backs them." Achituv's words, unusual for the head of the secretive Shin Bet, were later substantiated at length by a committee of jurists appointed by Israel's attorney general and headed by his deputy.[41]

It seems that the Begin government had taken consistent actions that would inevitably produce violence between Jews and Arabs in the occupied territories. Not only had the government let it be known that it eventually intended to annex the West Bank and Gaza, but the most radical Jews of all, Gush Emunim's and Kach's zealots, were allowed to take up residence in the heart of the Arab population.[42] Although the support of the Begin government was considered insufficient by some of the Gush members, who organized a terrorist underground whose members were subsequently convicted of committing murders, attempting assassinations of Arab leaders, and planning attacks on holy sites, the Begin government was considerably more generous toward Gush Emunim than any previous Israeli government.[43]

It ought to be emphasized that many religious people in Israel opposed Gush Emunim, its use of the Jewish religious traditions to support nationalist causes, and its general philosophy. Important rabbis, such as Chief Rabbi Untermann, specifically stated that the territories should be traded for peace. On the whole, the Gush was unsuccessful among members of the religious kibbutzim, and many religious intellectuals vehemently opposed it. In 1975 the latter organized in a movement called Oz Ve'Shalom (Courage and Peace) to block the nationalist erosion within the religious camp, which was reflected in the appearance of the Gush. Although Oz Ve'Shalom had among its leaders some of Israel's most prominent intellectuals (including Professor Ephraim Auerbach, president of the Israeli Academy of Sciences), it never became a mass movement, nor did it gain the political clout of the Gush. Oz Ve'Shalom, as well as individual religious thinkers such as Yishayahu Leibovitz,[44] maintained that the Gush/Begin positions were un-Jewish, nonhumanitarian, and destructive. They emphasized the moral degradation involved in these positions and argued against mixing religion with politics (let alone using religion for political purpose), as well as against what they saw as false messianism.

Members of Gush Emunim and other West Bank settlers had the greatest impact in terms of human rights when they acted as vigilantes by taking the law into their own hands and committing acts of violence against the inhabitants of the territories. Although on occasion it was declared by leaders of the settlers that they had no intention of initiating actions to maintain their own security, recognizing that this was the role of the army,[45] in fact the settlers as individuals, and sometimes as groups, often reacted on their own to Arab attacks or even initiated violence in the territories. On numerous occasions settlers arrived at Arab towns, villages, and refugee camps and randomly committed acts of violence and destruction, often attacking not only the Arab residents but also Israeli soldiers trying to restore order. Some Israeli commentators believe that because the settlers realized that Jews were not settling the West Bank in large numbers, extremists among them were trying to encourage an Arab exodus as an alternative.[46]

Numerous violent attacks by settlers on Palestinians have been dealt with ineffectively, or not at all, by the army, the police, and the judicial system. In an article published in 1982, Knesset member and law school professor Amnon Rubinstein reported that settlers often refused to answer questions put to them by the police regarding incidents in the West Bank, a phenomenon also documented in the Karp Report. Wrote *Ha'aretz* about the situation: "The police do not dare question or arrest Jewish suspects, fearing a violent confrontation with the settlers."[47]

Even prior to the beginning of the Intifada, there were numerous reports of settler attacks leading to deaths, severe injuries, and serious property damage. Such reports were written by Palestinians,[48] Israelis,[49] and others.[50] Benvenisti and others reported on a pattern of continuous and ever-increasing severe attacks by Jewish vigilantes. These involved opening fire, smashing windshields of parked vehicles belonging to Arabs, burning houses, and beating passersby. Severe attacks occurred on the eve of the Intifada when settlers in large number attacked the town of Kalkilya and the Deheishe refugee camp. Although these attacks followed the death of a Jewish woman caused by a gasoline bomb, they were nevertheless classical vigilante actions.

Many observers of the events in the territories noted that vigilante activity by the settlers went unpunished in the vast majority of cases. Not only had settlers refused to cooperate with police and IDF investigations, but in many cases they refused to obey orders of Israeli soldiers and officers and sometimes attacked them physically. Although the penalty code for the Palestinians became more and more severe, this was not the case for the West Bank Jewish settlers.

The sense of power among the settlers, leading to violations of human rights, can be explained by several factors. First, their membership in the security forces, such as service in the IDF's Territorial Defense Units. As a result of such service, the settlers were well armed. Benvenisti estimated that on the eve of the Intifada the settlers possessed no fewer than 10,000 firearms of all types, as well as other military equipment, including radio sets and vehicles.[51]

Second, the settlers had developed tremendous clout within Israel's political system: some politicians, especially on the extreme right, supported the settlers wholeheartedly; others feared them. On occasion, the Israeli political and security system responded radically due to the pressure of the settlers.[52]

Third, the strong ideological belief system of many of the settlers, especially those belonging to Gush Emunim, has led to excesses. The settlers have developed an ideology based on the belief that they act for a higher good and on behalf of the entire nation. Some have shown themselves unlikely to be dissuaded by humanitarian considerations.[53]

Beginning in December 1987, with the start of the Intifada, the rate and intensity of acts of settlers' vigilantism increased dramatically, so much so that many in Israel and elsewhere came to believe that "vigilante action by Jewish settlers could push the country to the brink of civil warfare."[54] Settlers attacked not only Arabs but also IDF personnel (including high-ranking officers), political opponents, and members of the international and national media. Some Knesset members argued that the settlers had established "an armed militia" that carried out, on a daily basis, actions to punish, terrorize, and take revenge against the Arab inhabitants.[55]

Organized violent activity against Arabs by Jewish settlers, especially individuals associated with (and often leaders of) Gush Emunim, was not a new phenomenon. In July 1985, members of a group known as the Jewish Underground in the Territories or the Jewish Terror Group were convicted by an Israeli court for an attempt on the lives of three Arab mayors (in retaliation for a Fatah attack on Hadassah House in Hebron in May 1980, in which six settlers were slain), an attack on the Islamic College in Hebron in which three students were killed (July 1983, in response to the murder of yeshiva student Aaron Gross), a plot to blow up the Dome of the Rock on Temple Mount in Jerusalem in preparation for the rebuilding of the Temple, and a plan to attack Arab buses in East Jerusalem with explosives. In response to the arrest, conviction, and imprisonment of the perpetrators, a lobby of more than twenty Knesset members from the religious parties, Tehiya and the Likud, was organized to assist in the early release of the convicted men, all of whom were associated with Gush Emunim.[56]

Other groups of radicals have operated in Israel and in the territories as well. The Lifta Group tried to blow up the Dome of the Rock. Members of the group were brought to trial. A group known as TNT, representing extreme religious-nationalistic views, planted grenades in churches and mosques in Jerusalem, opened fire on Arab buses, and committed violence against Arabs and Jews. Additional groups were established after the beginning of the Intifada.

One of the features common to all of these groups has been not only their violent and conspiratorial nature but also their inclination to disregard the human rights of the Arabs in Israel and in the territories, and, on occasion, of Jews who disagree with their goals or methods. Thus, the Kach party (established by the late Rabbi Meir Kahane) has openly sought the expulsion of all Arabs from Israel and the territories, and some of its positions have been adopted by others in Israel (e.g., Moledet).

Yet, it must be emphasized that the ideas represented by Kahane have not been adopted by most Israelis. The Israeli political system, which reacted to the Underground and Lifta groups by legal means, reacted to Kach politically: Kahane was not allowed to run in the Knesset election in 1988 and, as a result, lost his seat.[57]

On the whole, the settlement activity in the West Bank and in the Gaza Strip resulted in widespread violation of human rights in the territories. The close contact between Jews and Arabs, within the context of an ongoing military occupation, precipitated continuous, relentless conflict. The connection between settlement and human rights violations has been intimate, immediate, and quite negative.

3

๛

Measures of
Enforcement and Punishment

THE prolonged Israeli occupation of the West Bank and the Gaza Strip, accompanied by an increasingly vigorous settlement policy —especially since 1977, when Likud emerged as the dominant political force in Israel—has generated increasingly active resistance from the inhabitants of the territories. The paradox has been that although Israel has succeeded brilliantly in defeating the military challenge put to it by the Arab states, as well as the one presented by the Palestine Liberation Organization, the stubborn refusal of the inhabitants of the West Bank and the Gaza Strip to accept the occupation as a fait accompli has hardened as the occupation has stretched in time and deepened in obtrusiveness. Although some of these processes remained hidden for a long time, the explosion of December 1987, the Intifada, made them apparent to the whole world.

The determined resistance of the Palestinian inhabitants of the territories to quiet acceptance of the de facto annexation of the West Bank and Gaza led to a harsh Israeli response. The harshest possible legal response, the imposition of the death penalty, was for all intents and purposes canceled by Israel, but other tough legal measures were not. Although widespread and indiscriminate shooting at rioters and demonstrators was not sanctioned by the Israeli government, other severe penalties were adopted and extensively applied.

In this chapter, three of the harshest penalties against convicted, and often suspected, persons in the territories will be considered: the policy of expulsion or deportation, the policy of detention (especially administrative detention), and the policy of house demolition or sealing.

The policies on deportations, detentions, and demolition have a few characteristics in common. First, these have been among the most powerful punitive measures in the arsenal of the Israeli military authorities. Second, these punitive measures have generated worldwide attention resulting in "bad press" for the Israeli authorities. Third, the implementation of all three policies has led to condemnations by many in Israel and abroad as violating the norms of international law and reasonable procedures of due process. Finally, an argument has been made that these policies, especially deportation and administrative detention, have been used against political activists and not exclusively against those indicted or even suspected of terrorist activities or security violations.

It must be emphasized at the outset that none of these arguments remains unchallenged. Some analysts have suggested that although Israel's policies have indeed been tough, they have been considerably softer than the policies adopted by other democracies in times of war and crisis. Other analysts have observed that the press has tended to apply a double standard to Israel and to judge it too harshly. Some international lawyers have defended Israel's policies as conforming to the legal standards of the international community. These counterarguments deserve serious attention when discussing the human rights situation in the territories.

This chapter will examine these arguments and counterarguments regarding deportations, detections, and demolitions in the territories. It also will assess the effectiveness of these measures as political tools and evaluate the world's response to them. Above all, the chapter will assess the argument that those measures constitute a systematic deviation from fundamental human rights and evaluate it against the counterargument that sees these measures as necessary for maintaining the security of the state of Israel.

Expulsion

One of the most controversial policies of the Israeli authorities has been that of expulsion or deportation of Palestinians from the territories. Both the Israeli authorities and the Palestinians have perceived deportation as an extremely severe punishment. Between 1967 and the mid-1980s about 2,000 persons were deported from the territories.[1] The policy has been subject to dramatic fluctuations reflecting different and changing views of its effectiveness. Thus, although no new deportation orders were issued in 1989,[2] in January 1992, following the killing of several Israeli civilians, the deportation of twelve Palestinians was ordered. Although none of the twelve was charged with the killings, they had been accused by the government of inciting violence. All deportation orders were eventually canceled, however, and the twelve Palestinians were sent to administrative detention.

On December 17, 1992, the government deported (to Lebanon) 415 Palestinians alleged to be associated with two fundamentalist Muslim organizations. The deportation order followed a series of Palestinian attacks in which a number of Israelis were murdered. In an important ruling on the deportation policy, the Israeli High Court of Justice decided (5973/927) that although the authorities may issue deportation orders against individuals, general or collective orders of the type issued by the government are illegal. Moreover, the HCJ stated that each individual has a right to be heard before an expulsion order is carried out.

The 1949 Fourth Geneva Convention, to which Israel is party, explicitly prohibits deportation of protected persons from occupied territories. ARTICLE 49 of Geneva IV states in its opening paragraph: "Individual or mass forcible transfers, as well as deportations of protected people from occupied territories to the territory of the Occupying Power or to that of any other country, occupied or not, are prohibited, regardless of their motive."

Despite the apparent clarity of that provision, the military government has used expulsion as a weapon in its punitive arsenal almost continuously since 1967. The Israeli HCJ has refused to block the deportations even though not only the international community but even some Israeli authorities on human rights and international law have emphasized that ARTICLE 49 clearly bans any type of expulsion.[3] Opponents of the deportation policy have argued that individuals have been deported not for personal involvement in acts of terrorism but for political activity.

Israeli newspapers have reported that some of the deportees have had long-standing reputations as political moderates. For example, in 1986, Akram Haniyeh, the editor of the Jerusalem paper *a-Sha'ab*, was expelled. An editorial in the *Jerusalem Post*, published under the title "Expulsion—for What?," stated that Haniyeh was deported for political, not terrorist, activity.[4] The *Post* thought that the authorities knew a trial would be inconvenient and embarrassing, and therefore chose a deportation, essentially a nonjudicial process. In 1988 a well-known moderate and professor of physics at Birzeit University, Dr. Taysir Aruri, was served with a deportation order. Over 1,100 of the world's leading physicists, including sixteen Nobel laureates and more than sixty members of the U.S. National Academy of Sciences, appealed the decision. These are only two cases in what the opponents of the expulsion policy considered a large category of political deportees with well-known moderate views.

The international community has been almost unanimous in condemning the deportation policy. Condemnation of the practice has come from human rights bodies, individual governments, and global organizations such as the United Nations. On November 16, 1979, the U.N. General Assembly approved, 132–1, a resolution urging Israel to cancel the deportation of the Nablus mayor, Basam Shaka'ah. On January 5, 1988, the Security Council unanimously adopted Resolution 607, which condemned the deportation policy on the basis of the Fourth Geneva Convention.[5] The annual U.S. Department of State reports on human rights have consistently criticized the deportation policy.[6]

The frequency of deportations from the territories has changed quite dramatically throughout the years of Israeli rule over the West Bank and Gaza Strip. Whereas this instrument was used heavily in the first decade of occupation, its usage declined somewhat in the late 1970s and had virtually been suspended by the early 1980s. In the mid-1980s, the measure was reintroduced, and since the beginning of the Intifada, it has been used quite extensively. Sometime during 1989, a decision was made by the Israeli government to suspend its use. It was renewed, with vigor, in 1992.

In general, there are relatively minor differences between various sources in assessments of the number of deportees. According to official Israeli figures, between 1967 and 1977 as many as 1,180 persons were deported from the territories.[7] Lesch's total figure of deportees for the same period is 1,151 persons.[8] A Palestinian source estimated the number of deportees during the first decade of occupation at 1,156.[9]

In the context of numerical fluctuations and the factors that may determine them, it is interesting to note that between 1980 and 1985 few, if any, deportations occurred.[10] When Labor, under

Yitzhak Rabin, took over the Defense Ministry, the deportations were reinstituted. Prior to Likud's ascendance to power in 1977, deportations were heavily used by Labor. One explanation was the enhanced pressure from the Israeli right wing, especially the settler movement. The Labor government apparently felt the need to demonstrate toughness in dealing with the Palestinian challenge in the territories: frequent deportations were established as a political instrument.

The frequency of deportations has increased significantly since the beginning of the Intifada. However, the pace is still lagging far behind the level established in the late 1960s and the early 1970s.[11] Whereas only nine Palestinians were deported in 1987, an increase of 300 percent (thirty-six deportees) was registered in 1988.[12] By July 1989, the number of deportees since the beginning of the Intifada had reached fifty-five. On August 17, 1988, as many as twenty-five Palestinians were served with deportation orders, the largest number since the occupation began.[13] On December 17, 1992, 415 Palestinians were deported to Lebanon, a new record.

The legality of the deportation policy has been challenged vigorously since 1967, especially because it is explicitly prohibited by the 1949 Geneva Convention.[14] The legal instrument used by the military government to deport individuals from the territories has been the Defense (Emergency) Regulations introduced by the British government in Mandatory Palestine in 1945. The regulations gave the high commissioner for Palestine and the British military authorities enormous powers, frequently used against the Jewish underground groups that fought to free the country of its foreign rulers. The leaders of the Jewish community in Palestine bitterly denounced the regulations.

The legality of the DER as a foundation for the Israeli security measures in the territories has been challenged on a number of grounds. It was suggested that the British revoked the regulations prior to their departure from Palestine and that the Jordanians never accepted their applicability to the West Bank (and sometimes, as in the case of deportations, had enacted specific provisions contradicting the DER). Because the occupant may not change the existing law in an occupied territory, the argument goes, the DER cannot be applied now to the West Bank. Some analysts have thought that Geneva IV "clearly supersedes earlier non-Israeli legislation," such as the DER, and makes it illegal.[15]

The Israeli government has rejected this position: it has considered the DER as part of the law in the territories. To eliminate any doubt, the military government issued Order 224, ARTICLE 3 of which specifically and unequivocally stated that the DER applies to the territories.[16]

The Israeli government has used Regulation 112 of the Defense Emergency Regulations as the legal foundation for the deportation policy. Regulation 112 authorized the high commissioner for Palestine to deport any person from the country. Although it was canceled in Israel proper in 1980, on the grounds that it was cruel and infringed on basic rights, equivalent action was not taken in the territories.[17] Nevertheless, even the Israeli human rights organization B'Tselem, which has consistently criticized the Israeli government's policies in the occupied territories, stated that ARTICLE 112 of the DER is still in force there because similar orders were enacted in the West Bank by the Jordanians and there were no legal revisions in Gaza.[18]

ARTICLE 49 of Geneva IV and Israel's DER 112(1) as it is applied to the territories are obviously incompatible. Nevertheless, some jurists, in Israel and elsewhere, have defended the practice of deportation, even in the face of worldwide criticism.[19] A number of arguments have been introduced. First, in an official decision the Israeli High Court of Justice ruled that ARTICLE 49 of Geneva IV relates solely to mass deportations and not to cases where individual persons are expelled.[20] This argument rests on the assumption that ARTICLE 49 was specifically and exclusively written in response to the experience of World War II, during which millions of people were deported from their native lands. The point of this argument is that to compare Israel's selective deportation policy with the monumental, horrific experience of World War II is to offer an invalid comparison and ignore the different contexts involved.

Second, Chief Justice Meir Shamgar argued that deported persons were saboteurs, members of terrorist organizations, and persons engaged in acts against state security and public order; therefore, they deserved expulsion.

Third, Shamgar and others argued that if the choice for the Israeli authorities is between keeping saboteurs and terrorists in administrative detention for an unlimited period and deporting them to a neighboring Arab state, deportation is to be preferred on humanitarian grounds. Thus, the deportation policy was defended as relatively humane.

Fourth, supporters of the deportation policy defended the practice of expelling individuals to Jordan, common especially in the early days of the occupation. They maintained that such expulsion was compatible with ARTICLE 49 of Geneva IV because individuals were not deported to the territory of the occupying power (Israel) or to the territory of another country (the West Bank and Jordan were under the same sovereignty).

Fifth, those who justified expulsion often fell back on the argument that the Israeli government and the military authorities in the territories are not bound by any of the provisions of Geneva IV (see chapter 1).

These five pro-expulsion arguments, and similar ones, have not been accepted by the vast majority of the international community. As for the first argument, although it is true that ARTICLE 49 was introduced in response to the experience of World War II, it explicitly prohibits both individual and mass deportations. This was clearly stated by Justice Gabriel Bach in a minority opinion challenging the majority in HCJ 785/87. ARTICLE 49 constitutes an absolute ban on forcible expulsion of protected persons. Justice Haim Cohn of Israel's High Court of Justice went even further when he argued in a minority opinion that deportation was contrary to customary international law.[21]

The second argument, focusing on the nature of the deportees as terrorists and the security function of the deportation, proved equally problematical: (a) ARTICLE 49 does not allow the expulsion even of "saboteurs and terrorists" (although it clearly allows their detention); (b) although it could be argued that at least some deportees were involved in violent activities in the territories, numerous sources report that a large number of deportees have been neither saboteurs nor terrorists, but social and political leaders in the occupied territories; (c) ARTICLE 49 specifically states that deportations are banned "regardless of their motive": the justification of expulsion in terms of maintaining "security and public order" is invalid in terms of ARTICLE 49.

The third pro-expulsion argument, that deportation is to be preferred to long detention, runs into two possible counterarguments. First, even if deportation is more humane than detention, ARTICLE 49 still outlaws the former but not the latter. Second, the argument that deportation is to be preferred to imprisonment could be substantively challenged: families can meet detainees on occasion, but much less so deportees. It seems that most, or at least many, deportees would have preferred to be detained rather than expelled.

Mustafa Qan'a, a Palestinian deported in January 1991, described the deportation as an "execution."[22]

The fourth pro-expulsion point, that deportation to Jordan is legally acceptable, is problematical on a variety of counts. A straightforward reading of ARTICLE 49 leads to the conclusion that the deportation of persons from an occupied area to the area of any state, including the state of which the occupied territory is part, is unacceptable, regardless of the sovereignty question. Beyond this legal reading of ARTICLE 49, it is important to recognize that whereas in the early days of the occupation Jordan was indeed the only country to which individuals were expelled, other countries, especially Lebanon, subsequently became deportation destinations.[23] Contextually, it seems that the legality of the Israeli expulsion policy cannot rest on the "Jordanian argument."

The fifth pro-expulsion argument, which focuses on the applicability of Geneva IV, was discussed at length in chapter 1. Geneva IV applies to the territories, but because it was not incorporated by the Knesset into Israel's domestic law, a plaintiff cannot resort to it in an effort to block a specific deportation order. The Israeli judicial system, headed by the HCJ, does not have the means to respond to an appeal against a deportation order even though Israel is internationally committed to Geneva IV.[24] The legal instrument used by the military government to deport individuals from the West Bank is the DER; the argument is that these regulations are still part and parcel of the legal system there, as they were under the British and the Jordanians. Yet, some analysts have argued that the Jordanian law, inherited by the occupying power (Israel) in 1967, explicitly prohibited deportations.[25] A Jordanian legislative ban enacted in 1953 forbade the deportation of a Jordanian citizen from the kingdom.[26]

The legal problems associated with deportation have been so serious that important Israeli jurists such as Dinstein and Cohen have felt compelled to reject the government's position on that question.[27] Segments of the Israeli public and media have done the same, as have many foreign governments and numerous international organizations. Nevertheless, the HCJ has rejected the argument that the policy was fundamentally illegal, and has refused to block any deportations.

The deportation policy has been perceived as problematical not only from the perspective of international legality but also from the perspective of a more general, accepted legal procedure: some observers have felt that due process has not been maintained in regard to deportations and have emphasized that the deportation process has been based mostly on administrative decision making rather than on a judicial process. This decision-making process, in the hands of the military commanders of the West Bank and the Gaza Strip, it requires some examination.

The expulsion process begins with the issuance of a deportation order signed by the appropriate area commander. The candidate for deportation and his or her attorney are not permitted to see the file or the evidence that led to the deportation order.[28] The subject of the order is immediately placed under arrest. If the detainee requests, an appeal committee to reconsider the deportation order is formed. The three committee members, one of whom has a legal background, are appointed by the area commander who issued the deportation order. The committee, which discusses the appeal behind closed doors, has only advisory and nonbinding powers. To date, in only few cases, including that of Nablus's mayor, Basam Shaka'ah, has the committee recommended the cancellation of a deportation order.

Erez Israeli described the deportation procedure: "The [appeal] board operates in a way contrary to the principle of assumed innocence which underlies all modern jurisprudence . . . the board's review is conducted behind closed doors, and the would-be deportee and his/her attorney are faced with military government representatives on both sides of the bench. The review bears no resemblance to regular criminal proceedings. The military government is under no obligation to call witnesses or to observe any of the stringent rules of evidence applied in a normal trial. The evidence is submitted in writing and is customarily kept confidential, so that neither the person slated for deportation nor the defense attorney can challenge the reliability of the evidence or its sources."[29]

Once the appeal committee makes a recommendation, the prospective deportee may appeal to the Israeli Supreme Court. Like the committee, the Court is extremely unlikely to overturn the expulsion order: to date it has supported the decisions made by the area commander except in one case in which it ordered the IDF to return three deportees to the territories to complete their hearing before the committee. The limitations on intervention are built in: the Court's function (as the Court has interpreted it) is merely to ascertain that the proper deportation procedures, as specified in the

DER, have been implemented. It does not deal with the actual evidence or with the question of whether the prospective deportee is a danger to security and public order.

From the perspective of due process, it is important to note that in the deportation process, charges are not brought against the deportee, no trial is held, the allegations are usually very general, evidence to substantiate these allegations is secretly submitted by the military government, and the deportee and his or her attorney are routinely denied access to evidence.[30]

As previously stated, if and when a prospective deportee submits an appeal against the decision to deport him or her, both the appeal committee and the High Court of Justice have severely limited powers to change the order. The committee is merely advisory, and the Court deals with the deportation order solely on procedural grounds. Essentially, the Court's only function is to make sure that the military commander acted within the limits of the powers granted to him by the DER and of international law, which the Court believes to allow deportations. Within such parameters, it is not surprising that the HCJ has not overturned a single deportation order.

Various considerations seem to have been at the basis of the deportation policy. At times, deportation has been employed as a severe punitive act. On other occasions, the military government has seemed to respond to pressure from the settler community, especially following significant Palestinian attacks on Israelis or large-scale clashes between the settlers and the local population.[31] Third, expulsion has been widely used as a tool to prevent the emergence of an indigenous Palestinian leadership in the territories. Community leaders, journalists, lawyers, trade unionists, student activists, politicians, and others have been expelled to maintain political control over the local population. Among the deportees have been many persons with a distinctly and well-known moderate position on the prospects of an Israeli-Palestinian settlement.[32]

Some analysts have argued that in expelling Palestinians, Israel has violated ARTICLE 9 of the UDHR, which prohibits the arbitrary arrest, detention, or exile of an individual. This argument is difficult to assess in regard to expulsion because the evidence against Palestinian deportees is never made public.

Politically, the deportation policy has not been an effective security measure. The policy proved not only to be problematical from the perspective of human rights but essentially a useless political tool as well, arousing animosity toward Israel in the territories and generating worldwide condemnation.

Administrative Detention

A very large number of Palestinians have been the subject of administrative detention orders since 1967 and particularly since the beginning of the Intifada in December 1987. According to international sources, more than 5,000 Palestinians were in administrative detention between December 1987 and the middle of 1989.[33] Israel's military advocate general (MAG) said in a press conference on October 19, 1989, that more than 9,000 administrative detention orders had been issued since the beginning of the uprising, as part of a wave of 40,000 arrests during this period.[34] B'Tselem reported that over 14,000 administrative detention orders had been issued between December 1987 and September 1992.[35] On November 5, 1989, it was announced by the spokesman for the IDF that as of that date, the army held 9,009 persons: 2,943 convicted; 2,918 in the midst of legal proceedings; 1,354 awaiting trial; and 1,794 in administrative detention.[36] According to data in the files of the police, 4,000 additional persons were detained by the police. As of November 1989, there were about 13,000 Palestinians in Israeli prisons. According to the 1989 human rights report issued by the State Department, IDF figures indicated that as of January 1, 1990, the number of Palestinian detainees in IDF prison facilities was 9,138.[37] By the end of September 1992, the number of Palestinians in administrative detention had declined to 185.[38]

Most of the detainees have spent six months in prisons or detention centers—many have spent longer periods in custody. The vast majority of the Palestinian detainees have been sent to the specially constructed detention center at Ketziot, a camp known for its harsh conditions.[39] In general, since the start of the uprising, the use of administrative detention has become extremely widespread; the number of those empowered to issue administrative detention orders has increased, and "detainees' rights have suffered serious erosion as procedural safeguards which did exist [prior to the Intifada] have been dropped."[40] For example, in August 1989, the authorities decided to allow the imposition of administrative detention for twelve months instead of six.[41] Furthermore, district military commanders were authorized to order administrative detention, a right previously given only to the area commander.[42]

Also called preventive detention, administrative detention is the internment of individuals through administrative, rather than judicial, proceedings; under the military government in the territories, the military commanders of the West Bank and the Gaza Strip, or persons authorized by them, have the power to order the detention of any individual without charging the person with the commission of a specific crime.

The justification for using administrative detention has always been that it is a measure necessary to prevent persons thought to be dangerous from committing acts that may endanger the security of the state. The preventive nature of the measure, rather than its punitive nature, has always been the basis for its employment. Israeli analysts, and others, have emphasized that administrative detention is legal under international law only if it is preventive; it cannot be a measure designed to punish for an act done in the past but must be an instrument for preventing a suspect from committing an illegal act in the future. If a person is suspected of an actual violation of the law, he or she must stand trial.[43]

Administrative detention has also been used in cases where suspects may not have been convictable under conventional criminal law proceedings due to lack of sufficient evidence admissible by Israeli courts or in cases where, for security reasons, such evidence could not have been introduced in open court or even shared privately with the accused or his/her attorney.[44]

In the face of worldwide criticism of the extensive use of administrative detention, the Israeli authorities have emphasized that the internment of an individual through administrative means is "not intended as a political but as a security detention"; the reason for employing it "must always be suspicion of active engagement in or support for hostile terrorist activities and not mere political views."[45] In a public statement on January 26, 1986, Israel's attorney general declared that an administrative detention order can be issued only for reasons of state or public security. Administrative detention is intended only to prevent the perpetration of illegal acts by the person(s) against whom the order is issued. This measure is resorted to only in circumstances where normal judicial procedures cannot be followed, and the limited and careful use of administrative detention is reasonable and in accordance with local and international law.[46]

These assertions—and the last one in particular—have been vigorously challenged, especially since the beginning of the Intifada, which brought a dramatic increase in the use of administrative detention. In terms of international law, administrative detention can be approached from the perspective of human rights or from that of the laws of war and belligerent occupation, which are more technical and specific.

ARTICLES 9 and 10 of the Universal Declaration on Human Rights are relevant to the issue of administrative detention in the territories. ARTICLE 9, which is reaffirmed and strengthened in Article 9(1) of the International Convention on Civil and Political Rights, states that "no one shall be subjected to arbitrary arrest or detention . . ."; ARTICLE 9(2) of the Convention on Civil and Political Rights states specifically that detainees must be informed at the time of their arrest of the reasons for their arrest, a controversial issue for the use of administrative detention in the territories. ARTICLE 10 of the UDHR, which deals with due process, declares that "everyone is entitled in full equality to a fair and public hearing by an independent and impartial tribunal in the determination of his rights and obligations and of any criminal charge against him." A defense of Israel's position on administrative detention is that it is not arbitrary and that most of the provisions of the UDHR are irrelevant insofar as they are designed to operate in time of peace.

With regard to administrative detention, the provisions of the law of war tend to be more sympathetic toward the security needs of the state detaining individuals than the human rights provisions, which tilt in the direction of the detainee's rights. In fact, despite the prevalent unease with the use of administrative detention, the measure is widely used in many parts of the world and in most countries in times of national emergency.

Within the context of the law of war, the single most important provision for the use of administrative detention is in ARTICLE 78(1) of Geneva IV: "If the occupying power considers it necessary, for imperative reasons of security, to take safety measures concerning protected persons, it may, at the most, subject them to assigned residence or to internment."

It ought to be quickly noted that the internment of protected persons is left to the discretion of the occupant. At the same time, the occupant may detain persons only on the basis of "imperative reasons of security" and not for political reasons. It may also be argued that the occupant is answerable to the more general provisions included in the Universal Declaration on Human Rights and other such conventions, especially with regard to issues such as due process.

ARTICLE 78(1) of Geneva IV has served as one of the most important legal justifications for the use of administrative detention by the Israeli military authorities in the West Bank and the Gaza Strip. Israeli jurists, critical of other punitive measures, found ARTICLE 78 of Geneva IV to be a valid legal foundation for administrative detention.[47] It has been emphasized that although the Geneva Convention requires detention to be executed according to a regular procedure, emphasizes the right of appeal for detainees, and mandates a periodic review (if possible, every six months) of the internment decision, it does not ban detention altogether; in fact, it authorizes it.

Nevertheless, detention is not an absolute right of a government. It is closely regulated, especially in a situation of belligerent occupation. In the official commentary on ARTICLE 78, prepared by the International Committee of the Red Cross, important principles in regard to internment in the occupied territories were laid down: "In occupied territories the internment of protected persons should be even more exceptional than it is inside the territory of the parties to the conflict; such measures [internment] can only be ordered for real and imperative reasons of security: their exceptional character must be preserved."[48] Moreover, administrative detention could be used, according to the official commentary, only "[w]hen other measures have proved inadequate."[49] Although the decision of whether to detain or not to detain is the occupier's, this measure must be used only when it is necessary, imperative, and unavoidable.

In terms of internal Israeli law, administrative detention in the West Bank has been regulated since 1967 mostly through Military Order no. 378, which incorporated Regulation 111(1) of the Defense Emergency Regulations and empowered the area commander of the West Bank or person(s) authorized by him to detain individuals in the territories. In 1979 a new law, the Emergency Powers (Detention) Law, was enacted in Israel proper, replacing the Defense Emergency Regulations. The 1979 law limited the authority to impose detention to the minister of defense and the maximum period of detention to six months. This liberalization applied only to the state of Israel.

Nevertheless, on January 11, 1980, Military Order no. 815 was issued, amending ARTICLE 87 of Order no. 378 and bringing it, and the procedures governing administrative detention on the West Bank, into line with the new (1979) Israeli law. Military Order no.

1229 of March 1988 further revised the administrative detention practice in response to the Intifada conditions. It expanded the right to issue administrative detention orders to persons other than the area commander of the West Bank[50] and limited the right of appeal. Moreover, in August 1989, the IDF amended the 1988 order and extended the maximum period of each detention order from six to twelve months.[51] In December 1991, the maximum period of each order was reduced to six months.[52]

There has been an Israeli effort to establish a detention process compatible with the requirements of Geneva IV. The regulations regarding administrative detention originally required an automatic judicial review every six months, but this provision was not always maintained. Furthermore, in instructions prepared by the military advocate general, the army was ordered to use administrative detention as a last resort and as a preventive rather than a punitive measure. In addition to the board of appeals required by Geneva IV, Israel established regional advisory committees, also appointed by the area commander, to deal with detention cases of nine months or over. An additional avenue for appeal and review was opened by the willingness of the Israeli High Court of Justice to deal with individual cases of administrative detention.[53]

Despite these efforts, the Israeli practice of administrative detention has not been free of severe criticism. A 1989 U.S. Department of State document on human rights stated that secret evidence is often used as grounds for administrative detention, that appeals to the HCJ are invariably unsuccessful, that in "many cases individuals appear to have been detained for political activities," that even Israeli officials have confirmed that in some instances release of a detainee depends upon the behavior of the people in the area in which the detainee lives, and that detainees have been transferred from the occupied territories, which "in view of the United States contravenes the Fourth Geneva Convention."[54]

The State Department statement identified what the U.S. government sees as a series of problems relating to due process, the punitive and political nature of this particular security measure, and legal problems in the way detention is administered. Amnesty International reported that detainees are rarely given the reasons for their detention when they are arrested. After their arrest, the information made available to them is "almost invariably insufficient for them and their lawyers to be able to effectively exercise their right to challenge the detention order."[55]

Among the many complaints about administrative detention, questions of legality, the rationale for detention, the procedures under which Palestinians are detained, and the conditions of imprisonment seem to dominate. Some analysts have noted that although ARTICLE 78 of Geneva IV authorizes detention of protected persons, ARTICLE 6 states that except for a number of specified provisions (not including ARTICLE 78), the convention shall cease to apply in occupied territories "one year after the general close of military operations." It was apparently expected by the writers of Geneva IV that within a year of the beginning of an occupation, the strict methods of control provided for by the convention will not be needed.[56] In reply to this point, it could be argued that when Geneva IV was written, no one expected a belligerent occupation to last as long as Israel's control over the territories has.

A more substantive assault on Israel's administrative detention practices has been that ARTICLE 78 permits the occupying power to detain protected persons only "for imperative reasons of security." With the internment of thousands of individuals, including some persons known as politically moderate and even people committed to nonviolence,[57] many commentators found it increasingly doubtful that all Palestinian detainees actually pose real security danger to the state of Israel. Administrative detention has been widely perceived as an instrument for curbing freedom of expression, association, and political activity. The extensive use of the measure seems to have eroded the requirement that it be used sparingly and as an exceptional instrument. Many observers believe that administrative detention has become more and more punitive. Upon reviewing administrative detention in the territories since late 1987, Amnesty International observed that "the broad formulation of the grounds of administrative detention has allowed this measure to be abused to detain people on account of nonviolent political beliefs and activities."[58]

The procedures governing administrative detention have also proven problematical. Some observers have felt that these procedures are clearly set against the detainee and favor the state. For example, the defendant has to initiate the appeal proceedings, proving that the detention order is improper.[59] Yet, the accused is "confounded in his efforts to meet that burden by the fact that the evidence supporting the detention order is typically withheld on security grounds."[60] To complicate matters for the detainee and his or her attorney, the charges are, according to Amnesty International, always too general.[61] Under the circumstances, argues Orentlicher, the result of a challenge of a detention order is "all but a foregone conclusion."[62]

The practice of administrative detention has been criticized from the perspective of the conditions under which Palestinian detainees are kept, often for extended periods of time. Several specific points have been raised in this context:

1. Although Geneva IV clearly requires that administrative detainees be detained in the occupied territory in which they reside, most Palestinians, especially since the beginning of the Intifada, have been interned in Israel proper;[63] furthermore, administrative detainees are not always kept separate from criminal prisoners, as is required by Geneva IV.[64]

2. Detainees have repeatedly complained of unsatisfactory hygienic conditions and sanitary facilities, the lack of adequate medical attention, beatings and other physical abuse, collective punishment (even for minor offenses), and "culturally humiliating forms of punishment."[65] These complaints have been documented by international organs. According to the Lawyers Committee for Human Rights, some administrative detainees have been forced to perform labor that exceeds the administrative, maintenance, and domestic work permitted by Geneva IV.[66]

3. The focus of much of the criticism of Israel's treatment of detainees has been the detention facility at Ketziot. Even the Israeli HCJ recommended the appointment of an advisory committee to monitor the conditions there.[67] A long list of complaints about this particular detention camp have been published by Israeli and Palestinian human rights groups, Amnesty International, the Lawyers Committee on Human Rights, U.N. agencies, and others.

The Lawyers Committee found that the location of the Ketziot facility "fails to comply with the standards of the Fourth Geneva Convention," as does the treatment of those interned there.[68] The facility is located in the Negev Desert in southern Israel. The weather conditions in this region are rather severe, especially during the long summer, when temperatures are extremely high. The detainees also suffer from serious overcrowding.

Despite the criticisms, a number of jurists have vigorously defended not only Israel's right to use administrative detention in the territories but also the specific practices adopted in detaining Palestinians. Several arguments have been offered in this context:

1. Some observers have found that, on the whole, "Israel has made use of administrative detention in a controlled manner,"[69] not excessively and indiscriminately. Dershowitz tried to demonstrate this point by comparing the Israeli use of administrative detention with the use of the very same measure against 109,650 Japanese-Americans during World War II.[70] Cohen emphasized that administrative detention is used against specific individuals and not against population groups.[71] Certainly, prior to the Intifada, administrative detention was used more sparingly than after the beginning of the uprising.

2. Some jurists have argued that every state, including democracies, has recourse to administrative detention in times of national emergency or war. Such measures were used in Quebec in 1970–71, against the IRA in Northern Ireland, to combat the Basques in Spain, and even against antiwar demonstrators in the United States.[72] The uprising in the territories could certainly be looked upon as a genuine national emergency.

3. Israel's policy defenders have argued that the majority of detainees were, in fact, engaged in terrorism or incitement to civil disobedience but often could not have been brought to trial due to Israel's strict rules of evidence and security considerations. Thus administrative detention was required.

4. Some defenders of administrative detention have argued that it ought to be judged in the context of other security measures: "administrative detention is to be preferred to deportation or house demolitions, although not to prosecution under regular court procedure."[73]

5. Despite some arguments to the contrary, defenders of administrative detention maintain that the practice has sufficient safeguards to offset the initial decision to detain an individual and keep administrative detention as limited as possible. According to the IDF, approximately 30 percent of detention orders were either canceled or shortened in 1989 as the result of an appeal.[74]

6. Finally, the argument has been offered that the occupier has a fundamental right to use administrative detention as a means of keeping order in the territories under its control.[75]

Despite these arguments, Amnesty International and most international observers believe that administrative detention has been used too often and too extensively in situations where regular criminal proceedings had to be employed. Furthermore, they feel

that the evidence should be shared with detainees and their lawyers, and that the practice of administrative detention has flaws in
terms of due process.[76] Even official Israeli reports sometimes con-
firm that the human rights of detainees are frequently violated. The
Landau Report (October 1987) found that the Shin Bet (Israel's
security service) has often violated the rights of detainees. Confessions have been extracted through illegitimate pressure and then
submitted to the courts as admissible evidence. Because Shin Bet
testimony is crucial in cases brought to court, and more so in cases
of administrative detention, the Landau Report cast serious suspicion on this practice.

It is important to note that the Israeli political system has not
been completely unsympathetic to the plight of Palestinian detainees. The HCJ called for close supervision of the Ketziot facility.
The Landau Report criticized the security forces in the territories
(although it also endorsed the use of moderate physical pressure
against detainees). Measures have been taken to curtail violence
against detainees by their jailers.[77] Yet, the real function of administrative detention as a control mechanism has remained politically
too important for the practice to be eliminated or even seriously
curtailed. This is the context in which the 1989 extension of administrative detention from six to twelve months ought to be
understood.

In general, it seems that political concerns, more than pure
security considerations, have driven the policy of administrative
detention since 1967. These political concerns explain the fluctuations in the number of detainees through the years. Between 1980
and 1985 there were no administrative detainees in Israeli prisons
(due to a clear political decision rather than unexpected improvement in the security situation). In 1985 there was a conscious decision on the part of the new defense minister, Yitzhak Rabin, to
renew the use of administrative detention. The outbreak of the
Intifada led again to a decision to extensively employ administrative detention as a means of reestablishing control over the population or as a means of punishing the rebelling inhabitants. This is
the background to the extremely large number of administrative
detentions since December 1987.[78]

The number of Palestinians arrested since 1967, and particularly since December 1987, has been very large. Some sources estimate that about 200,000 security prisoners and detainees, 20
percent of the population, have passed through Israeli prisons.[79]

According to some Israeli sources, basing their estimates on official Red Cross reports, there were about 1.5–2 million pre-Intifada arrests on security grounds in the territories.[80]

The Intifada signaled not only an increase in the number of detainees but also an overall toughening of the administrative detention policy. Although at the beginning of the riots there was an inclination on the part of the military authorities to try people on criminal charges, in March 1988, there was apparently a decision to shift to administrative detention as a major control and punishment method. In fact, the large number of new detainees forced the authorities to open new facilities specially designed for administrative detainees. The Ketziot (Ansar III) Military Detention Center was constructed to handle the unprecedented number of new detainees.[81]

The uprising also resulted in changes in the provisions governing administrative detention. On March 17, 1988, the authorities issued Military Order 1229 for the West Bank and Military Order 941 for the Gaza Strip, which amended the existing policy on administrative detention. The new orders extended the power to issue detention orders to all officers with the rank of *aluf mishne* (colonel) and above. This power was previously reserved to the area commanders of the West Bank and the Gaza Strip.

The new orders temporarily suspended the prompt and automatic judicial review of administrative detention orders (conducted by a military judge within ninety-six hours of the arrest). They established a new procedure according to which an appeal must be initiated by the detainee and was no longer automatic.[82] Detainees could now appeal to a three-member Advisory Appeals Committee authorized to make recommendations to the military commander of the area.[83]

The new, nonbinding nature of the appeal process was strongly criticized in Israel. The authorities responded on June 13, 1988, by amending Military Order 1229 through Military Order 1236, which abolished the three-member Advisory Appeals Committee and replaced it with a single military judge empowered to make binding decisions and capable of confirming, canceling, or reducing administrative detention sentences.[84] According to official Israeli figures, as of August 1988, more than 1,400 appeals had been lodged and more than 400 of the detention orders had been reduced or canceled. At the same time, Amnesty International noted that appeals were sometimes heard "weeks if not months after the arrest."[85]

From a human rights perspective, the possibility of an effective appeal is a positive sign, as is the ability of the system to respond to public criticism, as it did through Military Order 1236. Yet, the preceding order, no. 1229, indicates erosion of the inhibition in using administrative detention. The erosion is seen not only in administrative and military circles but also in judicial ones. Two decisions issued by Israeli judges in 1988 questioned the distinction between political activity and terrorist activity as a basis for administrative detention. The judges stated that sometimes political activity is more dangerous than terrorist activity; therefore, some political activities warrant administrative detention. The lawyer Amnon Zichroni saw this new thinking as endangering freedom of speech. Another lawyer, Adam Fish of the Association for Civil Rights in Israel, noted that until then, endangering the state and the public had to involve physical danger.[86] Referring specifically to the administrative detention of one important Palestinian leader, Judge Vinograd said that Faisal Husseini's nonviolent actions were more dangerous than the ones he could have carried out actively.

Beyond the technical revisions in the administrative detention provisions, the greatest change in this area has been that following the outbreak of the Intifada, all sections of the Palestinian society (and not, as before, only prominent figures in the community and individuals involved in military activity) have been impacted by the policy. Among the administrative detainees since December 1987, there have been persons involved in riots and demonstrations and individuals accused of membership in illegal organizations (PLO, the territories' popular committees, religious groups, etc.): detainees have been accused of direct involvement in violent acts, but often of incitement to violence, transfer of funds to finance the challenge to Israel, political leadership, and other forms of indirect involvement.

The administrative detention policy has emerged, along with deportations and house demolitions, as one of the most controversial practices of the military authorities in the West Bank and Gaza. The ability of military officials to detain persons for long periods of time without a trial or even a formal charge has created the potential for widespread abuse. Thus, a person may be detained administratively on improper grounds and accused of ill-defined security offenses. Moreover, during the interrogation stage a detainee may be physically abused, especially because in this stage (which precedes the judicial review carried out following eighteen days of arrest), access to counsel is routinely denied.[87]

The Israeli system of administrative detention has not been wholly devoid of safeguards against extreme abuse. For example, police warrants must be secured after four days of arrest for each and every detainee. Yet, since the information regarding the detainee is in the hands of the General Security Service, "the value of this layer of protection depends upon the good faith of the Shin Bet."[88] The Lawyers Committee argued that several factors suggest the Shin Bet is all too ready to use detention powers for political purposes and for punitive functions. Detainees are often held close to the full period authorized prior to judicial review (eighteen days), then released without charge or even interrogation. No charges have been filed against the majority of the West Bank residents who have been detained.

In a system in which people may be arrested and held for long periods of time without a charge or judicial review, and all within the context of a fierce conflict, the potential for serious problems is substantial. According to the procedures, detainees may be held incommunicado for up to two weeks without a visit from the representative of the International Committee of the Red Cross, and without access to a lawyer for thirty days. To some observers, this practice invites abuse.[89] Israeli, Palestinian, and international sources concluded even prior to the Intifada that physical abuse of detainees is quite common.

On the basis of a special study of administrative detention in the territories, Amnesty International observed that it "falls short of international human rights standards."[90] The organization thought that the grounds for detention are so broad that even those who nonviolently exercise their right of freedom of expression are often detained. The massive use of administrative detention led observers to the conclusion that hundreds of people have been mistakenly detained.[91] Baruch Bracha, an Israeli law professor, commented on administrative detention that he has "the clear impression that in anything relating to the security of the State, the proper balance between security considerations and human dignity, justice and fairness is violated."[92]

One of the problems of administrative detention has been the place of detention. Most of the Palestinian detainees have been sent either to the Ketziot detention center or to the Meggido prison, near Afula. Both of these facilities are located in Israel proper. The U.S. Department of State and others have expressed the view that this practice violates ARTICLE 76 of Geneva IV, which does not allow the detention of protected people outside the occupied territory.[93] In 1988 the HCJ dismissed a petition brought before it by Ketziot detainees and held that the provisions of Geneva IV could not be enforced by an Israeli court because they have not been enacted into Israeli law.

In addition to administrative detention, the military authorities in the territories have used other restrictive measures, including house and town arrests. The basis for these measures has been ARTICLE 86 of Military Order 378 and ARTICLE 78 of Geneva IV.[94] Although house or town arrest is legal in terms of the provisions of Geneva IV, this measure is acceptable only in case of crucial security concerns.[95]

In the period between 1980 and 1985, when administrative detention was cut to a minimum, town arrest became more common. At the end of 1982, fifty-seven people in the West Bank had been placed under such restriction; in August 1984, the number of restricted people was fifty; and in 1985 it rose to seventy.[96]

International criticism of the practice focused on the nonviolent activity of many restricted persons. It was felt that people were punished for their political opinions. In 1984 Amnesty International published a report on town arrests and restriction orders in the territories. It felt that even though an appeal was available to restricted persons, their chances for success were minimal: full and precise reasons for restrictive orders were rarely given ("security reasons" was the formal but general cause for restriction). The evidence was consistently withheld from the restricted person and his or her lawyer(s), and so forth. The report of the Center for Peace in the Middle East in Tel Aviv concluded that town and house arrests were used not as a means of enhancing security but as a means of punishment.[97] The Center noted that in terms of human rights, restricting orders could easily destroy a person's career, work opportunities, and family and social contacts.

House Demolition

In addition to deportation and administrative detention, house demolition has been used by the military government in the West Bank and the Gaza Strip. Like the other two measures, house demolition has intensified and expanded as a result of a March 1988 package of sanctions approved by the Israeli government.[98]

House demolition has been criticized by many governments, protested by human rights organizations, and repeatedly challenged by international jurists. Even Israeli commanders put in charge of implementing this measure recognize that it is an especially harsh punishment.[99] Critics have argued that it is an administrative measure, carried out without a legal process, and that it inflicts an irreversible collective punishment. Some commentators have even argued that "this method of punishment is unique to Israel and is not employed in any other place in the world."[100]

Cohen distinguishes two categories of house demolition:[101] (1) punitive demolition, in which a house used by terrorists as a base of operations against Israeli soldiers or civilians is blown up;[102] (2) preventive demolition, in which house(s) is or are being demolished to prevent future use by terrorists.[103]

Houses in the territory have been demolished, by the use of explosives or bulldozers, or sealed off (completely or partially). Sealing off a home has sometimes been done when the residence of the accused person is an apartment in a house tenanted by a few families or when the dynamiting of a house might render neighboring houses unsafe.[104] The demolition of houses often causes damage to neighboring residences, and in such cases the IDF has often compensated for the damage.

A house may be demolished if the person suspected of a security offense owns it, if a relative of that person owns it, if the security offense occurred on the premises, or if the owner of the house knew about the presence of a saboteur or sabotage material in the residence. The application of the punishment to persons other than the suspect has traditionally been a major cause for international outcry. According to one Israeli source, in about 70 percent of the cases, the demolished house belonged not to the suspect but to his or her parents.[105] Others have commented, however, that in practice, only homes in which the suspected saboteur actually lives are demolished.

Figures as to the number of houses demolished vary according to the source. On December 16, 1969, Defense Minister Dayan stated in the Knesset that 516 houses had been demolished, expropriated, or sealed off between June 1967 and December 1, 1969.[106] In this early period Arab sources, supported by Israeli human rights groups, already believed the numbers to be substantially higher. Both the PLO and Jordanian sources maintained that in the late 1960s, 5,500–7,100 houses were demolished.[107] The Israeli League for Human and Civil Rights tended to agree that the number of houses razed ran into the thousands. The 1978 annual report of the

International Committee of the Red Cross states that 1,224 buildings had been demolished or sealed off since 1967,[108] a figure accepted by Knesset member Dedi Zucker and the Tel Aviv-based International Center for Peace in the Middle East.[109]

Like deportations and detentions, house demolitions have fluctuated. In the late 1970s and early 1980s, there was a tendency to use house demolition minimally.[110] The beginning of the Intifada signaled a sharp increase in demolitions. In 1988 between 145 and 154 houses were demolished.[111] According to Israeli sources, between December 1987 and July 1989, about 230 houses were blown up or bulldozed, and 102 more were sealed and made unusable.[112] B'Tselem reported that during the first year of the Intifada, 130 houses were demolished in the West Bank and the Gaza Strip, during the second year the number increased to 156, declined to 90 in the third year, and further declined to 47 in the Intifada's fourth year.[113]

Regardless of the exact figures, it is clear that, in general, the Intifada intensified house demolition and broadened the guidelines for its use. Whereas prior to the Intifada, the tendency was to destroy houses of persons involved in actual violence, Israeli reports indicate that on April 5, 1988, three houses belonging to individuals suspected of incitement were demolished in El Yammun.[114] Houses of youngsters accused of stone throwing also have been demolished,[115] and, according to some reports, so have houses of people accused of resisting arrest.[116] On October 31, 1988, a house belonging to the grandmother of a suspect in the throwing of a Molotov cocktail was demolished.[117] At least eleven houses in the territories were demolished while suspects were still at large.[118] Efforts to convince the HCJ to prevent some demolitions (e.g., of houses rented by suspects, homes of stone throwers, etc.) proved unsuccessful.

House demolition has been extremely controversial from a legal point of view. In terms of internal law, the authorities have based their house demolition policy on Regulation 119 of the Defense Emergency Regulations, arguing that in both the West Bank and the Gaza Strip, the Mandate legislation still holds. The HCJ has accepted this position despite many challenges (897/86), and has rejected the argument that house demolition is a collective punishment (698/85). In terms of international law, the Israeli authorities have relied on ARTICLE 53 of Geneva IV and ARTICLE 23(g) of the Hague Regulations, arguing that both empower the occupant to destroy property.

ARTICLE 53 of Geneva IV states that "any destruction by the Occupying Power of real or personal property belonging individually or collectively to private persons, or to the State, or to public authorities, or to social or cooperative organizations, is prohibited, except where such destruction is rendered absolutely necessary by military operations." Similarly, ARTICLE 23(g) of the Hague Regulations allows destruction of property only in cases "imperatively demanded by the necessities of war," an even more confining definition than the one included in ARTICLE 53 of Geneva IV. The two documents state categorically that private property ought not to be destroyed unless war or military operations necessitate such destruction.[119] The Hague Regulations are binding as part of customary international law,[120] and Geneva IV is a binding multilateral treaty that is generally accepted by the entire family of nations.[121]

In its interpretation of ARTICLE 53, the International Committee of the Red Cross states that destruction of property is allowed only if it is "absolutely necessary—i.e. materially indispensable for the armed forces [of the occupant] to engage in action, such as making way for them." The International Committee also states that "this exception to the prohibition [on the destruction of property] cannot justify destruction as a punishment or determent, since to preclude this type of destruction is an essential aim of the article."[122]

In addition to the provisions dealing with house demolition from the perspective of the law of war, the law of human rights has something to say about the matter. ARTICLE 17(2) of the UDHR states that "no one shall be arbitrarily deprived of his property." Some analysts have argued that the procedures governing house demolition in the territories are arbitrary; however, this is a controversial claim. A few arguments justifying demolitions have been offered through the years:

1. Often there is indeed a military necessity—as required by Geneva IV—to destroy houses from which terrorists operate.[123]

2. The definition of military necessity is left in ARTICLES 53 and 23(g) to the discretion of the occupant.

3. House demolition is essential for effectively deterring terrorism, especially because capital punishment is not used in the territories.[124] In other words, house demolition ought to be evaluated in view of the alternatives for combating terrorism and not merely in and of itself.[125]

Those who feel that house demolition is essentially unacceptable have advanced a series of counterarguments:[126]

1. Most house demolitions are not "absolutely necessary by military considerations" or "war," as required by the relevant international conventions. They are carried out not in the heat of battle but after a saboteur or armaments are found, or following an incident in which a person connected to the residence has been allegedly involved. The blowing up of a house is typically unrelated to military operations or war.[127] According to von Glahn, the military necessity has to be "very urgent and vital," and "a genuine military emergency" must exist to justify any destruction of property.[128] House demolition as punishment or deterrent is unjustified.

2. Some observers argue that the destruction of houses as reprisals against the harboring of guerrillas and weapon concealment is also unjustified, and that the language of ARTICLES 53 and 23(g) seems to support this position.[129]

3. Procedurally, house demolition, as administered in the West Bank and Gaza Strip between 1967 and July 30, 1989, has been widely perceived as highly problematical. In almost all cases, it has been executed swiftly, apparently to increase its punitive character and deterrence effect. In many cases, the owner, the residents, or both, of the home did not even have time to gather all their belongings, let alone appeal the decision. According to some sources, the rapid execution of house demolition decisions has deprived the affected person of an effective procedure to appeal to the military and civilian authorities, despite the formal commitment of the IDF to allow appeals and judicial review.[130] Stated one international observer: "Although in principle persons potentially subject to demolitions can petition the Supreme Court for relief, in practice they rarely have sufficient notice to do so."[131] According to the International Center for Peace in the Middle East, due process is not being maintained.[132]

4. House demolition is an extremely severe punishment for the individual who allegedly committed a crime and his or her family, and it is imposed without a trial or formal charge. Furthermore, the owner or owners of the demolished house is or are usually not allowed to rebuild it; therefore, house demolition is an irreversible punishment of indefinite duration.

5. There is no evidence that house demolition deters violence in the territories; in all likelihood it increases violence. General (res.) Aryeh Shalev, a former commander of the territories, found that the number of Molotov cocktails thrown at IDF units in the territories often rose following a large number of demolitions. Sha-

lev concluded that over time the deterrent effect of house demolition was reduced: it increased the opposition to Israeli rule, and
the Palestinians found ways to counteract the demolition effect.[133]

6. House demolition almost invariably involves collective punishment because the house in which the alleged offender resides is
often a family residence. ARTICLE 33 of Geneva IV forbids collective punishment or reprisals against the occupied population.
Cohen believes that house demolitions have not only punitive but
also "collective character,"[134] and that they violate ARTICLES 53 and
33 of Geneva IV. House demolition affects not only or even mainly
the alleged offender, who often is in prison at the time of the demolition and likely to spend many years there, but also members of his
or her family, who become homeless as a result of the demolition.[135]

The collective nature of the punishment has proved since 1967
to be one of the most controversial aspects of the house demolition
policy, in view of ARTICLE 33's clear language: "No protected person may be punished for an offense he or she has not personally
committed. Collective penalties and likewise all measures of intimidation or of terrorism are prohibited." B'Tselem reported that the
average number of persons living in houses demolished by the IDF
was about eleven.[136]

Despite the overwhelming condemnation of house demolition,
the authorities have openly stated that it is an instrument of punishment and deterrence and not the result of military necessity. Even
the High Court of Justice, in accepting house demolition, stated
(HCJ 434/79) that "regulation 119 calls for an extraordinary *punitive measure* whose main purpose is *deterring* similar actions."
There can be no question that when house demolition was expanded in response to the Intifada, it was done punitively.[137] The
IDF chief of staff, General Dan Shomron, openly stated that "the
significance of house demolition as a deterrent cannot be over-
looked."[138] The same position was expressed by Defense Minister
Rabin.[139]

The collective nature of house demolition is complicated by
the issue of home ownership. Demolition has been applied to a
house in which the alleged terrorist lives, even if he or she does
not own it: In such situations, large numbers of innocent persons
are bound to be affected.

The internal and external pressure on the Israeli government
regarding house demolition led to a significant change during the
summer of 1989. This change dealt with at least some of the criti-

cisms aimed at the Israeli authorities in regard to house demolition. On July 30, the HCJ ruled, as a result of a petition by the Association for Civil Rights in Israel, that Palestinians accused of security offenses and whose homes have been condemned to demolition must be given time to appeal through the military and civilian courts before the army demolishes their homes.[140] The Court stated that the individual should be given the time to obtain a lawyer, file an appeal, and plead the case at the Supreme Court before the demolition is carried out. Owners of houses condemned to demolition now have forty-eight hours to appeal to the area commander and an additional forty-eight hours to appeal to the HCJ.[141]

The HCJ ruling is especially important in the context in which house demolition became an increasingly common phenomenon influenced not only by security but also by political considerations. In some cases, such as the Beita incident (April 1988), large numbers of homes were demolished because of political pressures from the settlers. Some settlers called for the destruction of entire villages in which people who had thrown Molotov cocktails reside, but their demands were not met by the government.

The meaning of the 1989 HCJ ruling on demolition is that the Israeli judiciary, which traditionally tended to stay out of the house demolition controversy, finally asserted itself and came down on the side of an orderly appeal process. This is another example of the ability of the Israeli legal system to respond to the human rights crisis brought about by the Intifada. We have seen this ability to respond to other punitive measures, including deportations and administrative detention.

It could be argued that the level of response by the HCJ has not been sufficient. In late 1991 B'Tselem reported that "the High Court has to this day rejected all but two petitions against the demolition of houses."[142] Nevertheless, even the rare willingness of the HCJ to intervene could be significant. Since the July 1989 ruling—allowing an appeal before a demolition is carried out—the number of house demolitions has declined significantly. Israeli security sources have stated that the right to appeal to the HCJ renders the punishment of demolition less effective.[143]

4

ᏇᏇ

Justice under Occupation

THE application of the Israeli legal system to the territories
through the military government in the West Bank and Gaza Strip
has been among the most controversial aspects of the occupation.
Defenders of what might be called "Israel's judicial policy" have
pointed out that Israel has maintained the rule of law in the territories, that it quickly restored the normal function of the local courts
and has allowed them to exercise their traditional powers without
interference, that it has maintained its basic obligations as the occupant in accordance with the relevant international standards, and
that it has done all of this in the face of a severe and continuous
challenge by the local population, the PLO, and the neighboring
Arab countries.[1] Opponents of Israel's policies have argued that
Israel has established the superficial appearance of a fair system
of justice, but in reality this system is a "sham," "charade," and
"theater."[2]

This chapter will try to assess the activity of various courts in
the territories since their occupation in 1967 and will dwell on the
military court system and the Israeli High Court of Justice. It will
describe and analyze the legal process in the territories, including
such stages as arrest, investigation, and interrogation. Sections will
deal with the right to a lawyer, the extralegal activity in the West
Bank and Gaza, the use of excessive force, and collective punishment, and discrimination in the application of the law. Although
obviously not all aspects of the legal condition in the territories can
be covered, those most relevant to human rights will be analyzed.

An authoritative analysis of the "justice system" in the territories is difficult to achieve. First, a belligerent occupation of the kind Israel has maintained in the territories since 1967 necessarily entails an extremely complicated legal system, which includes elements of at least three distinct frameworks: the law of the sovereign, the law of the occupant, and the applicable rules of international law. Second, the unusual length of Israel's occupation makes the legal foundation on which it rests even more complex, especially from the perspective of human rights. It could even be argued (see Chapter 1) that the human rights obligations of the occupant have grown and deepened as the occupation has lengthened. Third, the highly controversial nature of the Israeli control in the territories makes scholarly analysis rather difficult: terminologies are biased, data are debatable, assumptions are challengeable, and so forth. Nevertheless, a detailed examination of the various legal institutions and processes operating in the West Bank and Gaza is crucial for understanding the status of human rights in these areas.

The Courts in the Territories

Three different court systems currently exist on the West Bank:

1. The local Palestinian courts have jurisdiction over relationships among the Arab inhabitants of the area and issues of civil wrongs between local Arabs and Jewish settlers.[3]

2. The local Jewish courts have exclusive jurisdiction over the Jewish settlers in the area. These courts are empowered by emergency regulations, enacted by the Knesset, to deal with offenses committed by Israelis in the territories: the court in Kiryat Arba has authority over the southern half of the West Bank, and the court in Ariel has responsibility for the northern West Bank.[4]

3. The military court system has jurisdiction over all security matters and issues related to water, land, and taxes.

According to the principles of international law governing belligerent occupation, existing local courts should continue to function in occupied territory. The Israeli authorities have maintained that this principle remains intact and that they have allowed the continued existence and free functioning of the local West Bank courts. According to some Israeli jurists, the local judiciary system remains almost entirely "free from intervention by the military administration."[5] Some Israeli interpreters, however, tend to be more critical. For example, the Association for Civil Rights in Israel has pointed out that the independence of the local courts is undermined because the military commanders of the territories can fire judges.[6]

In a comprehensive study of the legal system in the territories, the Palestinian jurist Raja Shehadeh called attention to what he perceives as a few major problems (a perception shared by others) with the way the local courts operate. First, the local courts have been "usurped of many of their powers": their jurisdiction has been restricted to West Bank Palestinians and their internal affairs.[7] With very few exceptions, the Jewish settlers are not subject to the power of the local Palestinian courts.

Second, Shehadeh believes that the "independence of the West Bank judicial system has been undermined by the Israeli authorities":[8] a committee of Israeli officers appoints the judges and decides their promotions, salaries, and transfers. Thus, the courts are not free of the heavy and continuous influence of the military government. According to the Association of Civil Rights in Israel, most of the judges in local West Bank courts have been appointed since 1967, and the power of the area commander over them "undermines, in theory and in reality, the independence of the judiciary."[9] The dependence of the local courts and their inferiority is demonstrated when cases tried by them are occasionally transferred to military courts in the midst of the legal proceedings.[10]

Third, the local courts are known for their lack of efficiency, serious corruption, low salaries of judges, chronic shortage of manpower, and other ills. Palestinian jurists have expressed the view that this situation leads to "serious perversion of justice."[11]

Israeli civil courts in the territories have jurisdiction over Israelis residing in the West Bank and Gaza Strip and over foreign tourists visiting there, but not over the local Arab residents. Although Israeli settlers are ostensibly subject to the territorial law in force in the West Bank (that is, the Jordanian law and the Israeli security enactments), in actuality they have the rights and duties of residents of Israel.[12] This situation is problematical: the separate legal system for Israelis in the territories underlies the fact that Arabs and Jews in the West Bank and Gaza are subject to different laws and are tried in different courts. For all intents and purposes, the Israeli settlements in the territories are extensions of the state of Israel. Although the Arab courts theoretically have territorial jurisdiction, settlers never appear before them in criminal matters and rarely in civil matters.[13] In criminal matters, settlers may be tried before military courts, Israeli civilian courts (in the territories or in Israel), or settlement courts established by the military commander of the region.

The legal situation in the territories is quite ambiguous. There is no law or military order stating that an Israeli citizen cannot be tried before a local court in a criminal matter; however, it never happens.[14] In civil matters, Israelis may appear before a local court in rare cases. In contractual matters, the parties may agree in advance which court is competent to hear disputes. In the absence of an agreement, an Israeli or a Palestinian court may have jurisdiction. Although in cases of civil wrongs (such as torts), the local courts have jurisdiction over all persons in the territory, Shehadeh argues that "in practice it is not possible [for a Palestinian] to start legal proceedings against a Jewish settler whatever the subject of the case."[15] The separation of the settlements from the rest of the West Bank and the refusal of the settlers to cooperate with the legal authorities, documented by official Israeli sources,[16] prevent the application of the law in civil matters as well as in other matters.

Most important in terms of the analytical focus of this book, it is essential to note that legal norms and legal institutions in the West Bank and Gaza operate not on a territorial but on a personal basis. Put differently, the norms that apply to Israeli Jews in the territories are different from the ones that apply to Palestinian Arabs residing there. The Knesset has enacted laws that extend the application of the Israeli legal norms to Jewish settlers but not to their Arab neighbors. At the same time, the military government has issued more than 1,400 orders that apply to the Palestinian population in the West Bank and Gaza but not to the Jewish settlers. The two sets of legal norms resulting from these developments have been entirely different from the outset.

From the perspective of the human rights of the local Palestinian population, the most important legal institution is the military courts. The norms of international law and the regulations governing belligerent occupation entitle the occupying power to establish military courts with jurisdiction over the local population in the occupied area.[17] Israel's military courts in the territories operate in accordance with Military Order no. 378 of 1970, which is titled "Order Concerning Security Matters (Judea and Samaria)";[18] prior to 1970, the military courts operated in accordance with Military Order no. 3 of June 8, 1967.

The military court system is governed by the president of the court, an officer appointed by the area commander on the recommendation of the military advocate general (MAG).[19] A military court may consist of three judges, one of whom, who has legal training, serves as president, or a single judge with legal training.[20] In either case, the judges and the prosecutors in the military courts are invariably military officers appointed by the area commander upon the recommendation of the MAG.[21]

Both types of military courts have general jurisdiction over all offenses, but they differ with regard to their punitive powers. A single judge may not impose a prison term exceeding five years, but his decision does not require the approval of higher authority. On the other hand, a three-judge panel may impose the maximum sentence for the crime at hand, but its verdict has traditionally required the approval of the area commander.[22] Since the establishment of an appeals court, the area commander's approval has not been sought.

The activity of the military courts has become controversial. One of the traditional complaints in regard to them has been the lack of the right to appeal their decisions to higher courts. However, a convicted person has been given the right to appeal to the area commander by contesting either the conviction or the sentence.[23] It has been noted that although the area commander has been given extensive powers to overrule a conviction, change the sentence, or even order a retrial, his intervention has been rare.

Originally, the High Court of Justice resisted pressure to order the establishment of an appeals court to hear cases decided by the military courts. It even issued an opinion that there is no duty to establish an appeals court, which had been the position of some international jurists.[24] The High Court of Justice later shifted toward the recommendation for the establishment of an appeals court. Such a court was finally established, at the suggestion of the HCJ, at Ramallah in April 1989.[25]

Prior to the creation of the appeals court, Israel's attorney general expressed the view that the establishment of such a court in the territories was desirable.[26] According to the MAG, as of October 1989, twenty-five cases had been brought before the court of appeals. Fifteen defense appeals and seven prosecution appeals were accepted.[27] The establishment of an appellate court constituted a positive development in the legal situation in the territories.

Many observers thought that the absence of an appellate court to review decisions of military courts constituted a violation of both the Universal Declaration on Human Rights (UDHR) and the International Covenant on Civil and Political Rights (ICPR). ARTICLE 11(1) of the UDHR states that "everyone charged with a penal offense has the right to . . . all guarantees necessary for his defense"; the right of appeal is often thought to be one of these necessary guarantees. According to some, the absence of a special tribunal empowered to hear appeals might "induce a laxity in the court's application of law and procedure" and could be regarded as a breach of ARTICLE 11(1) of the UDHR.[28] The establishment of an appellate court was a move to correct this problem.

The direct involvement of the area commander in the appeals process highlights what some observers have seen as a second major problem with the operation of military courts in the territories: the issue of their independence vis-à-vis other governmental authorities. The right of the defendant to a trial before an independent court depends on three conditions: (a) the court must be independent of other governmental branches; (b) the court must be independent of private pressure groups or public opinion; and (c) the court must be independent of the parties involved in issues before it. These conditions can hardly be fully met in the territories, where the military judges are dependent on the executive branch for appointments and promotions; are influenced by Israeli public opinion, which often demands severe penalties for Palestinians; and are dependent on one of the parties (the MAG). Unfortunately, these conditions of dependence are a built-in feature of any occupation regime.

The independence of the judges is unquestionably one of the most fundamental principles of law. In every progressive legal system, there is a series of guidelines designed to guarantee the court's independence. The military judges in the territories belong to the IDF Legal Corps and are subject to its decisions. About 20 percent of the judges are career officers; their activity as military judges is part of their service. The rest of the judges are lawyers on reserve duty. They also are appointed by the IDF Legal Corps and may be fired by it. The Israeli daily *Hadashot* wrote about the judges' independence: "[t]he judges are dependent hierarchically on the Military Commander of the region, who holds in his hands all the governmental powers—the legislative, the executive and the judifical. The Area Commander is the one signing recommendations for appointment of judges and he can also, theoretically, fire them, although to date he has not taken advantage of his power. . . . Can a judge whose livelihood and professional future are in the hand of the legal system, deal fairly with an accused person who is brought before him by that very system?"[29]

Although many of the military judges are experienced jurists—lawyers, civilian judges, government attorneys, university lecturers[30]—there is still a major problem or at least a perception of a problem with the independence of the judicial system. It is true that the area commander is unlikely to remove a judge without the recommendation of the MAG; this point has been emphasized by a former MAG, Brigadier General Amnon Strashanov.[31] Furthermore, there are other guarantees in the system. For example, judges are promoted by the Legal Corps, not by the Area Commander. Yet, the fact that the military judiciary in the territories acts as an integral part of the military government brings into a question its ability to be independent. The courts often convene within the compounds of the military government and there is an ongoing, continuous social link between the military government personnel and those who serve as part of the judiciary in the territories.

A journalist interviewing the MAG described this situation as a "symbiosis" and asked Brigadier General Strashanov bluntly: "What kind of justice are we talking about?" The military advocate general replied that the symbiosis was indeed a problem, and that separation between the military government and the judicial branch was necessary.[32] A military judge on reserve duty stated that there is "complete symbiosis" between the prosecution, the judges, and the lawyers in the territories, "with the [Palestinian] accused on the sidelines."[33] Added the same judge, Aryeh Koks: "Since the separation of powers is a basic principle of every legal system, its absence constitutes one of the essential reasons that the legal element in the territories is impure."[34] Also Amnesty International has expressed concern about the independence and impartiality of the military judges, emphasizing that the existence of an independent and impartial judiciary is critical for the right to a fair trial.[35]

In its comprehensive study of the military judicial system in the West Bank, B'Tselem emphasized what it called the "severe problem of dependence of the military judicial system." The human rights organization focused on both judges and prosecutors and stressed that they belong to the same military unit, the Legal Corps, on whose goodwill they depend for their promotion. Officers who serve as judges are often promoted to other senior positions within the Legal Corps; there is also a "role reversal" in which individuals shift from prosecution roles to adjudication roles or vice versa. In any event, all officeholders within the Legal Corps are dependent on the military advocate general for promotion. According to Golan, the situation "creates a problem of unhealthy judicial dependence and commitment of judges to a system that promotes them."[36]

The independence of the judiciary from other governmental branches is essential for the rule of law, because the law must be upheld impartially.[37] The UDHR, ARTICLE 10, emphasizes the principle of "an independent and impartial tribunal," and the ICPR, ARTICLE 14(1) does so in even more detail. Both documents do not specifically apply to belligerent occupation. Nevertheless, if we take them at face value, the all-important Military Order 378 is problematical, because it authorizes the area commander to appoint judges. Al-Haq finds that although "the procedure appears to be designed to establish the appearance of a formal 'separation of powers' between the legally qualified judiciary and the executive and legislative authority," which is in the hands of the area commander, the procedure is inherently biased against the Palestinians.[38] Insofar as both the area commander and the military advocate general are IDF officers and answerable to the chief of staff of the IDF, and ultimately to the minister of defense, separation of powers does not seem to exist. At the same time, it could be argued that the provisions of the independence of the judiciary were not created for situations of occupation.

The qualification of the military judges raises a third objection by many observing the military courts. Some judges must be legally qualified; others (such as those who do not serve as presidents on a three-judge panel) do not require any legal training whatsoever. The "legal" judges are recommended by the MAG; the others are not. In fact, the "nonlegal" judges may be of any rank, educational qualifications, or experience. The appointment of nonprofessional judges enhances the danger of partiality, dependence of the courts on other authorities, and incompetent application of the law. Nevertheless, the competence problem is less serious than the independence problem. The major defect of the military court system remains that its subordination to the area commander.

The assessment of the quality of justice in the territories is often depends on the subjective perspective of the evaluator. Defense attorneys, human rights activists, and most journalists covering the territories have often expressed the feeling that the military courts favor the prosecution. For example, when the defendant appears without a lawyer, the judges have occasionally participated in the cross-examination and tended to assist the prosecutor. In general, military judges accept the evidence submitted by the military government, which reflects the version of the police, the IDF, or the Shin Bet. The testimony given by Arab witnesses, including the accused, tends to be rejected. A Palestinian human rights organization stated that "some defense lawyers feel that whatever the official burden of proof is said to be, in practice they need to prove the innocence of their clients beyond a reasonable doubt, if they are to obtain their clients' acquittal."[39]

Critics of the military legal system in the territories also have emphasized procedural improprieties in the territories' military courts. It has been argued that defense lawyers have occasionally been denied the right to make representations in court. One lawyer reported that although he had represented 700 detainees since December 1987, he had attended only three hearings regarding extension of detention.[40] In a bitter national conflict, where the judiciary is an arm of the military government, such deviations are to be expected. The Lawyers Committee on Human Rights noted in a report (February 1993) that "many reputable international and local human rights organizations have reported on the continuing failure of the military justice system to provide a fair trial, in accordance with international standards, to defendants from the Occupied Territories."[41]

The operation of Israel's military courts in the territories reminded one Israeli journalist of comments made in the pre-1948 era about the modus operandi of British military courts in Mandatory Palestine. In 1946 Ya'acov Shimshon Shapira, who later became Israel's justice minister, said of the British courts that they were "military tribunals masquerading as a court of law while they are nothing more than advisory councils on legal matters to the general." Dov Yosef, another future justice minister, said about the British system of justice in Palestine: "The cardinal principle that a man is innocent until proven guilty has been abolished in this country."[42]

One of the major difficulties with the activity of the military courts is the distinction made between Jewish settlers and Palestinian residents of the territories. According to guidelines issued by the Israeli police and approved by the attorney general and the

IDF military advocate general, military courts may try local inhabitants who violate IDF security orders or the local laws (if the
violation is security related). Military courts also may try visitors
from Israel. Despite the law, "in reality, only the Palestinian inhabitants, and sometimes visitors, are tried by the military courts. Residents of Israel and Jewish settlers in the territories are tried in
Israeli courts," not by the military courts.[43] This arrangement un-
derscores the legal duality existing in the territories.

Although the justice system in the territories is plagued with
numerous problems, some improvements have been recognized
even by those usually critical of that system. B'Tselem noted that
the caseload of individual courts had been reduced over the last
few years as a result of the appointment of additional judges and
prosecutors, and the opening of new courthouses.[44] Similarly, the
incidence of appearances in court of witnesses and accused persons
has risen.[45]

On the macro level, it is clear that the Palestinian inhabitants
do not have confidence in the military courts' ability to "deliver"
justice. Yet, the Israeli government has made another judicial level
available to the Palestinian population: the High Court of Justice.
Since 1968 the High Court of Justice, the supreme judicial body in
Israel, has ruled on petitions submitted to it by people residing in
the territories.

The controversy surrounding other aspects of Israel's activity
in the West Bank and Gaza also arises on questions relating to the
role of the High Court of Justice in the territories. In general, any
court's jurisdiction is restricted to the territory of the state. Yet, the
High Court of Justice has convincingly argued that because the
officers of the IDF, the military government, and other Israeli organs are agents of the state of Israel, the High Court of Justice
should be entitled to review the legality of their actions wherever
they may be carried out.

Nevertheless, the Court's jurisdiction in the territories has
been quite narrow, sometimes as a result of Israel's judicial traditions and sometimes as a result of the Court's own choice. As explained in chapter 1, the Court has chosen not to apply the 1949
Fourth Geneva Convention to the territories: acts by the military
government violating Geneva IV have not been examined in light
of the Convention. Furthermore, in the absence of a constitution in
Israel and provisions for judicial review, the Court lacks power to
review primary legislation. Therefore, the HCJ could not invalidate

laws passed by the Knesset as they relate to Israel or the territories. Finally, the court has accepted the government's position that accused persons may not see the evidence accumulated against them. For example, in 1986 the minister of defense decided to expel Akram Haniyeh, the editor of the East Jerusalem daily newspaper *A-Sha'ab*. The Israeli secret services claimed to have 311 documents proving Haniyeh's involvement in "terrorist activities," but Haniyeh and his lawyers were denied access to these documents, which were declared "classified material." The HCJ ruled this procedure to be legal under the provisions of the "emergency regulations," and the secret documents were admitted as evidence.[46] The self-imposed restraints on Court intervention in the fundamental legal situation have been far-reaching.

Despite these limitations, the High Court of Justice declared itself competent to review the actions, if not the legislation, of the military government. The Court's Law (1957) and the later Hok Yesod: Hashfita (Basic Law: Adjudication) allow the High Court of Justice to examine the legality of state officials' actions. The basis for the Court's decisions is personal and not territorial: it is competent to deal with the actions of government officials wherever they may be. The attorney general and the government of Israel accepted this limited Court authority, and most Israeli jurists have seen it as an extremely positive development, in the sense of creating a channel for judicial supervision of the military government's activities.[47]

Although critics of the occupation have argued that the constraints imposed on the High Court of Justice have made the Court's impact on the legal status of the residents of the territories marginal,[48] the access to the Court contributed to the self-restraint of the military government.[49] At the same time, the Court has recognized the overwhelming power given to the military government by international law and has rarely deviated from its reluctance to intervene on behalf of the local population. One of Al-Haq's lawyers wrote about this situation: "As long as the military governor is the sole unchecked legislator in the West Bank, and his orders are viewed as beyond the scrutiny of the High Court, access to the High Court becomes worthless, because his essential authority remains unchallenged and any reverses suffered by him [the governor] are quickly remedied by subsequent 'legislation.' "[50]

Although in some cases, such as the establishment of a settlement in Elon Moreh, when an appeal to the High Court of Justice has produced a reversal of the authorities' action, the High Court has accepted restrictions that have permitted it to avoid some of the thorniest issues generated by the prolonged occupation. As demonstrated in chapters 2 and 3, some of these issues—land control, administrative detention, house demolition, expulsion—have had an overwhelming impact on the status of human rights in the territories. Although the self-imposed restraint of the High Court of Justice has reflected the traditional position of the Court within the Israeli legal framework, it has proved dysfunctional for the promotion of human rights in the West Bank and Gaza.

The government has sometimes made what may be seen as inconsistent use of the High Court of Justice. On the one hand, the Israeli government and the Court allowed the Palestinian inhabitants of the territories access to the Court, pointing out repeatedly that no other occupier has done that. Thus the accessibility of the Court gave the occupation a liberal image. On the other hand, the government insisted that even international conventions signed and ratified by Israel do not apply to the territories unless they have been explicitly incorporated into Israeli domestic law by the Knesset. Thus, although the Arab residents have gained access to the Court, they have not been given all the legal tools to fight for their rights once they arrive there. This paradox has never been resolved satisfactorily.

The High Court has adopted a distinction between customary international law, which it now sees as binding on the government, and lawmaking conventions, which it perceives as nonapplicable by courts in the absence of specific domestic legislation incorporating them.[51] Despite this position, the attorney general has occasionally agreed that the Court should decide a case as if Geneva IV applies. This position seems to be inconsistent: whenever the position of the government is weak—as in the establishment of Jewish settlements in the territories, which contradicts ARTICLE 49(6) of Geneva IV—the attorney general simply refuses to accept the applicability of Geneva IV to the territories.[52]

The High Court has given the government wide latitude, especially when the authorities claim "security considerations" as a basis for an act, as in cases of confiscation of private land. A few other factors also contribute to the marginal utility of the Court in defending human rights in the territories: the reluctance of the population in the territories to give the occupation legitimacy by appealing to the Court, especially because of the perception that there is low probability of success; expenses involved in appealing to the High Court of Justice, which are clearly beyond the means of most of the residents of the territories; and the inaccessibility of the High Court of Justice to Arab lawyers who reside in the West Bank and Gaza.[53]

The High Court of Justice has proved useful, on occasions, for obtaining orders to halt actions by the military government, for restraining the military government in situations where it has not followed its own procedures, and for ruling on cases where the litigant has proved an irrelevant motive (e.g., Elon Moreh) or arbitrary action on the part of the authorities. On the whole, it would be wrong to maintain that the High Court of Justice has positively supported the government's policies in the territories (as in the case of the settlement policy): in most cases it has simply refrained from taking a decisive position against the government, perceiving itself to be procedurally incompetent to do so.

The Israeli lawyer Avigdor Feldman, who specializes in human rights and civil rights cases, found the High Court of Justice unresponsive to the reality of the West Bank and Gaza: "Reading the Court's decisions dealing with the territories creates the impression of lack of sensitivity and total absence of sympathy and empathy between the High Court and the inhabitants of the territories." According to Feldman, the court is "dealing with people whose lives have nothing to do with it, and whose language and culture are foreign to it; there is no link of communication between the Court and the inhabitants." He believes that the Court could have been more selective in using what he calls "the legal violence in its disposal" against the Arab inhabitants of the territories.[54]

Not everyone sees the willingness of the High Court of Justice to open its doors to Palestinians as a positive step. Avishai Ehrlich, a sociologist at Tel Aviv University, systematically and quantitatively studied the decisions of the High Court. He argued that by allowing the Arab inhabitants to submit cases, the Court replaced the appeals court in Ramallah, which operated in the territories during the Jordanian period.[55]

The Israeli lawyer Amnon Zichroni interprets the Court's motivations as more benign. The goal of the Court was positive: to prevent arbitrariness stemming from the unlimited power of the occupier, and to supervise the governmental and army personnel beyond Israel's boundaries. Yet, like Shehadeh and others, Zichroni believes that the activity of the High Court of Justice has some inherent weaknesses. One frequently mentioned problem is that the Court has accepted the military orders issued by the military government as primary legislation; it cannot strike them down as either unconstitutional or in violation of international law, unless they violate the Hague Regulations. Other problems are related to the modus operandi of the Court. The HCJ decides on the basis of deposition and written evidence, without hearing witnesses. With such limitations, it cannot check whether, for example, "security considerations"—which are often claimed by the government—are valid or not. The tendency of the High Court of Justice has been to accept government depositions without question. In general, Zichroni believes that the High Court of Justice has lost power with time; Ehrlich's position is similar.[56]

Professor Leon Sheleff of Tel-Aviv University's School of Law pointed out that although the HCJ opened its doors to the inhabitants of the territories, in reality they have only been able to "gather crumbs of partial successes and procedural victories." Sheleff found a dramatic difference between the Court's activism in promoting civil rights inside the Green Line (Israel proper) and its reluctance to intervene on behalf of the inhabitants of the West Bank and Gaza Strip (which Sheleff calls "judicial passivity").[57]

At the same time, the HCJ has shown on occasion the capacity for effectively intervening on behalf of human rights in the territories. In July 1989, following a petition submitted by the Association for Civil Rights in Israel regarding the right to appeal before a house is demolished, the Court ruled that houses in the territories cannot be demolished without allowing the injured parties to petition to the High Court. B'Tselem saw this important decision as reflecting "a trend in the courts to subject the military government's use of its extensive powers to judicial scrutiny."[58] At least part of the decline in house demolitions over the last few years can be explained by the Court's intervention.

The Legal Process

Having discussed in some detail the legal institutions that have operated in the territories since 1967, this section will focus on the legal process in the territories, especially the approach taken by the military government and the various security services to persons suspected of security offenses. Special attention will be given to the suspect's treatment during arrest, investigation, and interrogation. The analysis will focus on the human rights implications of the existing procedures and practices.

Arrests

Arrest powers in the territories were extensive prior to the Intifada. Section 78 of Military Order no. 378 (1970) empowered any policeman, soldier, or member of the General Security Services (GSS) to arrest, without warrant, anyone who has committed or is suspected of committing a security offense. B'Tselem, the Israeli human rights organization, noted in its *Annual Report for 1989* that although in "any reasonable legal system" the cause for arrest is based on the seriousness of the offense and the probability that the suspect was responsible for it, these criteria do not apply in the territories. Even the slightest suspicion that a person has violated the law may lead to an arrest. Military Order no. 378 lists a variety of offenses that may lead to arrests, including some that B'Tselem found "amorphous," such as "acts that *may* violate public order." The organization emphasized that even minimal suspicion can lead to the arrest of a person in the territories, and that suspicion does not even have to be "reasonable."[59] "The problem is rooted in the ease with which it is possible to decide to detain an individual," noted a later B'Tselem report.[60]

Initially a suspect may be detained for four days. An officer may extend the detention for two additional periods of seven days each —eighteen days in total. Only following this period must a detainee be brought before a judge to extend his or her detention.

The meaning of this procedure is that in the territories a person may be detained without an order from a judge or an appearance before a judge for a full eighteen days. In Israel proper, a suspect must be brought before a judge within forty-eight hours of detention, and the police have to request an extension of the arrest from the court.

The relative ease with which a person can be detained in the territories—either for investigating a crime or for punitive reasons —has drawn much critical attention. Even an official Israeli commission, the Landau Commission, which investigated the Shin Bet, recommended that the period of detention without court authorization be shortened from to eight days, because long arrests violate the suspect's human rights. Although the government officially adopted the commission's recommendation, nothing was done to effect the recommended change.[61] Only the detention period for minors and those accused of less serious offenses (such as stone-throwing) was shortened, with the maximum time prior to appearance before a judge fixed at eight days.[62]

At the time of arrest, detainees usually are not told why they have been arrested. This is despite a recommendation of the HCJ (726/88) that at the time of arrest detainees be given an accurate and detailed statement of the reasons for the arrest.[63] Amnesty International found the arrest practices in the territories inconsistent with international law, including the requirements of Geneva IV and the International Convention on Civil and Political Rights.

Once the suspect is brought before a military judge (usually at the end of the eighteen-day period), the court may extend the arrest for six months prior to a trial. In many cases, however, the detention ends prior to the eighteenth day and the detainee is released without having been brought before a judge. In some cases, the detainee is not even interrogated or told why he or she has been arrested. This situation has led some observers to conclude that many arrests are the result of error, arbitrariness, or an attempt to harass the population.[64] It is obviously very difficult to assess this claim in the context of a large-scale popular uprising.

The broad arrest powers and their widespread use is problematical from a human rights perspective. ARTICLE 9 of UDHR and ARTICLE 9(1) of the ICPR state that "no one shall be subjected to arbitrary arrest or detention." Yet, it has been very widely reported that following incidents in the West Bank and the Gaza Strip, it has been the practice to make large-scale arrests. This means that many persons unrelated to the disturbances are detained. In numerous situations, "suspects," sometimes numbering in the hundreds, have been dealt with harshly while in this type of detention. Some sources have estimated that hundreds of thousands of Palestinians have been arrested since 1967; and since December 1987, the frequency of arrests has increased sharply. The military advocate general said in October 1989 that since the beginning of the Intifada, about 40,000 arrests had been made in the territories, and that 18,000 Palestinians had been tried.[65]

ARTICLE 9(2) of the ICPR requires that any arrested person be informed at the time of arrest of the reasons for the arrest. Yet, the military orders in the territories do not require that this be done. In late 1986, the legal adviser to the military government of the West Bank informed a Palestinian lawyer that he had issued instructions requiring soldiers to give reasons for the arrest of any detained person.[66] The U.S. State Department human rights report for 1989 stated (p. 1436) that "detainees are often not told the reasons for their detention." The legality of an individual arrest, a writ of habeas corpus, cannot be contested in military courts. On the other hand, petitions to release on bail are examined, although they are rarely successful in the case of security detainees. In Israel proper, the release of detainees on bail is much more extensive.[67]

During the eighteen days following the arrest, and prior to appearance before a judge, the detainee is often in complete isolation and without access to legal representation of any kind. Lawyers sometimes are not allowed to visit their clients prior to the completion of interrogation. The same restrictions apply to representatives of the Red Cross. After the filing of indictment papers, the detainee may stay in prison until a verdict is rendered. In the territories, there is no limit on the duration of pretrial imprisonment. In Israel proper, the authorities may hold a person for a period not exceeding one year, unless a justice of the Supreme Court prolongs the period.[68]

In general, the IDF does not inform a detainee's family that he or she has been arrested. Despite the fact that the army's own Military Order 378 (ARTICLE 78a) requires immediate notice of any arrest to members of a person's family and the location of the prison where the detainee is held, the families are rarely given any information. Under pressure from the High Court of Justice, the IDF issued new orders designed to deal with this matter, but B'Tselem found that these orders have not been implemented.[69] According to the U.S. Department of State report for 1989 (p. 1436), "the problem of delayed notification [to families of detainees] continues." B'Tselem reported in May 1990 on certain improvements in this regard. Lists of detainees have been posted in the civil administration office. Furthermore, the IDF has printed postcards notifying families of the detention of their loved ones. Nevertheless, the number of recipients of these postcards is still very small, and "thousands of families hear about the detention of their loved ones only through rumors."[70] Overall, the increase in the number of detainees caught the army unprepared, but there seems to be some effort to remedy the situation.

Investigations

An important element in the operation of the Israeli legal system on the West Bank and Gaza Strip is the criminal investigations carried out by the police. Like the arrests and interrogations of suspects, police investigations have been recognized by various analysts to be plagued by serious problems that often stem from the political conditions in the territories. Some in the Israeli legal establishment have boldly identified the miscarriage of justice associated with the way many police investigations are conducted. Recommendations for improvements have been made.

On April 29, 1981, the Israeli attorney general appointed a panel headed by his deputy, Yehudit Karp, to examine law enforcement in the territories. The formation of the commission was in response to a petition by fourteen law professors, who expressed concern about irregularities in law enforcement in the territories and cited numerous cases in which violence committed by Israeli settlers against Palestinians had not been thoroughly investigated. The panel included representatives of the police, the chief military prosecutor, and the regional prosecutor. Although the Karp Report was completed in May 1982, its findings were not published until February 1984. Public pressure, media coverage, and requests by Knesset members finally compelled the government to publish the findings.

The Karp Report examined seventy files of police investigations and found that fifty-three of them "have reached a dead end." In a random sample of fifteen cases, the committee found that the police investigation was "either poor or contained substantive defects." The committee concluded that there was "a failure on the part of the police to investigate incidents in Judea and Samaria in which Jewish settlers had been accused of harassing and intimidating the local populace."[71] In particular, the Karp Report took "a very grave view of the slow pace of investigation in cases of death from shooting." The committee noted several cases in which police investigation of settlers stopped in response to direct pressure from the military government, and stated its clear impression that the settlers systematically refused to cooperate with the police.

Gideon Alon, writing for the Israeli daily *Ha'aretz* (February 9, 1984), described the thirty-three-page report as "an extremely severe indictment" of the authorities. He noted the report includes data indicating negligence, apathy, ineptness, cover-ups, refusal on the part of the settlers to cooperate with the legal authorities and a policy of discriminating between Arab and Jewish lawbreakers. Haim Ramon, M.K., saw the report as "painting an horrendous picture of settler gangs attacking Arab residents."[72] Moshe Ben-Zeev concluded that the Karp Report confirmed that in the territories "there are different regimes to different populations."[73] The *Jerusalem Post*, in a powerful editorial (February 9, 1984), stated that "the Karp Report bears out the initial suspicion that a systematic miscarriage of justice is being perpetrated in the West Bank. Jewish settlers . . . take the law into their own hands and refuse to cooperate in police investigations. The police, deferring to the army, fail to stand on their rights and the army tends to look benignly on those it views as its soldiers [the settlers]. The result is that files are closed without anyone being booked."

Although the Karp Report is written in moderate language,[74] it decisively demonstrates that the police authorities have not sufficiently investigated numerous violent incidents on the West Bank, particularly incidents in which settlers have harmed Arab residents. Many criminal acts have not been reported to the police or, when reported, have remained uninvestigated. In some cases, the military government has pressured the police to release Jews arrested for investigation. In general, investigations have deliberately been conducted slowly and inefficiently.[75]

The issuance of the Karp Report was a courageous act by Israel's legal authorities. A reading of it indicates that its purpose was merely to give examples of what the committee has seen as widespread lawlessness and discrimination in the territories. Said *Ha'aretz:* "This is merely the very tip of the iceberg. Today the reality in the territories is tenfold more severe."[76] Pinchas Inbari wrote in *Al Hamishmar* that although the Karp Report was written in legal language and it uncovered police omissions, one should read a hidden political message between the lines: the events described in the report were not exceptions due to negligence but part of the policy in the territories.[77]

The situation in the territories has not improved since the publication of the Karp Report. In fact, it has probably deteriorated as a result of the intensification of the Israeli-Palestinian conflict in the West Bank and Gaza Strip and the increase in the number of settlers in the territories.

Interrogations

Following arrest, Palestinian detainees are usually interrogated. In some ways, the interrogation stage is the most critical one for the detainee and the one when his or her human rights are most threatened. During this stage, the detainee is highly vulnerable to pressures of all kinds. According to many sources, the pressures are designed to force the detainee to confess a crime he or she may or may not have committed.

Interrogations are normally carried out by members of the General Security Service, commonly known as the Shin Bet. After a suspect confesses, a policeman is brought in to record the confession.[78] There is a strong incentive for the interrogators to elicit a confession, because the case against alleged security offenders often relies on it. More than 90 percent of the convictions in military courts operating in the territories are based on the defendant's confession;[79] therefore, the pressure to obtain a confession is part and parcel of almost every investigation.

The situation is so structured that the Shin Bet has powerful reason to obtain confessions from detainees. The many means at its disposal and the extreme vulnerability of the suspect during the interrogation stage have been considered by analysts to be a recipe for abuse and human rights violations. The vulnerability of the detainee is a function of at least two factors:

1. During the interrogation phase, detainees arrested on security grounds are often held incommunicado. The isolation makes the detainee extremely vulnerable.

2. Throughout the interrogation, the detainee is denied access to legal counsel. Therefore, he or she is largely uninformed as to options, including the right to remain silent during the interrogation.

According to numerous sources, physical and psychological mistreatment of detainees during the interrogation is common. It has been documented by Palestinian (Al-Haq), Israeli (B'Tselem), American (State Department annual reports), and international sources (e.g., the United Nations and Amnesty International). Moreover, it is included in journalists' investigations, numerous cases reported to lawyers and human rights organizations, and systematic inquiries such as the one conducted by B'Tselem between June and September 1990, in which forty-one Palestinians were interviewed about their experiences in Israeli detention centers.[80]

The most severe aspect of the interrogation stage has been accusations of torture. A 1991 Amnesty International report stated: "Once brought into detention centers for interrogation, detainees are typically subjected to forms of torture and ill-treatment."[81] The organization believes that torture and ill-treatment are "virtually institutionalized" prior to the detainee's appearance before a military court.[82] B'Tselem determined that there is a "modal period of interrogation" (lasting ten to eighteen days) in which ten different methods of torture and ill-treatment are used.[83] Diane Orentlicher, director of the International Human Rights Program of the Lawyers Committee for Human Rights in New York City, writes: "[t]wo weeks' *incommunicado* detention is a prescription, pure and simple, for abuse."[84]

The function and objective of the Shin Bet in the interrogation phase are to get information from the detainee and to extract a confession. With no effective monitoring of the Shin Bet and no effective protection of the detainee, pressures of all kinds, including physical torture, are inevitable, even though such methods are prohibited by both international law and domestic Israeli law. Although once the trial begins, the accused may argue that the confession was extracted through illegal means, with no witnesses to corroborate, the chances of removing the confession from the record are nil. Although Israeli law (which applies to all law enforcement officials in Israel and in the occupied territories) forbids the use of violence or threats to extract confessions, in practice the perceived necessity of getting information and extracting confessions prevails over the legal requirement to avoid ill-treatment and torture.

The Lawyers Committee for Human Rights thought that the practices of the Shin Bet during interrogations violate international standards. These practices include a variety of means designed to pressure the detainee to confess. The human rights reports of the Department of State described similar practices.

As in the case of the Karp Report regarding investigations and interrogations, there is substantiation of the widespread allegations even from an official Israeli inquiry commission. The Landau Commission, headed by former Supreme Court judge Moshe Landau, was set up after the Court ordered the release of a Circassian IDF officer, Izat Nafzu, who was convicted on the basis of false evidence and a confession extracted by Shin Bet agents.

Although torture is forbidden and punishable under Israeli law, and obviously unacceptable under international human rights law, the special commission found in 1987 that for at least seventeen years Shin Bet officers had used physical and psychological pressure to obtain confessions. Furthermore, Shin Bet agents had routinely perjured themselves by denying in court that such mistreatment had occurred.[85]

The information included in the Landau Report about torture

in Israeli prisons, particularly during the interrogation phase, is not new. A decade before the Landau Report, the London *Sunday Times* published ample and hard evidence of various methods of torture and their common use. A *Times* investigating team concluded that torture was planned, that it was organized as a "deliberate policy," and that it was designed to achieve three objectives: extract information, induce detainees to confess, and persuade the population in the territories to remain passive.[86]

Nevertheless, the importance of the Landau Report was that it was the first official acceptance of long-standing accusations of torture by Shin Bet agents and their lying about such practices in Israeli courts. Although many thought Israel had done the right thing in investigating, publicizing, and criticizing the interrogation practices of its own security services, others pointed out that the Israeli government did not use the publication of the report to stop the practice of torture. In fact, the Landau Report endorsed the use of "nonviolent psychological pressure" against security suspects and recommended that if such pressure fails, the use of a "moderate measure of physical pressure" be adopted. Details of the acceptable level of pressure were spelled out in a secret annex to the report, which was submitted to the prime minister but never revealed.

The Landau Commission recommended strengthening the supervision of the Shin Bet and possible retrials for those victimized by past Shin Bet practices. Yet, on the grounds that they were unaware of the regular and systematic Shin Bet practice of perjury, the report recommended that the political, judicial, and military authorities not be held responsible. It also recommended that no criminal action be taken against agents who committed perjury before the report was issued.

A few years after the publication of the Landau Report, B'Tselem expressed the view that the Shin Bet had not changed its ways in accordance with the Landau recommendations, even though the government formally accepted these recommendations.[87] Indeed, numerous complaints about Shin Bet mistreatment of detainees have been aired. B'Tselem reported on at least nine specific cases in which detainees died during interrogation.[88] The State Department human rights report for 1989 (p. 1434) mentioned ten such cases. In its follow-up to its original report on interrogation, published in March 1992, B'Tselem stated that "there has been little real change in the pattern of interrogation of Palestinian suspects."[89] B'Tselem also estimated the number of Palestinians interrogated at 5,000 per year.[90]

After reviewing the Landau recommendations, the Lawyers Committee for Human Rights sent a long letter (March 10, 1988) to Prime Minister Shamir protesting the "Shin Bet's longstanding, physically abusive interrogation methods." The letter stated that the methods were "still being used on a significant scale" and expressed the view that "the confessions resulting from these interrogations have formed the basis for virtually all prosecutions in the military courts." The committee dwelled on the practice of holding detainees incommunicado for two weeks before allowing them to meet a representative of the Red Cross and stated that this practice, which left the prisoner at the mercy of the interrogator, was universally recognized as "a prescription for abuse."

The Intifada brought a further increase in torture. Various reports informed the public that both men and women have become targets for torture. Female prisoners have complained of sexual threats and a variety of other types of torture. These reports led to the establishment of the Association for Female Political Prisoners in Israel.[91] This is another example of the response by the Israeli public to reports of human rights abuses. Yet, despite the public response, according to B'Tselem there was only one serious attempt by an official Israeli governmental authority to investigate the organization's allegations of torture: the IDF inquiry headed by Major General Vardi.[92]

The political context of interrogations in the territories makes systematic abuse virtually inevitable. Within the framework of Israeli rule over the territories, it is the function of the Shin Bet to maintain control of the population. Operationally, this means arresting and convicting those who actively oppose the occupation. Because there is rarely enough evidence to convict such persons, confessions are necessary. The only practical way to elicit confessions from resolute nationalists is through pressure and torture. Often evidence cannot be introduced in court because of security considerations; this situation also requires a confession. In brief, confessions and torture are part and parcel of political control in the territories. The more determined the opposition to the occupation, the greater the reliance on confessions and on torture during interrogation.

Plea Bargaining and the Right to a Lawyer

A military occupation's legal system is necessarily plagued by numerous problems. In the occupied territories the problems are reflected in the way plea bargaining is executed. According to some lawyers, over 90 percent of the cases are resolved through plea bargaining.[93]

In a plea bargaining situation, a detainee accepts responsibility for the act of which he or she is accused and receives a reduced punishment. The problem with plea bargaining could be that many of the accused persons entering into this deal do so not of their own free will but as a way of bringing their imprisonment to a quick end. Moreover, their willingness to enter into the deal may reflect their appraisal of the likelihood of acquittal, which is extremely low in the occupied territories.[94]

The vast majority of those brought to trial before the military courts in the territories are not released on bail (as most people accused of criminal offenses in Israel and other countries are) but are forced to wait for their trial in jail, sometimes for many months. Obviously, under such conditions a detainee has a natural tendency to admit to the crime, which shortens the pretrial detention and the expected sentence.

Furthermore, observers of the territories' military courts have reported that there is very often pressure from overworked judges to complete the trials as quickly as possible, and this pressure is focused primarily on the accused. According to Golan, who personally observed the proceedings in the Ramallah court for many months, the frequent request of the judge to "finish today" is direct pressure on the accused to confess. Every detainee knows that the way to avoid endless postponements of the trial—a period in which he or she will remain in prison under sometimes harsh conditions —is to look for a deal with the prosecution and to confess. "The temptation to give up on a trial in which guilt must be proven and to confess in order to get out of a difficult situation is extremely great and unfair."[95]

This situation has far-reaching implications in terms of the overall operation of the justice system in the territories, especially because it impacts on hundreds and possibly thousands of cases. Golan writes: "The lack of fairness is not only in that the detainee is deprived of any reasonable chance to have a full-fledged trial, but also in the strange twist in which punishment precedes conviction, replaces it and makes it unnecessary. The detainee is punished by the arrest, and only when he is ready to confess his release comes or at least a notice on the expected date of release. Punishment precedes conviction not only in reality but also as an institutionalized characteristic: the court decides merely when the punishment ends, not the question of guilt or innocence."[96]

Interestingly, the legal authorities in the territories interpret the plea bargaining situation much more benignly and even positively. Aryeh Pach, a military prosecutor in the West Bank (1971–74), wrote that plea bargaining demonstrates that "compromise with the Arab population may eventually apply not only in Military Courts, but outside them as well."[97] This is one more example of how the legal situation in the territories is open to different interpretations.

A second major problem in the territories' legal system is the common denial of contact with lawyers for security detainees. In the vast majority of cases, Palestinian detainees are not permitted to contact their attorneys even though, in principle, suspects have the right to see their lawyers.

The first meeting between a detainee and his or her lawyer is often held only twenty to thirty days after the detention,[98] when the authorities have to extend the detention and bring the prisoner, for the first time, before a judge. At this point, the interrogation phase has typically ended. If the detainee has already signed a confession, which is quite likely, the assistance of a lawyer may prove useless. Some sources, including Israeli and international ones, report that two months often elapse between a person's arrest and his or her being permitted to consult freely with an attorney.[99] Technically, it is possible to prevent a detainee from meeting with an attorney for a total of ninety days.[100]

In general, the effectiveness of legal counsel in the military justice system of the West Bank and Gaza Strip is limited because of the difficulty of contacts between lawyers and their imprisoned clients. The commander of the prison where a detainee is held may prevent a meeting between the prisoner and his or her attorney at any time for reasons of security (Military Order no. 29 for the West Bank and no. 410 for the Gaza Strip).

The practice in the West Bank and Gaza regarding the inherent right to consult a lawyer is rather problematical from a human rights perspective. ARTICLE 11(1) of the Universal Declaration of Human Rights states that "everyone charged with a penal offense has the right to be presumed innocent until proved guilty according to law in a public trial at which he has had all the guarantees necessary for his defense." It could be argued that one such guarantee is the right to competent and timely legal advice. This right is particularly important in view of the lack of familiarity of most Arab detainees with the Israeli legal system and the language used in Israeli courts, Hebrew.

ARTICLE 72 of Geneva IV specifically requires that "accused persons . . . shall have the right to be assisted by a qualified advocate or counsel of their own choice." However, some jurists maintain that ARTICLE 5(2) of Geneva IV limits ARTICLE 72 when it states that "where in occupied territory an individual protected person is detained as a spy or saboteur, or as a person under definite suspicion of activity hostile to the security of the Occupying Power, such person shall, in those cases where absolute military security so requires, be regarded as having forfeited rights of communication under the present convention."

It must be noted that ARTICLE 5(2) limits ARTICLE 72 only when it is necessary for "absolute military security." It seems that ARTICLE 5(2) cannot be applied en masse. In this sense, the military government's inclination to deny access to lawyers for long periods of time to practically all security detainees is highly problematical.

B'Tselem reported that in every Shin Bet interrogation the meeting of the accused with his or her lawyer is postponed until the end of the interrogation. Interestingly, in most cases where lawyers appealed to the High Court of Justice, arguing that there was no real justification for prohibiting a meeting with their client, the prohibition was quickly withdrawn. Even an indication of an intention to appeal to the HCJ is often sufficient to produce a meeting between lawyer and client. B'Tselem concluded that "it is reasonable to assume . . . that the 30-day ban on a meeting [between detainee and lawyer] has become a custom that in many cases does not have real security justification."[101]

Extralegal Activity

Having reviewed the activities of some of the judicial institutions in the territories, and the various aspects of the legal process, we now turn to what might be called the extralegal dimension of the justice system in the territories. The understanding of this dimension is important for assessing the overall quality of justice in the West Bank and Gaza Strip, especially since the beginning of the Intifada in late 1987.

Vigilantism

The intensification of the Jewish settlement effort in the territories during the 1970s led to the deterioration of the relationships between Arabs and Jews in the West Bank and Gaza. One symptom of that deterioration has been the increasing number of attacks by Arabs on Jews, and also an increasing number of attacks by Jewish settlers on Arab residents of the territories. Vigilantism, a form of violence in which settlers have taken the law into their own hands and carried out attacks on Arab inhabitants, has become common.

Vigilantism could be explained as an inevitable result of the expanded settlement program in the territories. This program generated tremendous anxiety among the Arab residents and was accompanied by increased violence against the settlers. The settlers felt that the government was not doing enough to protect them from Arab attacks. They responded by frequently taking the law into their own hands, not only by defending themselves but also by initiating attacks on their Arab neighbors.

The most dramatic vigilante activity since 1967 was the establishment of a group known as the Jewish Underground in the Territories or the Jewish Terror Group.[102] Many of the members of the group were associated with Gush Emunim's settlement effort in the territories, and some of them occupied leadership positions within the Gush. A few served as reserve officers in the IDF, and one was a career officer. In the subsequent trial of the members of the Underground, it was found that they were assisted by at least two officers serving in the headquarters of the civil administration in the territories.[103]

The Underground was responsible for violent actions including assassination attempts on the lives of three West Bank mayors serving on the National Guidance Committee, in retaliation for the murder of six settlers in Hebron, near the Hadassah House; an armed attack on the Islamic College of Hebron, which resulted in the killing of three students, in retaliation for the murder of a yeshiva student; a plot to blow up the Dome of the Rock on Jerusalem's Temple Mount; and an attempt to sabotage Arab buses in East Jerusalem.

Members of the Underground were finally caught and tried in an Israeli court. The three convicted of the murder of the Hebron students were sentenced to life imprisonment. Others received fairly light sentences and were released from prison after a rather short period of detention. A public lobby, headed by more than twenty Knesset members, was organized to assist in securing the release of all persons involved in the Underground activity.

Signaling an increased vigilantist activity, a few other violent groups have emerged in Israel and the territories since the mid-1980s. The Lifta Group planned the damage of the mosques on Temple Mount in Jerusalem (1984). Members of TNT, an organization that appears to have connection with Rabbi Kahane's Kach Party,[104] planted bombs in churches and mosques in Jerusalem, opened fire on an Arab bus, and so forth.

In addition to this kind of conspiratorial activity among right-wingers in Israel and in the territories, there have been numerous instances, both prior to and especially following the Intifada, in which individuals and groups of Jewish settlers have taken the law into their hands and committed acts of violence against Arabs in a more spontaneous and reactive manner. According to some sources, during the first year of the Intifada, settlers killed as many as fifteen Palestinians, often in response to rock-throwing.[105] The State Department annual human rights report noted that in 1989, Israeli settlers killed eleven Palestinians during "marches, patrols, retaliatory raids, and other incidents" (p. 1433). However, the report stated that the IDF condemned such vigilantism and attempted to stop it. This statement reflects the announced policy of the IDF.

Many observers have felt that the government has been lenient in its treatment of vigilante acts by settlers. The Karp Report and numerous other sources have documented the ineffective police handling of settler vigilantism. The courts have not shown any more zest in punishing those who have taken the law into their hands. On November 30, 1988, Israel Ze'ev, an Israeli settler, was found guilty of the shooting death of Judeh Taim, a Palestinian shepherd, in an unprovoked attack as Taim tended sheep on his land close to the settlement where Ze'ev resided. Although convicted of manslaughter, which carries a maximum sentence of twenty years, Ze'ev received only three years in prison.

This verdict was typical of many others in which the courts refused to impose a tough punishment on settlers committing violence against Arabs. When Nisan Ishgoyev killed a child in Nablus, Judge Uri Strosman imposed (February 22, 1988) such a lenient penalty on him that many editorialists attacked the court publicly, an unusual reaction. Strosman found Ishgoyev guilty of manslaughter, for which the maximum penalty is twenty years in prison. He sentenced him to six months of labor outside prison. Two Israeli policemen who witnessed the incident testified against Ishgoyev.[106]

The discriminatory nature of Judge Strosman's sentence was underscored by various commentators. A fairly typical response was that of Rubik Rosenthal: "A verdict that defends the killing of children at the hands of settlers generates a deep anxiety that next we will see the corruption of the judicial system. This system judges severely an Arab rock thrower and a Jew who steals or murders inside the Green Line [Israel], but will give moral support to the sacred militias in the territories."[107] Boaz Evron wrote that "the court's behavior indicates that the judicial system itself has become an appendage of the machinery of repression."[108]

It is interesting to mention in this context that in early 1988, nine Knesset members from five right-wing parties proposed new legislation (Release from Prison Law) that would "free a person from prison if he violated a law as a result of 'security distress' (*metzuka bitchonit*) or as a result of concern for the fate of the state and its inhabitants, with no intention to subvert the state's existence or with no membership in an organization hostile to the State." The purpose of the law was to force the release of the Jewish Underground prisoners (by then, they had spent five years in prison), two others who were convicted of killing Arabs, and a Kach member who shot a bazooka shell at an Arab bus in Jerusalem.[109] The legislation was never approved by the Knesset. Similarly, since the Intifada, the pressure of the settlers on the government has intensified, focusing on issues such as the broadening of rules for opening fire in the territories, expelling large numbers of Palestinians, and demolishing homes.[110]

In some quarters of Israeli society, there has been a feeling that the government has not been resisting the settlers' pressures or has chosen to look the other way in many cases of violence. Although government and IDF spokesmen have expressed disapproval of settlers taking the law into their own hands, no serious action has been taken to curb such behavior. In fact, the settlers have been heavily armed. The media have reported numerous violent raids by settlers on Arab villages and refugee camps, that have resulted in the destruction of property and crops, assaults on residents, and the widespread use of gunfire that occasionally has led to death.

Although some of the Israeli courts did not decisively intervene to stop vigilantism in the territories, the Supreme Court reacted more severely. In August 1988, the Court sentenced a settler to three years in prison for the killing of a thirteen-year-old Arab boy. The verdict was in relation to a 1981 incident for which the settler initially received a six-month prison term. In another case, the Court increased from three to eighteen months the sentence given to a man who set fire to a hut in Or Yehuda in which Arab workers were sleeping.

Settlers' vigilantism has been facilitated by several factors. First, almost all settlers are armed; therefore, they have the capacity to carry out violent actions in the territories. Second, many settlers serve in either the reserve or the regular forces in the West Bank. In their capacity as soldiers, they have further opportunity to use arms. Third, there is obvious and natural hostility between the Arab residents and the Jewish settlers in the territories: the likelihood of violent flare-ups between them is extremely high. Fourth, the Israeli military government has had, even according to Israeli sources, "a long and infamous history of intentionally looking the other way when settlers' activities are concerned."[111]

The nature of vigilantism in the territories is such that it is virtually impossible to know exactly how widespread it is. However, the Palestinian, Israeli, and international press have reported on it so often and so extensively that there is reason to believe it is quite common. Vigilantism had existed in the territories prior to the Intifada, and it included assault resulting in death[112] and numerous other forms of attack. Israeli soldiers returning from service in the territories not only have reported on vigilantism as a common phenomenon but also have emphasized that the authorities knowingly ignore the settlers' activities and that "the procedures for opening fire [are] more lenient for the settlers than for the IDF soldiers."[113]

In addition to settlers' vigilantism, there has been a flood of reports on soldiers or policemen clearly acting illegally. In particular, the Border Police have established a reputation for dealing harshly with the civilian population. One member of the Border Police reported: "[T]he truth is that we are not allowed to commit violence, but when violence occurs despite the prohibition, the authorities look the other way. They tell us that anyone who uses more than reasonable force will stand trial, but in reality there are no trials." The soldiers, along with many others, report that the Border Police constantly harass the population. It seems that the two Israeli groups prone to use violence against the Arab population, the settlers and the Border Police, have an affinity for each

other. One Border Policeman said to *Ha'aretz:* "[M]ost Magav-
nikim [Border Policemen] identify with the positions taken by the
settlers. I believe that almost all identify with the settlers."[114]

In general, the legal authorities in Israel have recognized the
problem of vigilantism in the territories.[115] Some observers have
perceived the problem as a reflection of the "double standard system of justice . . . under which Palestinian residents are punished
far more severely than Israeli soldiers and settlers for similar
crimes."[116] Put differently, some have pointed out that an Israeli
settler attacking an Arab resident in a vigilante action can be expected to be treated much more leniently than an Arab resident
attacking an Israeli settler. Settlers and soldiers charged with illegally killing Palestinians have very often been released on bail, an
unheard-of arrangement for Palestinians indicted for the killings of
Israelis. Also, the sentences given Jews for vigilantism have been
lighter than the ones given to Palestinians convicted of violent acts.
The West Bank Data Base Project found that settlers and soldiers
convicted of killing Palestinians were often sentenced to six to
twelve months, whereas Arabs received eight to ten years for
throwing gasoline bombs at Israeli vehicles.[117]

Excessive Force

An important aspect of the human rights situation in the territories has been the use of force by IDF soldiers and other security
personnel. Since the beginning of the Intifada, there has been increasing world attention focused on this issue, concentrating particularly on the number of deaths in the territories. In the Intifada's
first year 284 Palestinians died as a result of actions taken by Israeli
security forces; in the second year the number increased to 300;
and then it decreased dramatically in the third (127 fatalities) and
fourth years (91 deaths).[118] In the Intifada's fifth year (1992), however, a dramatic increase was registered: 158 deaths, the highest
number since the second year.[119] The number of fatalities, despite
its fluctuations, reflects a reality in which the resistance to the occupation continues unabated.

In addition to deaths resulting from actions taken by Israeli
security forces, there have been Israeli fatalities resulting from Palestinian violence and killings of Palestinians by Palestinians. The
world's attention has focused on the action of the Israeli forces.

IDF personnel have been widely accused in the media of unjustified shooting, the use of unreasonable force, and the extensive use of tear gas and live ammunition. In view of these accusations, one has to examine the question of the use of force contextually, empirically, and fairly: What place does the use of force have in maintaining law and order in the territories? Is it a necessary evil? Has force been used in a restrained fashion? These are some of the questions addressed in this section. They all have great relevance for human rights in the territories.

The Israeli human rights organization B'Tselem collected and published a vast amount of material about the use of force by IDF personnel in the territories. On the whole, B'Tselem believes that although the IDF has not completely ignored the problem of excessive force, it has not severely punished the perpetrators. According to B'Tselem, between December 9, 1987, and late April 1990, 646 Palestinians were killed in incidents involving IDF personnel,[120] and 802 were killed by the end of the fourth year of the Intifada.[121] According to official Israeli sources, 52 indictments (against 86 individuals) of Israeli soldiers and officers have been submitted. As a result of these proceedings, 63 soldiers have been convicted, 9 have been acquitted, and 14 files remain open. The military advocate general stated that in addition to indictments and trials in the IDF military courts, in the first two years of the Intifada, 500–600 soldiers had disciplinary charges brought against them in connection with incidents in the West Bank and Gaza.[122]

The severity of the punishment imposed on IDF personnel convicted of excessive use of force has been surprisingly low. According to B'Tselem's files, the six IDF soldiers and officers convicted for manslaughter by shooting received the following penalties:

1. Two soldiers received suspended sentences.

2. A captain, Alex Deutsch, was sentenced to three months in prison and six months' suspended sentence, which was later cut to two and one-half months by the area commander.

3. A soldier was sentenced to twelve months' imprisonment and twenty-four months' suspended sentence for causing the death of two Palestinians.

4. A corporal, Ya'acov Tamir, received one year in prison but was released after six months.

5. Another corporal, Eli Yedidia, received an eighteen-month sentence for shooting a rubber bullet at a Palestinian from a distance of 20 centimeters and for perjury.

On the basis of this information, the average period of imprisonment given for the unjustifiable killing of a Palestinian was about seven and one-half months. According to B'Tselem's figures, which are in general agreement with Palestinian and international ones, the pattern of leniency holds for offenses less severe than manslaughter. IDF personnel convicted of serious crimes against Palestinians and sent to prison were sentenced, on the average, to 4.3 months in prison; many received only suspended sentences.[123] Soldiers found to be using their weapons illegally and in violation of orders also received low sentences: one received two months' imprisonment; four others, one to six months' suspended sentences; and two were fined IS 200 (about $100) each.

The leniency toward IDF personnel has been even more pronounced when senior officers are involved in illegal, excessive use of force. An IDF colonel who shot at fleeing Palestinians and killed a villager from Bnai Naim (April 4, 1988) received a "severe reprimand." He was moved to another position within the IDF and then resigned. A reserve lieutenant colonel was found responsible for not preventing improper behavior in which detainees were taken to an orchard, stripped, and beaten, and a dog was incited to attack them. He was merely removed from his position.

One of the most famous cases involving a senior officer was that of Lieutenant Colonel Yehuda Meir, the military governor of Nablus, the largest city on the West Bank. Meir was accused of ordering (January 1988) his soldiers to assemble twelve Palestinian villagers, tie them up, and severely beat them. The officer, who in the meantime had been promoted to colonel, received a "severe reprimand" from the IDF chief of staff and left the IDF without standing trial. Following a petition by the Association for Civil Rights in Israel and four of the people who were beaten at Hawara, the High Court of Justice ordered on December 24, 1989, that Meir be put on trial. This decision was seen as a severe reprimand and a blow to the prestige of the military advocate general. In March 1990, Meir was charged before a special military court in Tel Aviv. He denied the charges and said that his actions were in accordance with the norms existing at the time throughout the IDF.[124] Nevertheless, the court found Meir's orders to be "patently illegal" and sentenced him to demotion to the rank of private. Many who praised the Meir conviction thought that he deserved a significantly harsher penalty.[125]

Another IDF colonel, the military governor of the Judea Region, received a reprimand for an action in which five Nahalin villagers were killed (April 13, 1989). A lieutenant colonel more directly involved in the Nahalin affair was removed from his position but assigned to a similar one in the Samaria Region.

In general, although the IDF has not ignored these clearly illegal actions, none of its senior officers has ever been imprisoned for ordering such actions, even if convicted. B'Tselem's *1989 Annual Report* noted that since the beginning of the Intifada, no officer with a rank above captain *(seren)* has been tried in a military court for a violation concerning an event in the territories.[126] Although since the publication of the 1989 report a few trials of high-ranking officers have taken place, punitive measures have been relatively lenient: demotions, reprimands, or removal from a position.[127] Human Rights Watch found that although the Israeli criminal justice system has shown willingness to expose abuses by the security forces, it has been reluctant to "mete out appropriate punishments."[128] The system, according to the organization, continues to "treat abuses by security forces with leniency."[129]

Soldiers carrying out illegal orders *(pkuda bilti-hukit)* or manifestly illegal orders *(pkuda bilti-hukit bealil),* an important distinction within the Israeli legal system, also have not been severely punished, even when their actions have led to death or severe injuries. Among the 500–600 soldiers tried for disciplinary violations, the average penalty was an eighteen days in prison.[130]

On a number of occasions well-publicized trials of soldiers have been held. In the so-called Golani Trial, the court itself described the development of a punitive policy. This policy directed soldiers to beat Palestinians as a deterrent against future activity. Soldiers were specifically ordered to beat detainees only on the limbs.

In the so-called Givati Trial A, the court described officers encouraging soldiers to break the law, rejecting the position (advanced by some senior officers) that what is prohibited by law in Israel might not be prohibited in the territories. The court stated that one cannot beat a suspect following arrest, and reminded the accused that in a democratic state, punitive action may be taken only by the judicial branch; this was a direct reference to the frequent use of beating as punishment. The court found that the orders were manifestly illegal *(pkuda bilti-hukit bealil),* the type of orders that a soldier can and must disobey.

In its human rights report for 1988 (p. 1378), the U.S. Department of State concluded that although the "Israeli authorities in some cases prosecuted or took disciplinary action against security personnel and settlers who killed Palestinians in violation of regulations . . . regulations were not rigorously enforced; punishments were usually lenient; and there were many cases of unjustified killing which did not result in disciplinary actions or prosecutions." The State Department report for 1989 observed that "only a relatively small number of incidents [leading to death and injuries] have resulted in prosecution and the sentences meted out have tended to be light" (p. 1433).

Amnesty International conducted a number of studies on the use of force in the territories. On the whole, it painted a harsher but not significantly different picture than B'Tselem and the U.S. Department of State. Amnesty International found that the use of force by the IDF has been excessive; intended to punish and intimidate; often indiscriminate (e.g., directed against people uninvolved in a demonstration); often used against those already in detention and or even against women, children, the elderly, and the wounded; and occasionally deadly.[131]

One of the most controversial issues has been the extensive use of beatings. The policy of the Israeli government toward beatings as a method for dealing with the Intifada has been inconsistent. In mid-February 1988, an Amnesty International delegation heard from General Amram Mitzna, the military commander of the Central Command, and thus the top IDF officer with powers over the West Bank, that the IDF policy allowed soldiers to use reasonable force to disperse violent demonstrations: Mitzna emphasized that there was no policy to beat people as a punitive or deterrent measure.[132] Yet, evidence indicated that severe beating of demonstrators was often used against fleeing Palestinians (a circumstance in which the beating was clearly punitive).

On January 19, 1988, Defense Minister Rabin announced what has been perceived as a policy on beatings. He stated that demonstrations would be prevented by "force, power and blows!" The function of this policy was not to reduce fatalities but to severely punish and effectively deter the population from continuing the Intifada. Amnesty International and others saw the Rabin announcement as "amounting to license to beat indiscriminately."[133]

The result of the new policy was a huge number of injuries in the territories. On January 25, about a week after Rabin's declaration, 200 people were admitted to the Al Shifa hospital in Gaza with broken wrists, arms, and legs. It was assessed that less than half of those in need of medical treatment arrived at the hospital out of fear of being arrested.

Israel and the territories were visited on February 4–12, 1988, by a delegation of the Physicians for Human Rights. The visitors, all practicing physicians, examined injured Palestinians and concluded that there was evidence of "a deliberate policy of systematic beating designed to disable and not to kill, to inflict maximum damage while reducing the risk of death."[134] Despite the physical evidence, Rabin and his assistants continuously stated that there was no policy of intentionally breaking bones, no beating for the sake of beating, and that persons were not beaten punitively (that is, after being detained). Nevertheless, the Israeli press reported justifications for the beating policy given by military officers. These statements reflected Rabin's initial declaration.[135]

The policy of beatings generated sharp criticism from members of Knesset. On February 23, 1988, Israel's Attorney General took the unusual step of writing a letter to the Minister of Defense. The letter advised Rabin that beating demonstrators to punish or humiliate them was illegal and that it was also illegal for soldiers to obey orders commanding them to do so. Attorney General Harish also stated that he had received enough complaints to convince him that the irregularities were not exceptional cases.[136] The Harish letter was another example of Israel's legal establishment trying to respond to the crisis in the territories.

Nevertheless, only a few soldiers involved in beatings have been prosecuted. Only in cases when severe brutality became public has prosecution resulted. IDF soldiers who ordered a bulldozer driver to cover four Palestinians with earth were tried. Yet, their commanding officer, who was convicted of assault and unbecoming conduct, was sentenced to a mere four months' imprisonment and to demotion. The sentence was later reduced to two months.

Severe beating of Palestinians has not been the only, or even the dominant, complaint against IDF personnel. The unjustified, hasty use of live ammunition against unarmed civilians has also been a topic of concern for the human rights community. Since the beginning of the Intifada, Amnesty International has issued a number of reports regarding the use of live ammunition by the IDF in the territories.[137] Other reporting organizations also have dealt with this issue extensively,[138] including in-depth reporting in the Israeli press.

The various reports indicate that hundreds of Palestinians have been shot and killed by live ammunition and many thousands injured. Palestinians have described the Israeli reaction to the Intifada as the unrestrained firing of live ammunition into crowds of protesters, crowds gathered at hospitals, and mourners at subsequent mass funerals."[139] Although the description of Israeli actions as unrestrained firing is an exaggeration, people shot on the West Bank and Gaza have not always been participating in violent demonstrations. Furthermore, many others have been shot not by IDF personnel but by settlers. The delegation of Physicians for Human Rights, which visited the territories in February 1988, reported observing an "essentially uncontrolled epidemic of violence by soldiers and police in the West Bank and Gaza Strip." It concluded that the frequency of assaults was such that "these episodes cannot be considered as aberrations or exceptions to established policy; they are close to being the norm."[140]

A close examination of the IDF guidelines regarding firing indicates that they have been liberalized since the Intifada. In March 1988, General Mitzna of the Central Command sent a letter defining the policy on the use of deadly force: to all security personnel serving in the West Bank: "As a general rule, live ammunition is not to be used against civilian population. However, it is permissible to open fire in those situations *where life is endangered* and the only remaining option is to use weapons."[141]

However, on March 21, 1988, Defense Minister Rabin said that orders on the use of live ammunition had been changed to permit soldiers to shoot directly at Palestinians who attacked them with gasoline bombs. And on April 3, 1988, Rabin confirmed that many of the confrontations between the IDF and the Palestinians were, in fact, initiated by the IDF, to "teach a lesson to those who start violence."[142]

The result of the new policy was a dramatic increase in the number of Palestinians killed by Israeli soldiers. The Physicians for Human Rights found that many of the injuries among the Palestinians have occurred not during Palestinian demonstrations but during unilateral and unprovoked army and police "sweeps" through refugee camps, villages, or neighborhoods under curfew. In those raids, many Palestinians uninvolved in the demonstrations have suffered injuries and death.[143]

In September 1988, the policy was further changed to permit the shooting of plastic bullets "to stop demonstrations or instigators of demonstrations in situations that do not threaten the lives of security forces and to increase injuries."[144] The IDF spokesmen claimed that plastic bullets are significantly less lethal than lead bullets, a claim challenged by many experts.

There are indications that IDF soldiers are currently authorized to fire at masked Palestinian suspects when they ignore an order to halt or are fleeing.[145] Al Haq reported that seventeen of the thirty-one Palestinians killed in October 1989 were masked.[146] The Department of State report observed that although the army authorities had tried to prevent anarchy by allowing shooting only on specific attackers, directing fire only at legs, in reality the situation was much less controlled. According to its human rights report, "IDF guidelines often were not followed," resulting in avoidable death and injuries.[147]

The State Department report on human rights practices for 1992 stated that although the IDF regulations permit using live ammunition only when soldiers' lives are in real and immediate danger, to halt fleeing suspects, or to disperse a violent demonstration, in practice members of the security forces use it in other cases.

It is extremely difficult to conduct accurate inquiries into the detailed circumstances of each occurrence in which live ammunition has been used. Yet, it is clear that since December 1987 the IDF has extensively used live ammunition. Although the IDF has a policy of investigating every case of fatal shooting, its investigations obviously do not enjoy the confidence of the Palestinians and are increasingly taken with a grain of salt by many in the international community. There is no independent monitoring of the IDF investigations.

Nevertheless, Amnesty International and others have collected testimony indicating many specific cases of what the organization has described as "unjustified killings." Amnesty International has concluded that in some cases "the authorities at a high level have actively condoned if not encouraged the use of live ammunition and unreasonable force by members of the IDF against Palestinians in the occupied territories.[148] The Physicians for Human Rights agreed.

The authorities in the territories have routinely claimed that the shooting of Palestinians resulted from soldiers finding themselves in "life-threatening situations." Yet, the Lawyers Committee on Human Rights stated in its letter to Prime Minister Shamir that the large number of fatalities and serious injuries among Palestinians, measured against the number of injuries among the IDF soldiers, "strongly suggest that this rationale has been abused in practice." The Lawyers Committee noted that although response to demonstrations had been a major responsibility of the IDF for at least several years prior to the Intifada, the IDF provided soldiers with virtually no training in riot control.

In general, it was found that IDF guidelines designed to minimize the killing of civilians "were often not followed. Soldiers frequently used gunfire in situations that did not present mortal danger to troops, causing many avoidable deaths and injuries."[149] The routine explanation that soldiers used guns to extricate themselves from dangerous situations was rejected by many who found that numerous Palestinians were killed while engaged in passive (if illegal) activities such as raising a flag or demonstrating.

One type of excessive force that has generated worldwide protest has been the tear gas against the civilian population. On June 1, 1988, Amnesty International issued a report on that topic. It found that tear gas had been overused since December 1987. It was used not only to disperse demonstrations but also as "a punitive measure, to harass and intimidate Palestinian residents in the occupied territories."[150] In numerous cases, the gas was used in residential areas, making it difficult for people to escape; on occasions, tear gas containers were thrown into homes, schools, mosques, and even health clinics and hospitals. The delegation of Physicians on Human Rights reached similar conclusions.

In its detailed report, Amnesty International noted that the IDF has used two types of gas in the territories: CN (chloroacetopheone) and CS (orthochlorobenzylidene malononitride). Both are manufactured in Saltsburg, Pennsylvania, by Federal Laboratories and exported to Israel for use in the territories.

The manufacturer's handbook describes CN and CS as nonlethal, riot control agents and states that there have not been any deaths recorded as a result of using them in the open air. The handbook warns, however, that if these agents are used incorrectly, they may cause serious injuries and even death. It emphasizes that under no circumstances should CN and CS be used in enclosed areas, and that those who are to use the agents must go through careful training.

In early May 1988, Federal Laboratories halted export of CS and CN to Israel in response to numerous reports of the misuse of these agents. According to Amnesty International, there were indications that the gas was used as a punishment for large numbers of persons, not exclusively for dispersing crowds. Although the gas was sometimes used to bring demonstrations to an end, it had been used against people not engaged in demonstrations. Palestinian sources asserted that on occasions tear gas was spread during the night over villages and camps involved in demonstrations during the day.[151]

It is important to note that Israeli sources were also concerned about the use of tear gas. A report issued by Israeli physicians and health workers after a visit to Gaza hospitals in May 1988 resulted in the IDF ban on the use of tear gas in enclosed areas.

The use of undercover IDF squads *(mista' arvim)* in the territories, a practice that started in 1988, also has been highly controversial. According to a 187-page report published in June 1993 by Middle East Watch (MEW) under the title *Licence to Kill*, these units were given permission to shoot at Palestinians even when no threat to themselves is involved. An IDF spokesman argued in response to the report that soldiers were bound by strictly defined open-fire orders, that all Palestinian deaths were investigated by military police, and that soldiers involved in wrongful shootings were punished.

According to MEW the undercover units had killed more than 120 Palestinians since 1988; a report of B'Tselem put the number at 70 (between December 1987 and April 1992).[152] B'Tselem found that "in a large percentage of the cases, it was possible to apprehend the suspects without killing them."[153] Furthermore, B'Tselem found that IDF undercover units were equipped with live ammunition only, and that a significant number of those killed by them were unarmed.[154] The organization ended its report by stating that "only a court is authorized to impose a death sentence on a person."[155]

Collective Punishment

Collective punishment is explicitly prohibited by the norms governing belligerent occupation. ARTICLE 50 of the Hague Regulations—a binding, customary international law that applies in the territories, according to Israel's High Court of Justice—states that "no general penalty . . . shall be inflicted upon the population on account of the acts of individuals." Similarly, ARTICLE 33 of Geneva VI (a convention that the HCJ has refused to view as applying to the territories but that the vast majority of other interpreters have seen as binding on Israel) states that "no protected person may be punished for an offense he or she has not personally committed." Although the occupying power is empowered to act when military necessity dictates an action, such action is limited, inter alia, by the prohibition on collective punishment. Although the laws of war permit the use of violent force to achieve military goals, humanitarian considerations (as reflected in ARTICLES 33 and 50) limit this force and call upon its user to direct it only toward the individual responsible for breaking the law or endangering the security forces of the occupier.

One of the major problems raised since 1967 in regard to the operation of the justice system in the territories is that of collective punishment: critics have argued that often residents are not punished for acts for which they are personally responsible but for the acts of others. The accusations have focused on measures such as house demolition,[156] the spraying of tear gas, the imposition of long-term (general) or night curfews, the closure of schools and universities, the prevention of movement in and out of an area, and mass arrests.

The closure of schools for long periods has been one of the most severe, comprehensive, and longest forms of collective punishment inflicted on the population. In the West Bank, the educational system in its entirety was closed from early 1988 to the end of July 1989. Universities and colleges were closed until the summer of 1990. The IDF explained the closure as a "security necessity," and maintained that the concentration of youth in schools leads to rock-throwing and other disturbances. Yet, a study comparing the number of disturbances while schools were closed and the number while schools were open, failed to establish a correlation.[157] Many observers believe that school closure was used not because of a security necessity but as a punitive measure.[158]

The imposition of curfews, often for extended periods, has been another measure identified as collective punishment. It has been carried out in accordance with the 1945 Defense (Emergency) Regulations, especially Order no. 124. At the beginning of the Intifada, curfew was used mainly to restore order following disturbances and to apprehend suspects. However, it has increasingly become a punitive and a preventive measure. In its preventive capacity, the curfew has been imposed on large areas and on days of great significance for the local population, when the authorities thought riots would erupt. In its punitive role, the curfew has been used extensively and has been accompanied by measures such as the suspension of telephone, water, and electrical services to large areas. Obviously the Israeli authorities have had at least a reasonable fear that without curfews, order in the territories would further deteriorate. On August 19, 1990, the HCJ dismissed an Association for Civil Rights in Israel (ACRI) petition asking for full or partial relief of curfews (HCJ 113/90).

During the Intifada there has been a very significant increase in the use of curfew by the authorities in the territories. Whereas in the first years of the Israeli military government in the territories, curfews were limited in terms of area and duration (normally lasting no longer than twenty-four hours), the uprising in the West Bank and Gaza has brought a massive use of this measure. During the second year of the uprising, about 1,600 curfews were imposed, and more than 10 percent of them were prolonged. Roughly 1 million people, about 60 percent of the total population in the territories, were placed under a prolonged curfew at some point during that year.[159] B'Tselem wrote about the extensive use of curfew that it "creates the impression that . . . it exceeds the legitimate operational needs of the governmental authorities" and that it is "frequently a form of collective punishment."[160] Human Rights Watch saw the imposition of curfews as "an act of collective punishment," which is "absolutely prohibited by international law."[161]

The bans on movement were frequently imposed as a form of collective punishment. Following riots, the residents of large areas in the territories not only were put under curfew but also were prohibited from going to Jordan. In view of the close relationships between the territories and Jordan, this was a rather severe penalty. The practice was discontinued by the IDF in response to an ACRI petition (660/89).

Politically, the use of collective punishment in the territories could be understood as a reaction of the Israeli authorities to what is generally perceived as a popular uprising. Some Israeli legal analysts denied the existence of collective punishment,[162] but such arguments were heard mainly prior to the Intifada. In a monograph about collective punishment. B'Tselem concluded (p. 54) that "the general impression is that the discretion as to the employment of these measures [curfews, closing of educational institutions, travel limitations, house demolitions, etc.] does not properly balance security considerations with considerations of basic human rights."[163]

The issue of collective punishment in the territories emphasizes the reality of a dual justice system in the West Bank and
Gaza. Collective punishment has been used extensively against
Palestinian Arabs but never against Israeli Jewish settlers. The territories have had two different legal systems—operating side by
side in the same area—and there have been dramatic differences
in the way the law has been applied. Palestinians caught throwing
rocks have received severe penalties, in some cases ten years in
prison. On occasion, the family residence of a rock-thrower has
been demolished, even if the act did not cause any damage.[164] The
throwing of a Molotov cocktail has led almost invariably to the
demolition of the family residence or to severe punishment.[165] On
the other hand, Israeli citizens who have violated the law in similar
ways (e.g., through throwing rocks at Arab cars) or even more severe ones (e.g., shooting at Arabs or systematically destroying their
property) have often gone unpunished. Even in the numerous cases
in which settlers have clashed with IDF soldiers, usually nothing
has been done to penalize the settlers.

According to the data presented by B'Tselem during 1988 and
1989, there were six violent events leading to the death of nine
Israelis at the hands of Palestinians. In four of the cases, suspects
were arrested and tried. In twenty-four additional violent events,
twenty-five Palestinians were killed in circumstances pointing to
Israeli responsibility. Of these twenty-four violent events, only one
legal case has been brought to conclusion, and the suspect tried
and convicted.[166] At the time of the preparation of B'Tselem's report
(December 1989), one additional case was in court. Twenty-two
cases were somewhere in processing, although many of them had
occurred close to two years prior to the writing of the report.

B'Tselem wrote about the double standard as follows: "It
seems that in cases of the investigation of death in which Israeli
citizens are involved, the picture painted by the Karp Report has
not changed over the last 7 years . . . the authorities have not shown
the appropriate zest and commitment to these type [sic] of investigations."[167] It seems that the authorities have not changed their
position despite a dramatic increase in violent actions on the part
of the settlers. Haim Ramon, M.K., reported that in May 1989 there
were eighteen cases of severe violence and hooliganism by settlers.
It is generally known that since the Intifada began, violence by
both sides has been a daily occurrence; however, the two sides
have not paid an identical price.

5

ഉ൦

Alternative Political Solutions

IN its first four chapters, this study dealt with various aspects of human rights in the territories occupied by Israel in the 1967 war. The political and legal environment of human rights in the territories was analyzed, the applicability of various conventions and standards of human rights was assessed, and the relationships between human rights and politics were investigated. The impact of the settlement effort and a series of enforcement measures on human rights was examined, as was the system of justice under the military government.

In this chapter, a summary and a future-oriented analysis will be offered. Following some general observations about the condition of human rights in the territories and Israel's performance in this field, an assessment of human rights within the context of a series of political-territorial solutions will be attempted. The study will conclude with general commentary about the conditions of human rights in the territories today and in the future.

General Observations

An occupation regime is typically characterized by a number of conditions. First, the military authorities act in the interest of the government that appoints them and rarely in the interest of the local inhabitants.[1] Second, public policy is made without consulting the occupied population and often against its determined opposition. Third, the courts appointed by the military government are loyal to it and lack sympathy for the local population. These

116

conditions are particularly apparent when the local population is involved, as it often is, in active opposition to the occupation.

These general observations on the character of an occupation regime fully apply to Israel's occupied territories. During certain periods, notably when the territories were under the ministerial responsibility of Moshe Dayan of the Labor Party, the occupation was relatively benign. Even then, however, the military government invariably acted in the interests of the Israeli government and rarely in the interests of the residents of the West Bank and Gaza Strip. On a series of issues, such as the all-important matter of settlement, the Israeli government and the military authorities consistently adopted public policy incompatible with the interests of the local inhabitants, who vehemently opposed these official policies. Although the military courts in the territories have not been in the forefront of violating the human rights of the Palestinians, they have not been able to prevent what some have perceived as an epidemic of violence and human rights violations in the territories. In some respects, the Intifada has brought about the collapse of the legal system in the territories.

Despite some of Israel's achievements in the area of human rights, perhaps its greatest failure in this area has been the establishment of a dual legal system in the territories. The transfer of a large number of settlers to the territories resulted in the emergence of two communities, governed by two different legal systems. Amnon Rubinstein, and others, have noted that a dual legal system violates the territorial principle, according to which "individuals living in a certain area ought to be ruled by the same legal system."[2] Amnon Zichroni, a well-known Israeli lawyer, has argued that "there has not been even one single case in which two different legal systems apply to two populations in the same territory" since the foreigners' colonies in China and the Capitulations of Europeans under Ottoman rule.[3] In no other area is the duality of the justice system as pronounced as in the operation of the courts in the territories.[4]

Above all, the creation of a dual system of justice was not accidental. It was a result of persistent political pressure on the government of Israel to allow the settlement of Israelis in the territories and to grant them an identical legal status to that of the residents of Israel proper. The Knesset, which like any democratic parliament responds to political pressure, enacted special laws for Israelis residing in the territories, and the military government issued orders applying only to the Jewish settlements. Military Order no. 783 (1979) established regional councils in Judea and Samaria, and Military Order no. 892 (1981) formed local councils. Similar powers were not given to the local Palestinian population, thus creating the duality. The combined effect of extensive lawmaking by the military authorities and the extraterritorial prescription of Israeli laws was the creation of what Eyal Benvenisti called "legal dualism."

Regardless of the intentions of the Israeli legislators, the Knesset's laws and the military government's orders created a sharp legal differentiation between Arabs and Jews in the territories. A Jewish settler residing in a town or a rural settlement in the West Bank lives, theoretically, under the authority of the military government and the Jordanian Law, which was the local code in the occupied territory in the pre-1967 era. Yet, in reality, this settler lives in accordance with domestic Israeli law: he or she votes for the Knesset and for Israeli regional and local councils; pays taxes as if living within the boundaries of Israel; and is tried before Israeli courts, not the West Bank military courts or the local Palestinian courts.

It ought to be quickly added that the application of two different sets of rules to two different groups of people in the territories is not racially determined. In this sense the often suggested analogy between Israel and South Africa is inappropriate and misleading. The distinction in the territories is not based on race, nor is it based on religion, cultural heritage, or ethnicity. The sole criterion for the differentiation between people in the territories is citizenship. All local "inhabitants" are Palestinian Arabs (of various religious affiliations), all "settlers" are Israeli Jews, and the two groups live under different conditions. The danger of a large-scale settlement effort in the territories is that what begins as a formal distinction based on citizenship ends in actual differentiation based on ethnic origin. Thus, the negation of human rights is a built-in feature of any settlement effort.

Despite the difficulties in maintaining a reasonable level of human rights in the territories—difficulties that are inherent in any occupation regime and are much aggravated by the settlement effort—the Israeli legal system has not been completely devoid of achievements in the area of human rights. A few official Israeli reports have uncovered, analyzed, and condemned major human rights violations in the territories (most notably the reports of the Karp Commission and the Landau Commission). Israeli courts have

convicted vigilantes (e.g., the Jewish Underground), and most Israeli politicians have publicly condemned them. Israeli officials—
Shin Bet head Avraham Achituv, Attorney General Yitzhak Zamir,
and Supreme Court Justice Moshe Landau, to name a few—have
criticized human rights violations as well. Furthermore, Israel has
eliminated the use of the death penalty in the territories, has allowed human rights investigations (although clearly not in complete freedom), and still has vigorous press coverage of human
rights violations in the territories. A number of Israeli human rights
organizations with legal expertise, individual attorneys, and distin-
guished law professors have played a significant role in promoting
the human rights of Palestinians in the territories.

The use of administrative detention has been used heavily since
the beginning of the Intifada, this has been done in the face of a
massive, popular rebellion. Most countries of the world use some
form of administrative detention in times of national emergency,
and this measure is permitted in ARTICLE 78(1) of Geneva IV. In
general, despite the feeling that many political activists (rather than
terrorists) have been detained, Israel has followed the procedures
established by Geneva IV. Boards of appeals have been established, and a substantial number of detention orders have been
canceled or shortened. Despite the authorities' inclination to
tighten the procedures governing administrative detention, they
have had to revise these procedures and allow the appointments of
judges who can (and often do) issue binding decisions regarding
the release of persons detained without justification. Such changes
have been a result of domestic and international pressure on the
Israeli government.

The use of another controversial measure, house demolition,
also has experienced the addition of restraints that did not exist
prior to the Intifada. In late July 1989, the High Court of Justice
ruled that Palestinians whose homes have been condemned to demolition must be given time to appeal the decision to the area
commander and then to the Court itself. This important ruling,
along with the April 1989 government decision to establish a military court of appeals in the territories, demonstrated once again the
ability of the Israeli political and legal system to react to criticisms
and to change.[5]

In general, the role of the High Court of Justice has been critical in guaranteeing at least some human rights in the territories.
Although one may criticize the Court for not doing enough, it must

be remembered that its constitutional role in Israel is rather limited. The Court has set limitations on the settlement effort in the territories,[6] although, in the final analysis, it could not have averted the political decision to allow and even encourage Israelis to settle there. The Court also has been active in areas more immediately linked to human rights. It urged an investigation into the conditions at the IDF detention center in Ketziot, has decided that house demolitions should be open to appeal, has looked into decisions to expel Palestinians from the territories, and so forth.

Indeed, the key to legal changes that could affect the future of human rights in the territories may be the attitude of the High Court.[7] So far, the Court has been reluctant to intervene in substantive decisions of the authorities, though it is willing to procedurally examine whether the authorities have reached their decision properly. In reaching a decision (say, to expel an individual from the West Bank), the military government must demonstrate relevant considerations. By examining the way the decision has been formulated, the Court may deal with the content or substance of the decision, but so far the Court has been reluctant to intervene. However, in the case of Elon Moreh, the Court decided in favor of the Palestinian plaintiffs by concluding that their land was confiscated for political purposes (even though the seizure was justified as a security need).

The level of intervention of the High Court of Justice on the side of those suffering from arbitrary decisions has been, to date, rather low. There have been practically no cases in which it has reversed a decision of a security authority in areas such as the expulsion of a person from the territories, the demolition of a house, the imposition of a curfew, and so forth. That is, if the authorities have decided to expel a person or destroy a home, and the argument has been couched in terms of "state security" (as it traditionally has been), the High Court of Justice has accepted the decision. In general, its intervention to date has been rather peripheral, although by no means meaningless.

The High Court of Justice could do more in the interest of human rights by expanding its review of the application of the law in the territories. Former Attorney General Yitzhak Zamir believes that this is exactly the direction in which the High Court of Justice is now moving. For him, the case of Elon Moreh (1979) was a genuine watershed.[8] The Court ruled that the decision of the military government to refuse the establishment of a regional bar association in the West Bank was illegal because it was not based on a proper balance between the relevant interests pertaining to the case. We may be witnessing a growing inclination on the part of the High Court of Justice to intervene in political decisions: the protection of human rights requires increasing flexibility in applying its authority to sensitive areas.

The concept of the "balance of interests" could be a key term for a fruitful role of the Court in dealing with human rights issues in the territories, because in the territories there are two almost entirely mutually exclusive, competing interests: the security of the state and human rights. So far, the security of the state has ruled supreme as the single guiding principle. The result has been frequent violations of human rights, with the High Court of Justice intervening only peripherally. In fact, it could be convincingly argued that certain elements of the legal system in the territories— including the protection of human rights—have disintegrated as a result of the Intifada. Only reinvigorating the role of the High Court of Justice could revive the legal system and establish strong protection of human rights, although in the final analysis a fundamental solution for the human rights problem in the territories ought to be sought in the political sphere.

Alternative Solutions and Human Rights

It is clear from the analysis included in this book that the Israeli legal system has not been able to offer a solution for the fundamental problems of the territories, including that of human rights. The legal system helped Israel to muddle through and to maintain a somewhat respectable record of human rights in the face of a popular rebellion. Yet, the legal system had very little to offer in the way of a fundamental solution to the political problems at hand. These problems have been the source of most of the human rights violations.

As the Intifada has demonstrated almost daily since December 1987, the legal system cannot help significantly in preventing the erosion of human rights in the territories. Typically, the legal system adjusts itself to the new circumstances rather than controlling them. A case in point is regulating the procedures for opening fire in the territories. Opening fire on demonstrators was allowed at the beginning of the Intifada only as a measure of "self-defense," but it quickly became a measure of "deterrence" and then of "punishment." A very small number of Israelis responsible for the deaths of Palestinians since the beginning of the Intifada—some say only 7 percent—have actually come to trial.[9] In short, the "shooting policy" has been a function of political considerations; the legal system has not shown, and probably could not have shown, the ability to significantly restrain it.

Israeli and Ehrenfeld state that "as long as Israel holds [the territories], it is bound to be confronted with inevitable infringements of human rights."[10] Although some observers today would replace "infringements" with "massive violations," Israeli and Ehrenfeld's point is well taken: human rights infringements or violations are built into the conditions of occupation. Put differently, even if one would give Israel high marks for its effort to maintain human rights in the face of a major political challenge, one is still bound to recognize that the condition of occupation itself leads to serious violations of human rights. In view of this conclusion, it is the obligation of the analyst to ask the following question: How would human rights fare under different political conditions, under alternative regimes? It is to this question that we now turn.

Analytically speaking, one may distinguish eight possible solutions to the Israeli-Palestinian conflict, most of which have been on the international and regional agenda since the 1967 war:[11]

1. Uninational Greater Israel with the expulsion of the Palestinians: this solution entails the establishment of a Jewish state in the entire area of western Palestine (pre-1967 Israel, the West Bank, and the Gaza Strip), accompanied by the expulsion of all or most of the Arabs from these territories. Radical right-wing groups and parties in Israel support such a solution, which is known in Israel as the "transfer."

2. Binational Greater Israel without the expulsion of the Palestinian Arabs: the establishment of a Greater Israel in western Palestine without forcing a fundamental demographic change. In Greater Israel, political control will reside exclusively in the hands of the Jews, but the population will continue to be mixed. This solution is supported by some elements within the Israeli right (e.g., the Tehiya Party).

3. Continuation of the status quo: the political situation of the West Bank and Gaza Strip remains undetermined while these areas continue to be under total Israeli control. Although no party to the conflict enthusiastically supports the continuation of the status quo, it is possible that countervailing forces will continue to neutralize each other and prevent a radical movement toward any solution.

4. Palestinian autonomy in the occupied territories, without Palestinian independence and under the control of Israel, Jordan, Israel-Jordan, or an international body. In 1978 Menachem Begin proposed this type of solution as a temporary arrangement. Some members of his party support it as a permanent solution.

5. Jordanian-Palestinian federal state, with or without border modifications, in the area of Jordan, the West Bank, and the Gaza Strip. Although the chances of effecting this type of solution now are quite low (following King Hussein's speech of July 31, 1988), the so-called Jordanian solution is not necessarily dead.

6. Two-state solution: Israel and Palestine, with Israeli sovereignty essentially in its pre-1967 borders and Palestinian sovereignty on the West Bank and in the Gaza Strip (with or without border modifications).

7. Binational Greater Palestine without the expulsion of the Jews: the establishment of a Greater Palestine in the area of pre-1967 Israel, the West Bank, and the Gaza Strip without forcing a demographic change in these areas. In Greater Palestine, political control will reside exclusively in the hands of the Palestinian Arabs.

8. Uninational Greater Palestine with the expulsion of the Jewish population from its territories (pre-1967 Israel, the West Bank, and the Gaza Strip). Radical Palestinians support this and the preceding solution, but their chances of effecting either in the foreseeable future are nil.

What would be the human rights implications of each of these political solutions? Although a precise answer is, obviously, impossible to give, a general outline could be drawn.

The human rights implications of solution 1, the establishment of a Greater Israel with the expulsion of the Palestinians, would be far-reaching, extremely negative, and indeed horrendous. Whatever might be the final status of the West Bank and Gaza Strip, their inhabitants would have a fundamental right to continue to reside in these territories because they lived there on the eve of the occupation.

Among individuals who support the idea of Greater Israel are those who believe that the Palestinians residing in the territories should be allowed to continue to live there. In other words, they propose a binational Greater Israel in which power would be in the hands of the Jews although the population would be mixed. In an effort to resolve the dilemma of establishing an undemocratic Greater Israel (in which the Palestinians would be devoid of any political power), some have proposed to allow the Palestinians in Judea, Samaria, and Gaza to vote for the Jordanian parliament. This solution (2) would also entail massive human rights violations. Benjamin Neuberger likened the option of enabling the Palestinians to vote for the Jordanian parliament to that of "enabling" Italian-Americans, Irish-Americans, and Mexican-Americans to vote in their countries of origin, or negating the right of American Jews to vote in the name of their "opportunity" to vote in Israel.[12]

It is quite clear that the establishment of a Greater Israel through the annexation of the territories under solution 1 (with expulsion) or solution 2 (without expulsion) would lead to significant deterioration of the human rights conditions in the territories. Either of these solutions would lead to a monumental confrontation between Arabs and Jews, and to much more serious violations of human rights than we have observed up to now under the status quo (solution 3).

In a situation of intense ethnic conflict, the creation of a binational solution or a one-sided uninational solution is a recipe for massive violations of human rights. A de facto binational Israel (solution 3, which is based on the status quo) or a de jure binational Israel effected through a formal annexation of the territories (with the Arabs staying in the territories, as Solution 2 suggests) would bring an end to democracy in Israel, a significant human rights violation. Such solutions would inevitably lead to violations of the fundamental human rights of the weaker national group. In a binational Israel, the small and shrinking Jewish majority would not be able or inclined to give up its monopoly over the government; it would have to resort to increasingly oppressive measures against the Palestinians. An Israel with a clear-cut Jewish majority can respect the rights of all its citizens, regardless of nationality, ethnicity, race, or religion; a binational Greater Israel cannot possibly do so, unless it ceases to be a Jewish state.

Although we can only speculate on the potential human rights impact of solutions 1 and 2, when it comes to solution 3, the continuation of the status quo, the accumulated data could help us to predict the future of human rights with a higher degree of certainty. There is little doubt that the continuation of Israel's rule over the West Bank and Gaza Strip would mean the continuation of intense Palestinian resistance to that rule and harsh Israeli response to this resistance. Despite the efforts of many individuals and groups in Israel to minimize human rights violations associated with the occupation, such violations will continue to characterize the status quo as long as it lasts. By definition, a military government is not a democratic one: it is not elected by the population, nor is it supported by it. Military rule is based on the negation of some of the most fundamental of all human rights: the rights to self-determination, participation in determining one's government, and so forth. The continuation of the occupation means a persistent and probably growing violation of human rights.

Solution 4, the establishment of a Palestinian autonomy in the territories under the overall control of Israel (or possibly a group of states such as Israel and Jordan), is a variation on solution 2, the establishment of a binational Greater Israel without a Palestinian "transfer." Although the establishment of meaningful autonomy could lower the level of human rights violations, and it ought to be considered as an immediate transitional step, it could not completely erase built-in, fundamental human rights violations. The population under autonomy will still not enjoy the right of self-determination, including the right to vote for and be elected to a government with responsibility for their country. From a human rights perspective, autonomy is an anachronistic solution, as it is from a purely political perspective.

In general, all the solutions that are based on the annexation of the territories to Israel (solutions 1–4) are fundamentally flawed from a human rights perspective. Whether Israel decides to continue its military control over the inhabitants, to expel all or large numbers of them, or to allow them to reside in the territories but with no political rights in Israel, the West Bank and Gaza Palestinians will remain without fundamental human rights. The interethnic conflict, which is built into all annexationist solutions, virtually guarantees a high level of human rights violations.

In the foreseeable future, the majority of Israelis would probably continue to oppose annexation with expulsion. However, the perpetuation of the occupation, accompanied by the intensification of the interethnic clash in western Palestine, may lead to a gradual change of heart on that question. A more significant group of Israelis would continue to support the idea of annexation without expulsion, but also without granting the Palestinians political rights (solution 2). The idea is, in fact, to eliminate the military government but not to change the substance of the political conditions in the territories, under which political power rests exclusively in Israeli hands. The Arabs in Judaea, Samaria, and Gaza are to remain under solution 2 without the right to vote or be elected, and without other fundamental rights. From a human rights perspective, this solution is as negative as the first.

To deal with the difficulties stemming from the idea of annexation (in all its versions), more liberal annexationists have proposed a variety of ideas: allowing the Palestinians in the territories to accept Israeli citizenship (following annexation), allowing them to vote for the Jordanian parliament, and so forth. From a human rights perspective, those options are deceptive. The vast majority of Palestinians in the territories oppose Israeli annexation and would refuse to accept Israeli citizenship, as have the vast majority of East Jerusalemites since 1967. If the majority of West Bankers and Gazans refuse to become Israeli citizens but at the same time are forcibly annexed by Israel, the status quo, a situation in which the Arab population has no share in power, will be sustained and perpetuated, despite the formal change in the status of the territories.

The idea of giving the Palestinians the option of voting for the Jordanian parliament is equally problematical. First, King Hussein announced in July 1988 that Jordan had given up all claims to the West Bank, thereby cutting off the political association between the two banks. But even if the king had not taken this step, the idea of allowing Palestinians to participate in Jordan's political life while residing in Greater Israel is both politically ridiculous and indefensible from a human rights perspective. People residing in a certain area have an inherent, inalienable right to take part in shaping the government that controls the area. To "allow" them such right in an adjacent area instead of the area of their residence is just as injurious to their human rights as to negate their voting rights altogether. In this sense, this idea is deceptive, especially if it is presented as a humanitarian solution to a political dilemma.

Israel can, in principle, annex the territories and grant full citizenship to the Palestinians in them. Yet, such a solution, while trying to respond to the argument that a Greater Israel cannot possibly be democratic, would surely bring an end to a Jewish, Zionist, and probably democratic Israel. The overwhelming majority of Israelis and virtually all important political forces in Israel vehemently oppose such a solution. A large Arab minority in Greater Israel, living side by side with a Jewish majority, would guarantee not only the continuation of the Israeli-Palestinian conflict but also its escalation. Such escalation would lead to further deterioration of human rights.

Says Neuberger (343): "Greater Israel and a liberal democracy together is an oxymoron, as are a Jewish state and a binational state. . . . Anyone who wants a state who treats all of its citizens equally and who respects human rights as promised in Israel's Declaration of Independence, must oppose the annexation of the territories." None of the annexationist solutions can guarantee even a bare minimum of human rights.

Solutions 7 and 8, the establishment of a Greater Palestine with Jews or without them, will be theoretically as negative as solutions 1 and 2. The dreams of some Palestinians of expelling the Jews (8) or "allowing" them to reside in Greater Palestine, where power would rest exclusively in the hands of the Arabs, is a mirror image to the dream of Greater Israel. Moreover, given the human rights conditions in most Arab countries, the human rights of Jews in Greater Palestine could very well be worse than a mirror image. Because solutions 7 and 8 are not politically in the cards in the foreseeable future, and because everything said about solutions 1 and 2 applies equally to them, there is little to add here about the likely status of human rights in Greater Palestine, if it ever comes into being. Suffice it to state that this status would be extremely negative.

Examining the future from the perspective of human rights, we are left, then, with only two political solutions, two regimes in which all residents of Eretz Israel/Palestine may achieve an acceptable level of human rights: a Jordanian-Palestinian federal state (solution 5) and the so-called two-state solution (6), in which Israel and Palestine would exist side by side. It is not the purpose of this analysis to compare the relative advantages and disadvantages of these two solutions from a variety of possible perspectives (economic, military, political, and so forth). Yet, from a perspective of human rights, either a two-state solution or a Jordanian-Palestinian state could, in principle, satisfy the human rights concerns raised in this volume. Either solution could enable all members of the national groups involved in this long-standing conflict to determine their own governmental institutions, to be ruled by consent rather than by coercion, and to be governed by individuals belonging to the national group. Although the status of many additional human rights within the polities emerging from either solution cannot be determined or predicted with accuracy, at least these fundamental principles of human rights could be guaranteed through a better political solution than the one existing under the status quo.

Summary

The point of departure of many analysts has traditionally been that national security takes priority over any other consideration, including human rights. The fundamental assumption regarding the supremacy of national security has served as a basis for public policy even in liberal democracies such as England and the United States—where, for example, people of German and Japanese descent, respectively, were detained without trial during World War II. In Israel, which has found herself in a severe national conflict with the Palestinians and her Arab neighbors, the assumption of the supremacy of national security has been particularly strong.

Although national security is necessary for national well-being and perhaps even for national survival, it is never an end in and of itself. Put differently, although national security is always a central goal of national existence, there are other important goals as well, including the maximization of human rights. In a liberal democracy, the polity loses its character, its raison d'être, unless it sustains and promotes human rights.

The confrontation between human rights and national security in Israel had been dramatic even prior to the 1967 war and the occupation of heavily populated Arab territories by the IDF. The Defense (Emergency) Regulations of 1945, which were incorporated by Israel when it came into being, were essentially antihuman rights. They enabled any military commander to detain a person thought to endanger public safety or security. Although the regulations regarding detention were changed in Israel in 1979, enabling only the minister of defense to detain a person, they have not changed in the territories. In fact, as explained in Chapter 3, the procedures for detention have become even harsher since the Intifada.

In general, although it may be possible to somewhat improve the status of human rights in the territories through legal means—for example, by expanding the role of the High Court of Justice as a legal supervisor in the territories—it seems that such improvement could not be more than marginal. Many jurists in Israel see judicial activism as a key to the improvement of the status of human rights in the West Bank and Gaza Strip.[13] Indeed, the High Court of Justice has shown increasing willingness to deal with human rights in the territories and even to examine security considerations. Yet, this involvement is still peripheral in terms of its overall impact on human rights, and is likely to remain so as long as there is an intense interethnic conflict in the territories.

Put differently, a fundamental, measurable change in the status of human rights can occur only through a political solution. The occupation and military government in the territories, on the one hand, and the preservation of human rights, on the other hand, are diametrically opposed to each other. According to former justice of the Israeli Supreme Court Haim Cohn, the control over the territories and violation of human rights are virtually identical.[14]

Moshe Negbi, one of Israel's best-known writers on legal issues, wrote on the occasion of the first anniversary of the Intifada that the uprising "shattered completely Israel's pretension to be one of those few states who respect the principles of the Universal Declaration of Human Rights not only theoretically, but also in reality. . . . Almost every measure taken by Minister of Defense Rabin in order to break the uprising contradicts the principles of the Universal Declaration."[15]

The comprehensive examination of human rights in the territories demonstrates that although Israel may not have violated the human rights of the Palestinians as other modern occupiers have violated the human rights of populations under their control, it has been unable to maintain an acceptable level of human rights in the territories. Although in relative terms Israel's human rights record is not as negative as some believe it to be, it is quite clear that the occupation has generated and sustained continuous violations of human rights. Only through a carefully crafted political solution, a negotiated settlement that takes the interests and aspirations of both parties into account, can the fundamental problem of human rights be resolved.

At the time of the completion of this essay, the parties to the bitter Israeli-Palestinian conflict seem to have finally understood this reality.

Appendixes
Notes
Bibliography
Index

Appendix A

The 1907 Hague Regulations Respecting
the Laws and Customs of War on Land

(Excerpts)

ART. 42. Territory is considered occupied when it is actually placed under the authority of the hostile army.

The occupation extends only to the territory where such authority has been established and can be exercised.

ART. 43. The authority of the legitimate power having in fact passed into the hands of the occupant, the latter shall take all the measures in his power to restore, and ensure, as far as possible, public order and safety, while respecting, unless absolutely prevented, the laws in force in the country.

ART. 46. Family honour and rights, the lives of persons, and private property, as well as religious convictions and practice, must be respected.

Private property cannot be confiscated.

ART. 50. No general penalty, pecuniary or otherwise, shall be inflicted upon the population on account of the acts of individuals for which they cannot be regarded as jointly and severally responsible.

ART. 53. An army of occupation can only take possession of cash, funds, and realizable securities which are strictly the property of the State, depots of arms, means of transport, stores and supplies, and, generally, all movable property belonging to the State which may be used for military operations. . . .

ART. 55. The occupying State shall be regarded only as administrator and usufructuary of public buildings, real estate, forests, and agricultural estates belonging to the hostile State, and situated in the occupied country.

It must safeguard the capital of these properties, and administer them in accordance with the rules of usufruct.

ART. 56. The property of municipalities, that of institutions dedicated to religion, charity and education, the arts and sciences, even when State property, shall be treated as private property.

All seizure of, destruction or wilful damage done to institutions of this character, historic monuments, works of art and science, is forbidden, and should be made the subject of legal proceedings.

Appendix B
Israel's Defence
(Emergency) Regulations, 1945
(Excerpts)

In exercise of the powers vested in the High Commissioner by ARTICLE 6 of the Palestine (Defence) Order in Council, 1937, and of all other powers enabling him, the Officer Administering the Government hereby makes the following regulations: . . . .

PART X.—Restriction Orders, Police Supervision, Detention and Deportation

108. An order shall not be made by the High Commissioner or by a Military Commander under this Part in respect of any person unless the High Commissioner or the Military Commander, as the case may be, is of opinion that it is necessary or expedient to make the order for securing the public safety, the defence of Palestine, the maintenance of public order or the suppression of mutiny, rebellion or riot.

109. (1) A Military Commander may make, in relation to any person, an order for all or any of the following purposes, that is to say—

(a) for securing that, except in so far as he may be permitted by the order, or by such authority or person as may be specified in the order, that person shall not be in any such area in Palestine as may be so specified;

(b) for requiring him to notify [regarding] his movements, in such manner, at such times and to such authority or person as may be specified in the order;

(c) prohibiting or restricting the possession or use by that person of any specified articles;

(d) imposing upon him such restrictions as may be specified in the order in respect of his employment or business, in respect of his association or communication with other persons, and in respect of his activities in relation to the dissemination of news or the propagation of opinions. . . .

110. (1) A Military Commander may by order direct that any person shall be placed under police supervision for any period not exceeding one year.

(2) Any person placed under police supervision by order as aforesaid shall be subject to all or any of the following restrictions as the Military Commander may direct, that is to say—

(a) he shall be required to reside within the limits of any area in Palestine specified by the Military Commander in the order;

(b) he shall not be permitted to transfer his residence to any other area in the same police district without the written authority of the District Superintendent of Police, or to any other police district without the written authority of the Inspector General of Police;

(c) he shall not leave the town, village or Sub-District within which he resides without the written authority of the District Superintendent of Police;

(d) he shall at all times keep the District Superintendent of Police of the police district in which he resides notified of the house or the place in which he resides;

(e) he shall be liable, whenever called upon so to do by the officer in charge of the police in the area in which he resides, to present himself at the nearest police station;

(f) he shall remain within the doors of his residence from one hour after sunset until sunrise, and may be visited at his residence at any time by the police. . . .

111. (1) A Military Commander may by order direct that any person shall be detained in such place of detention as may be specified by the Military Commander in the order. . . .

(3) Any person in respect of whom an order has been made by the Military Commander under subregulation (1) may be arrested by any member of His Majesty's forces or of the Police Force and conveyed to the place of detention specified in such order. . . .

111A. The High Commissioner, or any person generally or specially authorised in writing by the High Commissioner in that behalf, may by order require any person named in the order not to proceed from Palestine to a destination outside it, except under the authority of a written permit granted by such authority or person as may be specified in the order.

112. (1) The High Commissioner shall have power to make an order, under his hand (hereinafter in these regulations referred to as "a Deportation Order") for the deportation of any person from Palestine. A person in

respect of whom a Deportation Order has been made shall remain out of Palestine so long as the Order remains in force.

(2) The High Commissioner shall have power to make an order under his hand (hereinafter in these regulations referred to as "an Exclusion Order") requiring any person who is out of Palestine to remain out of Palestine. A person in respect of whom an Exclusion Order has been made shall remain out of Palestine so long as the Order remains in force.

PART XII. Miscellaneous Penal Provisions

119. (1) A Military Commander may by order direct the forfeiture to the Government of Palestine of any house, structure or land from which he has reason to suspect that any firearm has been illegally discharged, or any bomb, grenade or explosive or incendiary article illegally thrown, or of any house, structure or land situated in any area, town, village, quarter or street the inhabitants or some of the inhabitants of which he is satisfied have committed, or attempted to commit, or abetted the commission of, or been accessories after the fact to the commission of, any offence against these Regulations involving violence or intimidation or any Military Court offence; and when any house, structure or land is forfeited as aforesaid, the Military Commander may destroy the house or the structure or anything growing on the land.

(2) Members of His Majesty's forces or of the Police Force, acting under the authority of the Military Commander may seize and occupy, without compensation, any property in any such area, town, village, quarter or street as is referred to in subregulation (1), after eviction without compensation, of the previous occupiers, if any.

120. The High Commissioner may by order direct the forfeiture to the Government of Palestine of all or any property of any person as to whom the High Commissioner is satisfied that he has committed, or attempted to commit, or abetted the commission of, or been an accessory after the fact to the commission of, any offence against these Regulations involving violence or intimidation or any Military Court offence. . . .

132. (1) If any person, upon being questioned by a police officer or by a member of His Majesty's forces acting in the course of his duty as such, fails to satisfy the police officer or member of His Majesty's forces as to his identity or as to the purposes for which he is in the place where he is found, the police officer or member of His Majesty's forces may, if he suspects that person has acted or is about to act in any manner prejudicial to the public safety or the defence of Palestine or the maintenance of public order, arrest him and detain him pending enquiries. . . .

Appendix C
United Nations Universal Declaration of Human Rights (1948)
(Articles 1–21)

The General Assembly

Proclaims this Universal Declaration of Human Rights as a common standard of achievement for all peoples and all nations, to the end that every individual and every organ of society, keeping this Declaration constantly in mind, shall strive by teaching and education to promote respect for these rights and freedoms and by progressive measures, national and international, to secure their universal and effective recognition and observance, both among the peoples of Member States themselves and among the peoples of territories under their jurisdiction.

ARTICLE 1. All human beings are born free and equal in dignity and rights. They are endowed with reason and conscience and should act towards one another in a spirit of brotherhood.

ARTICLE 2. Everyone is entitled to all the rights and freedoms set forth in this Declaration, without distinction of any kind, such as race, colour, sex, language, religion, political or other opinion, national or social origin, property, birth or other status.

Furthermore, no distinction shall be made on the basis of the political, jurisdictional or international status of the country or territory to which a person belongs, whether it be independent, trust, non-self-governing or under any other limitation of sovereignty.

ARTICLE 3. Everyone has the right to life, liberty and the security of person.

ARTICLE 4. No one shall be held in slavery or servitude; slavery and the slave trade shall be prohibited in all their forms.

ARTICLE 5. No one shall be subjected to torture or to cruel, inhuman or degrading treatment or punishment.

ARTICLE 6. Everyone has the right to recognition everywhere as a person before the law.

ARTICLE 7. All are equal before the law and are entitled without any discrimination to equal protection of the law. All are entitled to equal protection against any discrimination in violation of this Declaration and against any incitement to such discrimination.

ARTICLE 8. Everyone has the right to an effective remedy by the competent national tribunals for acts violating the fundamental rights granted him by the constitution or by law.

ARTICLE 9. No one shall be subjected to arbitrary arrest, detention or exile.

ARTICLE 10. Everyone is entitled to full equality to a fair and public hearing by an independent and impartial tribunal, in the determination of his rights and obligations and of any criminal charge against him.

ARTICLE 11.—1. Everyone charged with a penal offence has the right to be presumed innocent until proved guilty according to law in a public trial at which he has had all the guarantees necessary for his defence.

2. No one shall be held guilty of any penal offence on account of any act or omission which did not constitute a penal offence, under national or international law, at the time when it was committed. Nor shall a heavier penalty be imposed than the one that was applicable at the time the penal offence was committed.

ARTICLE 12. No one shall be subjected to arbitrary interference with his privacy, family, home or correspondence, nor to attacks upon his honour and reputation. Everyone has the right to the protection of the law against such interference or attacks.

ARTICLE 13.—1. Everyone has the right to freedom of movement and residence within the borders of each state.

2. Everyone has the right to leave any country, including his own, and to return to his country.

ARTICLE 14.—1. Everyone has the right to seek and to enjoy in other countries asylum from persecution.

2. This right may not be invoked in the case of prosecutions genuinely arising from non-political crimes or from acts contrary to the purposes and principles of the United Nations.

ARTICLE 15.—1. Everyone has the right to a nationality.

2. No one shall be arbitrarily deprived of his nationality nor denied the right to change his nationality.

ARTICLE 16.—1. Men and women of full age, without any limitation due to race, nationality or religion, have the right to marry and to found a family. They are entitled to equal rights as to marriage, during marriage and at its dissolution.

2. Marriage shall be entered into only with the free and full consent of the intending spouses.

3. The family is the natural and fundamental group unit of society and is entitled to protection by society and the State.

ARTICLE 17.—1. Everyone has the right to own property alone as well as in association with others.

2. No one shall be arbitrarily deprived of his property.

ARTICLE 18. Everyone has the right to freedom of thought, conscience and religion; this right includes freedom to change his religion or belief, and freedom, either alone or in community with others and in public or private, to manifest his religion or belief in teaching, practice, worship and observance.

ARTICLE 19. Everyone has the right to freedom of opinion and expression; this right includes freedom to hold opinions without interference and to seek, receive and impart information and ideas through any media and regardless of frontiers.

ARTICLE 20.—1. Everyone has the right to freedom of peaceful assembly and association.

2. No one may be compelled to belong to an association.

ARTICLE 21.—1. Everyone has the right to take part in the Government of his country, directly or through freely chosen representatives.

2. Everyone has the right of equal access to public service in his country.

3. The will of the people shall be the basis of the authority of government; this will shall be expressed in periodic and genuine elections which shall be by universal and equal suffrage and shall be held by secret vote or by equivalent free voting procedures.

Appendix D
Fourth Geneva Convention Relative to the Protection of Civilian Persons in Time of War of August 12, 1949
(Excerpts)

ART. 2. . . . In addition to the provisions which shall be implemented in peacetime, the present Convention shall apply to all cases of declared war or of any other armed conflict which may arise between two or more of the High Contracting Parties, even if the state of war is not recognized by one of them.

The Convention shall also apply to all cases of partial or total occupation of the territory of a High Contracting Party, even if the said occupation meets with no armed resistance.

Although one of the Powers in conflict may not be a party to the present Convention, the Powers who are parties thereto shall remain bound by it in their mutual relations. They shall furthermore be bound by the Convention in relation to the said Power, if the latter accepts and applies the provision thereof.

ART. 6. The present Convention shall apply from the outset of any conflict or occupation mentioned in ARTICLE 2.

In the territory of Parties to the conflict, the application of the present Convention shall cease on the general close of military operations.

In the case of occupied territory, the application of the present Convention shall cease one year after the general close of military operations; however, the Occupying Power shall be bound, for the duration of the occupation, to the extent that such Power exercises the functions of government in such territory, by the provisions of the following ARTICLES of the present Convention: 1 to 12, 27, 29 to 34, 47, 49, 51, 52, 53, 59, 61 to 77, 143.

Protected persons whose release, repatriation or re-establishment may take place after such dates shall meanwhile continue to benefit by the present Convention.

ART. 27. Protected persons are entitled, in all circumstances, to respect for their persons, their honour, their family rights, their religious convictions and practices, and their manners and customs. They shall at all times be humanely treated, and shall be protected especially against all acts of violence or threats thereof and against insults and public curiosity.

Women shall be especially protected against any attack on their honour, in particular against rape, enforced prostitution, or any form of indecent assault.

Without prejudice to the provisions relating to their state of health, age and sex, all protected persons shall be treated with the same consideration by the Party to the conflict in whose power they are, without any adverse distinction based, in particular, on race, religion or political opinion.

However, the Parties to the conflict may take such measures of control and security in regard to protected persons as may be necessary as a result of the war.

ART. 33. No protected person may be punished for an offence he or she has not personally committed. Collective penalties and likewise all measures of intimidation or of terrorism are prohibited.

Pillage is prohibited.

Reprisals against protected persons and their property are prohibited.

ART. 49. Individual or mass forcible transfers, as well as deportation of protected persons from occupied territory to the territory of the Occupying Power or to that of any other coutnry, occupied or not, are prohibited, regardless of their motive.

Nevertheless, the Occupying Power may undertake total or partial evacuation of a given area if the security of the population or imperative military reasons so demand. Such evacuations may not involve the displacement of protected persons outside the bounds of the occupied territory except when for material reasons it is impossible to avoid such displacement. Persons thus evacuated shall be transferred back to their homes as soon as hostilities in the area in question have ceased. . . .

ART. 53. Any destruction by the Occupying Power of real or personal property belonging individually or collectively to private persons, or to the State, or to other public authorities, or to social or co-operative organizations, is prohibited, except where such destruction is rendered absolutely necessary by military operations.

ART. 55. To the fullest extent of the means available to it, the Occupying Power has the duty of ensuring the food and medical supplies of the population; it should, in particular, bring in the necessary foodstuffs, medical stores and other articles if the resources of the occupied territory are inadequate. . . .

ART. 64. The penal laws of the occupied territory shall remain in force, with the exception that they may be repealed or suspended by the Occupying Power in cases where they constitute a threat to its security or an obstacle to the application of the present Convention. Subject to the latter consideration and to the necessity for ensuring the effective administration of justice, the tribunals of the occupied territory shall continue to function in respect of all offences covered by the said laws.

The Occupying Power may, however, subject the population of the occupied territory to provisions which are essential to enable the Occupying Power to fulfill its obligations under the present Convention, to maintain the orderly government of the territory, and to ensure the security of the Occupying Power, of the members and property of the occupying forces or administration, and likewise of the establishments and lines of communication used by them.

ART. 65. The penal provisions enacted by the Occupying Power shall not come into force before they have been published and brought to the knowledge of the inhabitants in their own language. The effect of these penal provisions shall not be retroactive.

ART. 71. No sentence shall be pronounced by the competent courts of the Occupying Power except after a regular trial.

Accused persons who are prosecuted by the Occupying Power shall be promptly informed, in writing, in a language which they understand, of the particulars of the charges preferred against them, and shall be brought to trial as rapidly as possible. . . .

ART. 72. Accused persons shall have the right to present evidence necessary to their defence and may, in particular, call witnesses. They shall have the right to be assisted by a qualified advocate or counsel of their own choice, who shall be able to visit them freely and shall enjoy the necessary facilities for preparing the defence. . . .

Accused persons shall, unless they freely waive such assistance, be aided by an interpreter, both during preliminary investigation and during the hearing in court. They shall have the right at any time to object to the interpreter and to ask for his replacement.

ART. 73. A convicted person shall have the right of appeal provided for by the laws applied by the court. He shall be fully informed of his right to appeal or petition and of the time limit within which he may do so. . . .

ART. 76. Protected persons accused of offences shall be detained in the occupied country, and if convicted they shall serve their sentences therein. They shall, if possible, be separated from other detainees and shall enjoy conditions of food and hygiene which will be sufficient to keep them in good health, and which will be at least equal to those obtaining in prisons in the occupied country. . . .

Art. 78. If the Occupying Power considers it necessary, for imperative reasons of security, to take safety measures concerning protected persons, it may, at the most, subject them to assigned residence or to internment.

Decisions regarding such assigned residence or internment shall be made according to regular procedure to be prescribed by the Occupying Power in accordance with the provisions of the present Convention. This procedure shall include the right of appeal for the parties concerned. Appeals shall be decided with the least possible delay. In the event of the decision being upheld, it shall be subject to periodical review, if possible every six months, by a competent body set up by the said Power. . . .

Appendix E
International Covenant on Civil and Political Rights
Part I (Excerpts)

ART. 1.—1. All peoples have the right of self-determination. By virtue of that right they freely determine their political status and freely pursue their economic, social and cultural development. . . .

3. The States Parties to the present Covenant, including those having responsibility for the administration of Non-Self-Governing and Trust Territories, shall promote the realization of the right of self-determination, and shall respect that right, in conformity with the provisions of the Charter of the United Nations.

ART. 4.—1. In time of public emergency which threatens the life of the nation and the existence of which is officially proclaimed, the States Parties to the present Covenant may take measures derogating from their obligations under the present Covenant to the extent strictly required by the exigencies of the situation, provided that such measures are not inconsistent with their other obligations under international law and do not involve discrimination solely on the ground of race, colour, sex, language, religion or social origin. . . .

ART. 9.—1. Everyone has the right to liberty and security of person. No one shall be subjected to arbitrary arrest or detention. No one shall be deprived of his liberty except on such grounds and in accordance with such procedures as are established by law.

2. Anyone who is arrested shall be informed, at the time of arrest of the reasons for his arrest and shall be promptly informed of any charges against him.

3. Anyone arrested or detained on a criminal charge shall be brought promptly before a judge or other officer authorized by law to exercise judicial power and shall be entitled to trial within a reasonable time or to release. It shall not be the general rule that persons awaiting trial shall be detained in custody, but release may be subject to guarantees to appear for trial, at any other stage of the judicial proceedings, and, should occasion arise, for execution of the judgement.

4. Anyone who is deprived of his liberty by arrest or detention shall be entitled to take proceedings before a court, in order that the court may decide without delay on the lawfulness of his detention and order his release if the detention is not lawful.

5. Anyone who has been the victim of unlawful arrest or detention shall have an enforceable right to compensation.

ART. 10.—1. All persons deprived of their liberty shall be treated with humanity and with respect for the inherent dignity of the human person.

    2. (a) Accused persons shall, save in exceptional circumstances, be segregated from convicted persons and shall be subject to separate treatment appropriate to their status as unconvicted persons;

    (b) Accused juvenile persons shall be separated from adults and brought as speedily as possible for adjudication. . . .

ART. 12.—1. Everyone lawfully within the territory of a State shall, within [that] territory, have the right to liberty of movement and freedom to choose his residence.

2. Everyone shall be free to leave any country, including his own.

3. The above-mentioned rights shall not be subject to any restriction except those which are provided by law, are necessary to protect national security, public order (order public), public health or morals or the rights and freedoms of others, and are consistent with the other rights recognized in the present Covenant.

4. No one shall be arbitrarily deprived of the right to enter his own country.

ART. 14.—. . . 2. Everyone charged with a criminal offence shall have the right to be presumed innocent until proved guilty according to law. . . .

    3. (g) Not to be compelled to testify against himself or to confess guilt. . . .

5. Everyone convicted of a crime shall have the right to his conviction and sentence being reviewed by a higher tribunal according to law. . . .

ART. 17.—1. No one shall be subjected to arbitrary or unlawful interference with his privacy, family, home or correspondence, nor to unlawful attacks on his honour and reputation.

2. Everyone has the right to the protection of the law against such interference or attacks.

Appendix F

The Karp Report:
An Israeli Government Inquiry into
Settler Violence Against Palestinians
on the West Bank

(Excerpts)
(Released February 7, 1984)

Police Investigations

A. The head of the claims section at the Israel police national head-quarters, who is a member of the inquiry team, took on herself the rather difficult task of collecting, on an ongoing basis, the reports on complaints and investigations in Judea and Samaria (via the heads of investigation offices in the various Judea and Samaria districts), to keep track of how the investigations went and to report periodically to the team.

B. The Commission examined some 70 occurrences which were in-cluded in the reports, including psychological damage (the minority of cases), armed threats, threats, trespassing, assault, damage to property, and breaches of order. Of these 70 files, the investigation of 15 led to the files being passed on to the state's attorney with recommendation to prosecute; 33 of the files were closed; and the handling of 20 (in four of which, the investigation material had not been located) had not yet been completed. Only five of the files whose handling had not yet been completed are from March and April. The investigation of the remainder had been going on for more than six months, in some cases for more than a year (10 cases dealt with events which took place in April and May 1981, and four were opened in November and December 1981).

Experience has shown that protracted investigations of the above kind are not likely to have results, and one may therefore say that of the aforementioned 70 cases, 53 have reached . . . a dead end.

Approximately half of the 33 closed files were closed on the grounds of offender unknown; five were closed for lack of evidence; seven because no charge was brought; and three for lack of public interest.

The inquiry team did not examine the entire group of cases to the full, but random checks yielded 15 files in which the team thought that investigation was either poor or contained substantive defects. Some of them are cases whose handling was not completed, and some were closed in the wake of investigation, as was said above.

It should also be pointed out that in some cases, investigation was begun only following the Commission's request (this will be discussed below), and that in several cases it turned out that reports to the Commission were either defective (some 10 complaints were not included in the reports) or deviated from procedures established by the inquiry team (some 6 files). . . .

From the picture emerging from the collective total of the inquiry team's findings, one may conclude with reasonable certainty that the report's findings point to a situation which can neither be justified nor accounted for only by general constraints, and which clearly reveals special background characteristics, and a seriously problematic situation which stems from those charateristics. . . .

D. The above finding is based on the following:

1. The ratio between the overall number of files and those files which were closed without prosecution, and the percentage of files closed on the grounds of offender unknown.

2. The handling of many files went on for an unreasonable length of time, regardless of the sensitivity of the issue under investigation. The inquiry team takes a very grave view of the slow pace of investigation (and the pace of reporting) in cases of death from shooting. It should also be pointed out that even in those cases where the state attorney's office had given its commitment to the Supreme Court to conduct an effective investigation, the inquiry team's efforts to expedite handling were to no avail.

3. The aforementioned cases, which are the most conspicuous of those checked by the Commission, are enough to move the above conclusion from the sphere of estimation to that of fact. They will be detailed below in what may seem overelaboration, because this, in and of itself, will suffice to exhibit—without further explanation—the background, the characteristics, and the contradictions between commitment and reality. . . .

Investigation of Cases of Unnatural Deaths

A. The team had special difficulty following up police investigations of cases of gunshot wounds in which Israelis—not soldiers—had been involved, especially given the recent increase of such incidents. Police reporting in this sphere has been exceptionally slow. On injuries alone (not involving a complaint), there was no reporting and no investigating at all; and the police's position is (according to the head of the Judea investigations office and the police representative) that the police are incapable of following up these incidents. The team's inquiry, in any case, was basically deficient, because updated details of reports were received by the team after a great delay. The inquiry team received reports on two investigations into deaths—the case of the killing of a boy from Sinjil (March 15, 1982), and the case of the killing of a boy in Bani Na'im (March 24, 1982).

B. The inquiry's team's impression of the aforementioned cases was that the appropriate energy and required efficiency for investigations of this kind were not evident—and doubts arose as to the actual method of investigation. In the Bani Na'im case, investigation of the suspect did not commence until six days after the incident—while in the interim, a delegation of Israeli local residents had presented themselves to the police and explicitly declared that the residents would not cooperate with the police and would behave only as per instructions from the military government and the Minister. An arrest warrant that had been drawn up regarding one of the suspects was never served; and it is suspected that the police officers did not properly discharge their duties. (According to the report of the head of the Judea investigations office to the team, police officers had planned to serve the arrest warrant after midnight, and they reported that the suspect had not been at home—although the suspect claimed to have been at home.) The case was investigated in such a manner that the [District] Attorney had to return the file for completion of the investigation.

C. Regarding the murder of the youth in the village of al-Aroub (an incident from the end of April 1982)—the team has still not received details of the investigation; it appears, on the face of it, that there was an inconsistency of reporting between the various elements within the police —and the suspicion arises that the police did not efficiently follow through the investigation's leads that could lead to the identity of the person who fired the weapon.

Conclusions

... The above findings deal with 15 incidents which were investigated. They are only a portion of the entire group of 70 cases on which the team received reports. The inquiry team, as stated earlier, did not examine the entire group of cases to the full, and it therefore cannot determine with finality that the above findings characterize all investigations in the area under examination. However, a study of the details of these [15], and the fact (noted above) that of the 70 cases, 53 were closed without results, requires thought, if not concern. In any case, consideration should be given to whether the state attorney's office can indeed make a commitment in future before the court about conducting serious and effective investigations.

An analysis of the above requires that the following points be considered:

A. 1. The complaints submitted to the police centered mainly on the following: assault, damage to property, threats, armed threats, shootings, trespassing and closing off rights of way to fields and businesses in towns (among the complaints were also attacks on schoolgirls and an incursion into a private clinic for purposes of prayer).

A common denominator may be discerned here, which is that the backdrop to their occurrence is not the usual criminal delinquency; and save for instances of shooting for self-defense, they may be characterized as springing from the desire to demonstrate "rights" on the ground. In any case, they bear a sort of witness to an ugly atmosphere in the relations of Israeli residents of Judea and Samaria to the local populace. These things focus mainly on Hebron and the Shilo area.

2. In case 214/81 in Jerusalem district court, two Israelis were convicted on September 2, 1981 of attacking a Hebron Arab, trespassing, and deliberately damaging property, following the latter's refusal to allow them to enter real estate which the accused claimed was Jewish property.

In his verdict, Judge Goldberg noted the following:

In the instance before us, the accused at first only asked to enter an abandoned storey so as to demonstrate their presence in a non-violent manner; but when they encountered a refusal, they did not give up, but rather used force against the person who stood in their way. The accused's attachment to Jewish property cannot serve as justification for an act of hooliganism; and not by assaulting an elderly man and overturning crates of fruit at his stand will the accused bring about realization of rights to Jewish property. The Court cannot treat these actions indulgently . . . even if these are youths who have no past record.

These statements were cited in this context because they would appear to represent the character of most of the complaints which are the subject of our inquiry.

3. We will not have done our duty if, in describing the nature of these actions, we do not deal with the events which transpired during the curfew in Hebron in May 1980, following the murder of the settlers. True, these are incidents which occurred in the wake of trauma—and for this reason, we have no intention of presenting them as being usual, certainly not in their cumlative scope; but they are mentioned here as representing incapacity both to prevent acts of hooliganism towards Arab inhabitants and to investigate complaints in the sphere. . . .

B. 1. As a general finding, we can say that police activity to maintain public order and [ensure] the inhabitants' welfare in Judea and Samaria (at least in the sphere of Jewish-Arab relations) focuses on investigating in the wake of complaints. Incidents of lawbreaking when no complaints were lodged are not investigated. This holds true mainly regarding injuries resulting from shooting, but it is also true of simple criminal offenses. The inquiry team, in many cases, did not receive reports on police discoveries.

This is clear from episodes discussed earlier, principally those instances in which an investigation was begun as the result of a Supreme Court request or at the instigation of the inquiry team. One may therefore say that the police have not been honoring—as they might have been expected to do—the commitment given the Supreme Court regarding awareness of what goes on in sensitive areas, so as to prevent illegal actions insofar as possible. . . .

C. 1. The material submitted to the inquiry team clearly indicates that local residents refrain from complaining (Beit Hadassah, the Hebron school principal—aftermath to the Beit Hadassah affair, the assault on the guard at the Patriarch's Cave, et al.); and although the team hasn't any way to keep close tabs on events in the area via means other than police reports, one may conclude with a large measure of confidence that criminal occurrences take place in the area, [occurrences] which are not investigated, and whose scope isn't known to the inquiry team. In this context, the astonishing fact should be noted that in the Samaria district, the police reported on just two complaints in the space of half year.

2. The potential reasons for this absence of complaints may range from fatalism and [a] natural tendency not complain, to a lack of desire to come in contact with the authorities, to fear resulting from a threat or fear of an act of revenge, to drawing conclusions from a lack of results in previous complaints to the police or from police refusal to handle complaints.

While failure to report offenses is not typical only of Judea and Samaria —even in Israel, the number of complaints is far from reflecting all the offenses committed—the material presented to the team still gives substance to the fear that the pretext of alienation from the authorities (cf. The Arab proverb: "If the judge is your enemy, to whom can you complain?"), and fear of complaining due to the abovementioned fear of revenge, do indeed constitute a reason for failure to report. Another possible reason for failure to report, in the cases of gunshot wounds, is involvement by the wounded in incidents of stone-throwing or riots.

But besides all this, there is undoubtedly a direct correlation between the large number of investigations which end with case closed—and the large number of cases whose handling stretches over a long period—and the waiver of the right to complain. The real situation points to a vicious circle in which occurrences aren't investigated for lack of complaint, while complaints aren't submitted because of a lack of proper investigation. The rule of law and public order surely do not come out the winners in this matter. . . .

E. 1. The inquiry team didn't have the means for drawing comparisons, but its initial impression is that the number of cases in this sphere whose handling ended in closure of the case—on the grounds of offender unknown—exceeds the number acceptable in other spheres.

2. Of course, one must not overlook objective difficulties which exist in identifying suspects in occurrences of a certain type. Occurrences such as damage done at night, and gunfire from fleeing cars are, by their nature, difficult to solve. An additional difficulty occurs in incidents involving injury resulting from gunfire, since, as previously stated, the injured themselves face trial for involvement and therefore don't testify. These are objective difficulties that must be taken into account.

3. Another difficulty in connection with this, as previously mentioned, is that in CID investigations, the local residents are interrogated by the police, and material is passed on to it long after the incident, so that it's doubtful whether the investigation of the incident can be useful. The result is that witnesses from among the local population are not interrogated, and without such witnesses, it is necessary to begin from the assumption that there was a roadblock, stones were thrown, there was need to fire, the shots were actually fired in the air, and so it is difficult to reach any conclusions regarding identifying who fired. The difficulties increase in events ending in the death of an individual. Then, the question is asked whether in light of the loss of human life, there is reason to grant immunity to stone throwers or participants in riots, so that they will testify.

In the case of the death in Beni Na'im, the police decided not to grant immunity to the participants in the riots. Already at that stage, it was possible to say that the investigation was, therefore, one-sided and this has implications for the results.

4. Another phenomenon, relating to the non-identification of suspects, [is] that the complainants retract their statements that they can identify a suspect (such was the case in the Tomb of the Patriarchs incident, and the same for the uprooting of the vines in Kedumim). It is not for the team to establish the reason for this phenomenon, but the fear of the complainants should not be ruled out (fear of the threat in the case of the Jericho merchant). The inquiry team was not convinced that in the cases where complainants reneged on their willingness to identify a suspect, the police made real efforts to encourage the complainants to cooperate with them.

5. At the same time we can, without misrepresenting reality, point to a direct connection between the plethora of cases closed due to offender unknown, and failed investigations, either because the proper speed was not displayed when the event took place or the investigation occurred a long time after the event, or because no proper efforts were made to locate persons (and it is fitting to recall in this conection that during the Hebron curfew incidents, as mentioned earlier, all the cases of complaints of property damage, arson, assault, and others—numbering at least 13—were closed on the grounds that the offender was unknown). . . .

F. 1. The team formed the impression that the police investigations in the sphere of our interest were carried out in an ambivalent manner, as is evident from the results of the investigations.

This ambivalence stems not only from the natural complexity of the situation, and not only from the fact that the suspects in the abovementioned complaint files are not perceived by the police as offenders in the usual sense; it appears that the situation stems also, and mainly, from external interference on the part of military government personnel, in giving orders concerning the actual opening of investigations and related matters such as release from detention.

2. This was explained very bluntly to the inquiry team by the head of the investigations department in Judea, Superintendent Kalij, who provided examples. Similarly, he also explicitly stated in his report (of June 1, 1981) on the Beit Hadassah case:

The military governor of Hebron instructed the Hebron station chief not to handle the matter, as he would see to it that the military government repaired the damage. . . . In the first case, the complaint of *dendis* in the matter of the ceiling was not investigated properly, as the previous military governor had given instructions not to handle the case.

In his appearance before the inquiry team, Superintendent Kalij added that pressure was being brought to bear by the military government for the release of persons detained for questioning, pressures that led in a number of cases to their release. He said that when such pressures are applied directly, station chiefs are unable to withstand them, as they hesitate to enter into a confrontation with the governor and to act contrary to his directives. The result is release from arrest on irrelevant grounds and for reasons totally unrelated to the investigation. . . .

Appendix G

Landau Commission Report
on the Shin Bet, 1987

(Excerpts)

a. The Shin Bet, as a matter of policy, has been committing perjury in proceedings related to the admissibility of confessions since 1971.

b. The service committed perjury to conceal its interrogation methods and to ensure that the accused are convicted, since, in terrorism cases, the confession is the main instrument for conviction. The Commission terms this phenomenon in the Shin Bet "ideological criminality."

c. The use of the harsh interrogation methods and the commission of perjury was not meant to convict innocent persons.

d. The main responsibility for the commission of perjury lies with the three men who served as Shin Bet heads from 1971, especially the last two (Avraham Ahituv and Avraham Shalom) and with the service's legal advisers during this period. The Commission, however, does not recommend that any action be taken against them.

e. The political, judicial and military authorities did not know of the Shin Bet's practice of perjury and therefore are not to be held responsible for it.

f. The Commission agrees that limited and clearly delineated psychological and physical pressures may legitimately be exerted in the interrogation of those suspected of terrorism and has proposed precise guidelines for the Shin Bet to adopt. It rejected the justification advanced by the Shin Bet for the commission of perjury.

g. The Commission recommends that no criminal action be taken or be allowed against the Shin Bet operatives who committed perjury or employed illegal interrogation methods in the period before its report was published. The operatives, the panel said, could defend their illegal interrogation methods by the defence, which exists in the criminal code, of justification—that they were just carrying out orders—and of necessity— of preventing rampant terrorism. The perjury might also be defended by necessity, and, in any case, prosecution of operatives would wreak havoc in the Shin Bet.

h. The Commission recommends that external supervision and control of the service, by the Knesset, the prime minister, the cabinet and the State Comptroller, be strengthened and expanded.

i. The Commission recommends that the attorney general and the military judicial authorities take steps to permit retrials in [response to] all justified requests submitted in the wake of the report. It recommends that the appropriate guidelines be issued to allow prisoners sentenced in military courts in the territories, the right to retrial.

Notes

1. The Political and Legal Environment

1. See, for example, Alan Gerson, "Trustee-Occupant: The Legal Status of Israel's Presence in the West Bank," *Harvard International Law Review* 14 (1973): 1–49, in which the author specifically endorses the use of the term "West Bank" (1n. 1).

2. Moshe Drori, *Ha'hakika be'ezor Yehuda ve'Hashomron* (The legislation in Judaea and Samaria) (Jerusalem: Hebrew Univ. of Jerusalem, 1975).

3. Eyal Benvenisti, *Legal Dualism: The Absorption of the Occupied Territories into Israel*, (Boulder, Colo.: Westview Press, 1990).

4. U.S. Department of State, *Country Reports on Human Rights* (Washington, D.C.), is an annual publication. By the time of writing, the report for 1992 was published.

5. Al-Haq/Law in the Service of Man, *Punishing a Nation: Human Rights Violations During the Palestinian Uprising* (Ramallah: Al-Haq/Law in the Service of Man, 1988). Al-Haq continues to publish material on the human rights conditions in the territories.

6. Lawyers Committee for Human Rights, *An Examination of the Detention of Human Rights Workers and Lawyers from the West Bank and Gaza and Conditions of Detention at Ketziot* (New York: Lawyers Committee, 1988). See also Emma Playfair, *Administrative Detention in the Occupied West Bank*, Occasional Paper no. 1 (Ramallah: Al-Haq/Law in the Service of Man, 1989). The LCHR continues to publish important material, particularly on the work of the courts and lawyers in the territories.

7. Raja Shehadeh, *Occupier's Law: Israel and the West Bank*, rev. ed. (Washington, D.C.: Institute for Palestine Studies, 1989).

8. The Committee to Protect Journalists and Article 19, *Journalism under Occupation: Israel's Regulation of the Palestinian Press* (New York and London: The Committee and Article 19, 1988).

9. Yossi Sarid and Dedi Zucker, "A Year of Intifada," *New Outlook* 8 (Jan. 1989): 48–50. For a more comprehensive Israeli report, see International Center for

Peace in the Middle East, *Human Rights in the Occupied Territories 1979–1983* (Tel Aviv: International Center, 1985).

10. For the legal position of the Israeli right, see Yehuda Zvi Blum, "The Missing Revisioner: Reflections on the Status of Judea and Samaria," *Israel Law Review* 3 (1968): 279–301. The political right argues essentially that Israel is not an occupier because Jordan conquered the West Bank by aggression; Israel needed the area for security reasons; and in view of historical rights, Israel can now legitimately claim the area. Gerhard von Glahn and other scholars reject these arguments in view of the clear wording of the Fourth Geneva Convention, which, to them, implies the automatic application of Geneva IV to an occupied area (Gerhard von Glahn, *Law Among Nations: An Introduction to Public International Law*, 5th ed. [New York: Macmillan, 1986], 693). Very few people outside Israel support the right-wing contentions regarding the territories. See, for example, Jesse Helms, "Law and the Territories," *Jerusalem Post*, May 4, 1990.

11. Thomas S. Kuttner, "Israel and the West Bank: Aspects of the Law of Belligerent Occupation," *Israel Yearbook on Human Rights* 7 (1977): 166–221 (quote is from 174).

12. Nathan Feinberg, "The West Bank's Legal Status," *New Outlook* 20 (Oct.–Nov. 1977): 60–62. ARTICLE 51 of the U.N. Charter is the single most authoritative regulator of self-defense today; it does not authorize annexation of an aggressor's territory.

13. Gerson, "Trustee-Occupant."

14. For the position of the Labor-led government, see Shlomo Gazit, *Hamakel ve'Hagezer* (The stick and the carrot) (Tel Aviv: Zmora, Bitan, 1985), 25–26. For the position of the Likud-led government, see Ilan Peleg, *Begin's Foreign Policy, 1973–1983: Israel's Move to the Right* (Westport, Conn.: Greenwood Press, 1987).

15. This way of organizing the various positions is based on Drori, *Ha'hakika be'ezor*, esp. 24–31.

16. See Blum, "Missing Revisioner"; and Julius Stone, *No Peace-No War in the Middle East: Legal Problems in the First Year* (Sydney: Maitland Publications, 1969), 295, n. 60.

17. Such as Stephen M. Boyd, "The Applicability of International Law in the Occupied Territories," *Israel Yearbook on Human Rights* 1 (1971): 258–77.

18. Moreover, The Hague Regulations (ARTICLE 42) shed further light on the question of the applicability of international humanitarian law to the territories when they state that "territory is considered occupied when it is actually placed under the authority of a hostile army." ARTICLES 42–56 are of special importance: Gerhard von Glahn, *Law Among Nations: An Introduction to Public International Law*, 4th. ed. (New York: Collier Macmillan, 1968), 603. The legal actions taken by Israel since 1967 "were claimed to be in accordance with the framework of belligerent occupation under international law, more specifically, with the 1907 Hague Regulations. . . . [A]lthough Israel has never formally recognized that its status in the territories is that of belligerent occupant, it still justifies its acts there by resorting to the framework prescribed by international law" (E. Benvenisti, *Legal Dualism*, i).

19. See Diplomatic Conference for the Establishment of International Conventions for the Protection of Victims of War, *Geneva Conventions of August 12, 1949, for the Protection of War Victims* (Washington, D.C.: U.S. Government Printing Office, 1950), 164 (emphasis added).

20. Meir Shamgar, "The Observance of International Law in the Administered

Territories," *Israel Yearbook on Human Rights* 1 (1971): 262–77 (quote on 263). Reprinted in John Norton Moore, ed., *The Arab-Israeli Conflict,* vol. 2: *Readings* (Princeton: Princeton Univ. Press, 1974), 371–89.

21. Amnon Rubinstein, "The Changing Status of the 'Territories': From Escrow to Legal Mongrel" (Hebrew), *Tel Aviv University Law Review* 11, no. 3 (Oct. 1986): 439–56 (esp. 443); in English in *Tel Aviv University Studies in Law* 8 (1988): 59–79.

22. The Israeli position was ably summarized in Shamgar, "Observance." Shamgar's position is largely based on Blum, "Missing Revisioner."

23. U.S. Department of State, *Country Reports for 1988,* 1376, and *for 1989,* 1432. Prominent Israeli jurists accepted this position, notably Professor Yoram Dinstein: "The International Law of Belligerent Occupation and Human Rights." *Israel Yearbook on Human Rights* 8 (1978): 104–43. Dinstein believes that Geneva IV does not obligate all nations but does commit the signatories (of which Israel is one). The provisions of The Hague Regulations must be regarded as customary international law and are, therefore, binding on all states (106–7). Israel's High Court of Justice accepted Dinstein's position on The Hague but not on Geneva. See also Yoram Dinstein, *Dine Milhama* (Law of war) (Tel Aviv: Schocken Press and Tel Aviv University Press, 1983), 212 (HCJ 606/78, 390/79).

24. Esther Rosalind Cohen, *Human Rights in the Israeli-Occupied Territories, 1967–1982* (Manchester: Manchester University Press, 1985), 53.

25. Boyd, 260.

26. Cohen, 53–54.

27. Von Glahn, *Law Among Nations,* 4th ed., 693. According to von Glahn, both Geneva IV and The Hague Regulations are clear as to their own applicability to the West Bank and Gaza Strip. ARTICLE 42(1) of the Regulations states that "Territory is considered occupied when it is actually placed under the authority of the hostile army." This simple sentence avoids all reference to legitimate sovereigns, the previous legal status of the territory occupied, etc. (see von Glahn, 684–85). See also Geneva Convention, ART. 6, 166.

28. Diplomatic Conference, 174.

29. Ibid., 179.

30. Ibid., 181.

31. Ibid., 188.

32. *Israel Shelanu,* February 17, 1989.

33. Hillel Sommer, "But It Does Apply!" *Tel Aviv University Law Review* 11, no. 2 (Ap. 1986): 263–80 (esp. 264); Yoram Dinstein, "Settlements and Expulsion in the Administered Territories," *Tel Aviv University Law Review* 7, no. 1 (Sept. 1979): 188–94 (esp. 188–90), and *Dine Milhama,* 23–24.

34. Interview with Professor Yoram Dinstein, *Hair,* January 19, 1990. See also Yoram Dinstein, "Judicial Review over the Military Government in the Administered Territories," *Tel Aviv University Law Review* 1 (1973): 330–36 (esp. 330–32).

35. Ibid.

36. A. Rubinstein, "The Changing Status," 446.

37. Ibid., 448.

38. Lisa M. Fleischman. Appendix B (Legal), in *Committee to Protect Journalists,* 202.

39. Yoram Dinstein, "Medicine for Numerous Plagues," *Yediot Ahronot,* Feb. 10, 1988.

40. See, for example, a report on a discussion of the matter in U.N. Human Rights Commission; "Israeli Occupation Condemned, 4th Geneva Convention Reaffirmed," *HRI Reporter* 12, no. 2 (Winter 1988): 56.

41. Sommer.

42. Cohen, 29.

43. Cohen. For the text of these documents, see Walter Laqueur and Barry Rubin, eds., *The Human Rights Reader* (New York and Scarborough, Ont.: Meridan, 1979), 197–201; or *The International Bill of Human Rights* (Glen Ellen, Calif.: Entwhistle Books, 1981).

44. International Center for Peace in the Middle East, *Human Rights*.

45. Fleischman, 206; Louis Sohn and Thomas Buergenthal, *International Protection of Human Rights* (Indianapolis: Bobbs-Merrill, 1973), 518–19, 522.

46. Fleischman, 206–7.

47. Von Glahn, *Law Among Nations*, 5th ed., 684–85.

48. Cohen, 14.

49. Drori, *Ha'hakika*, 210.

50. Kuttner, 169.

51. Dinstein, *Dine Milhama*, 216–17.

52. Gerhard von Glahn, "The Protection of Human Rights in Time of Armed Conflict," *Israel Yearbook on Human Rights* 1 (1971): 208–27 (quote from 209).

53. Cohen, xvi (emphasis added).

54. Geneva IV, ART. 33; Hague Convention, no. 4 (1907), ART. 50.

55. Geneva IV, ART. 49. This provision has become especially important since the beginning of the Intifada, in light of ideas in Israel regarding mass "transfer" of the Arab population out of the territories.

56. Ibid., ART. 53.

57. Ibid., ART. 65.

58. Ibid., ART. 71.

59. Ibid., ART. 72.

60. Ibid., ART. 73.

61. Ibid., ART. 76.

62. UDHR, ART. 9.

63. Ibid., ART. 11.1. The demolition of houses of suspects in acts of terrorism, which normally occurs prior to a trial, is a clear violation of ARTICLE 11.1 of the Universal Declaration.

64. Ibid., ART. 13.

65. Ibid., ART. 17.2. See also Geneva IV, ART. 53; Hague Regulations, ART. 46.

66. Charles Humana, *World Human Rights Guide* (New York and Oxford: Facts on File Publications, 1986).

67. Humana's list, no. 5.

68. Ibid., no. 8. This human rights standard is important in view of accusations of frequent vigilantism on the West Bank and in the Gaza Strip by Jewish settlers.

69. Ibid., no. 13.

70. Ibid., no. 34.

71. Ibid., no. 35.

72. This classification is based on Michael Inbar and Efraim Yuchtman-Yaar, "The People's View on the Resolution of the Israeli-Arab Conflict," in Ilan Peleg and Ofira Seliktar, eds., *The Emergence of a Binational Israel: The Second Republic in the Making* (Boulder, Colo.: Westview Press, 1989), 125–42.

73. See, for example, Mark Heller, *A Palestinian State: The Implication for Israel* (Cambridge, Mass.: Harvard Univ. Press, 1983).

2. The Settlement Policy and Its Consequences

1. For a description of the Allon Plan, see Yerocham Cohen, *Tochnit Allon* (The Allon Plan) (Tel Aviv: Kibbutz Mehuad Publishers, 1972); Ilan Peleg, "Solutions for the Palestinian Question: Israel's Security Dilemma," *Comparative Strategy* 4, no. 3 (1984): 249–71; Meron Benvenisti with Ziad Abu-Ziad and Danny Rubinstein, *The West Bank Handbook: A Political Lexicon* (Jerusalem: Jerusalem Post, 1986), "Allon Plan," 406.

2. Avigdor Feldman, in *Koteret Rashit*, as reported in *The Other Israel* (Sept.–Oct. 1983), no. 3: 12.

3. American Friends Service Committee, *A Compassionate Peace: A Future for the Middle East* (New York: Hill and Wang, 1982), 21. According to Meron Benvenisti, *The West Bank Data Project: A Survey of Israel's Policies* (Washington, D.C.: American Enterprise Institute, 1984), 21, in 1977 there were 5,023 Jews in the West Bank. Giora Goldberg and Ephraim Ben-Zadok assess the average annual number of added West Bank settlers until 1977 at 300, and at 4,400 since 1977; see their "Regionalism and Territorial Cleavage in Formation: Jewish Settlement in the Administered Territories," *State, Government and International Relations* 21 (Spring 1983): 69–94.

4. Meron Benvenisti, *1986 Report on Demographic, Economic, Legal, Social and Political Development in the West Bank*. Jerusalem: Jerusalem Post; Boulder, Colo.: Westview Press, 1986.

5. Ibid., 49.

6. According to M. Benvenisti et al., between 1977 and 1983 the number of Jewish settlers in the territories increased from 5,023 to 27,500, and to 42,600 in 1984; see also Meron Benvenisti, "Know the West Bank," *Politika* (Hebrew), July 1985, 2–6. More than 100 settlements were established in the territories between 1977 and 1983. M. Benvenisti et al., assesses the number of West Bank Settlers in 1985 at 52,000.

7. Kuttner, 218.

8. Von Glahn, *Law Among Nations*, 5th ed., 692–93.

9. See, for example, letter from legal adviser, Department of State, of Apr. 21, 1978, in *International Legal Materials* 17 (1978): 777–79; excerpts from President Carter and others in *American Journal of International Law* 72 (1978): 138–39; *New York Times*, Feb. 17, 1978, A-2, and Apr. 24, 1979, A-1, A-4; and U.S. Department of State, *Country Report for 1988*, 1366–87.

10. See, for example, Resolution 32/5 of Oct. 28, 1977 (*New York Times*, July 15, 1979, p. A-7). The Security Council adopted a similar position (e.g., a resolution passed on March 1, 1980). For a summary of a position justifying Israel's settlements on the West Bank, see Justus R. Weiner, "The Settlements in Judea and Samaria: A Legal View," *Midstream*, Aug.–Sept. 1986, 24–26. Weiner argues that Geneva IV does not forbid Israel's settlement activities and that the convention is irrelevant.

11. Most spokespersons for the Israeli right have supported the settlement effort as a prelude to annexation.

12. Yoram Dinstein, one of Israel's best-known authorities on international law, wrote that the intention of ARTICLE 49 (of Geneva IV) was to "prevent a demo-

graphic change in the composition of the population in the occupied area" (*Dine Milhama*, 226). He believes that the establishment of Nahal (paramilitary) settlements is legal, because those can be seen as IDF bases. Citizens cannot be settled, but soldiers can. See also Dinstein, "Settlements and Expulsion."

13. M. Benvenisti et al., 139.

14. *Jerusalem Post*, Nov. 12, 1982, estimates 35,000 *dunams;* M. Benvenisti et al., 17, estimates the area at 50,000 *dunams.*

15. *Jerusalem Post*, Jan. 11, 1988.

16. Benvenisti et al., 116–17.

17. *Jerusalem Post*, Oct. 15, 1981; M. Benvenisti et al., 114.

18. Shehadeh, *Occupier's Law*, 36.

19. M. Benvenisti et al., 115.

20. Ibid.

21. Shehadeh, *Occupier's Law*, 23–24.

22. M. Benvenisti et al., 139.

23. For a detailed map of all "state lands" declared by the Begin government, see Meron Benvenisti, *The West Bank Data Project: A Survey of Israel's Policies* (Washington, D.C.: American Enterprise Institute, 1984), Map 7, 85. The same technique of land expropriation was used on Israeli Arabs, according to Ian Lustick, *Arabs in the Jewish State* (Austin: Univ. of Texas Press, 1980), 171.

24. Raja Shehadeh, *Haderech Hashlishit* (The third way) (Jerusalem: Adam Publishers, 1982), 91.

25. Shehadeh, *Occupier's Law*, 213. Shehadeh describes in detail some of the procedures used in land expropriation. He believes that irregularities in land transfers became especially "widespread in the late 1970s and early 1980s as the settlement movement accelerated" (215) and gives specific examples. Shehadeh describes a series of mysterious fires in the courts of Nablus (Dec. 20, 1984), Bethlehem, and Jenin, which destroyed files relating to land settlements (as many as 250 of which were in favor of Palestinians).

26. M. Benvenisti et al., 120–21; *Christian Science Monitor*, July 5, 1989.

27. M. Benvenisti et al., 140.

28. Shehadeh, *Occupier's Law*, 218.

29. This section draws heavily from Peleg, *Begin's Foreign Policy*, 117–22.

30. See ibid., chs. 1 and 2.

31. For many years, the Labor movement included radical nationalist elements. These were often associated with a party called Ahdut Ha'avoda (Unity of Work). Among the annexationists after 1967, there have been many important people with a socialist background. Among them are Haim Yachil, Natan Alterman, Eliezer Livneh, Zvi Shiloah, Moshe Shamir, and Yitzhak and Moshe Tabenkin.

32. Zvi Ra'anan, *Gush Emunin* (Hebrew) (Tel Aviv: Sifriat Poalim, 1980). The new theology of Gush Emunim was rooted in the writings of Rabbi Abraham Yitzhak Hachohen Kook, who saw Zionism as the beginning of redemption. His son, Rabbi Yehuda Zvi Kook, became the spiritual and intellectual father of the Gush and deeply influenced its activists and leaders. For the latter, see, for example, Yehuda Amital, *Hama'alot Mema'amakim* (The steps out of the depth) (Jerusalem: Agudat Yeshivat Har-Zion, 1974).

33. Even in 1985, Gush Emunim was estimated at 12,000 persons, more than half of them children, a total of only 3,000 families. See an interview with Nissim Zvili in *Politika*, no. 2 (July 1985): 19.

34. Danny Rubinstein, *Mi Leadonai Eli: Gush Emunim* (On the Lord's side: Gush Emunim) (Tel Aviv: Kibbutz Mehuad Publishers, 1981), 32.

35. Gazit, *Hamakel ve'Hagezer;* 175. Jews lived in Hebron until 1929.

36. Hannan Porat, one of the leaders of Gush Emunim, recognized its limited resources but emphasized its leadership role when he said: "Gush Emunim cannot settle Eretz Israel. We are merely the pioneers." *Jerusalem Post,* Mar. 27, 1981.

37. When the Knesset decided on withdrawal from the Sinai, an area not part of historical, biblical Eretz Israel, Gush Emunim led the struggle against the return of the area to Egypt.

38. *Jerusalem Post,* Mar. 27, 1983.

39. D. Rubinstein, *Mi Leadonai Eli,* 32–33, 89–91.

40. *Davar,* Aug. 19, 1983; Dan Margalit in *Ha'aretz,* Aug. 28, 1983, in reporting on Achituv's position, states that the Begin government supports the settlers openly to fuel the Arab-Jewish conflict in the territories.

41. *The Karp Report* (Washington, D.C.: Institute for Palestinian Studies, 1984). Information published to date confirms the impression that elements within the military government were highly supportive of the radical settlers on the West Bank. Major Shlomo Levitan of the military government said in the regional court in Jerusalem, where he was tried for helping the settlers in the assassination attempt on three Arab mayors, that following the event there was a "celebration" in the military government headquarters. "It was clear that the system knew who were the perpetrators but did not want to investigate. There was a silent agreement with the deed on the part of the security services," said Levitan. *Ha'aretz,* weekly ed., Oct. 24–25, 1984.

42. For example, in Hebron. See Zvi Barel in *Ha'aretz,* July 15, 1983. This policy was clearly provocative. It was designed to induce a radical Arab reaction, to be followed by additional acts of expropriation. Hebron served as the model. See, for example, *Jerusalem Post International Edition,* July 17–23, 1983.

43. In July 1985, about twenty settlers were convicted of membership in a terrorist organization. Three of them received life imprisonment for killing students on a Hebron campus. The Underground also was involved in an assassination attempt against three Arab mayors on the West Bank, planning the mass murder of Arabs on buses taking them to work in Israel (possibly as a way to cause panic and flight from the occupied areas), and the "rehabilitation" of the Harm el Sharif—the destruction of the two mosques on Jerusalem's Temple Mount as a prelude to the building of the Third Temple. The last act had, in the eyes of its perpetrators, great historic and theological meaning on the path to final redemption.

44. Yishayahu Leibovitz, *Yahadut, Am Israel, Vemedinat Israel* (Judaism, the Jewish people, and the state of Israel) (Jerusalem: Schocken, 1975).

45. *Foreign Broadcast Information Service: Middle East,* Feb. 3, 1985, under "Settler Council Chairman Comments."

46. David Kretzmer, "The Legal Status of Israeli Settlers on the West Bank," *Israeli Democracy* 1, no. 3 (Fall 1987): 16–18.

47. *Ha'aretz,* Apr. 5, 1982.

48. Shehadeh, *Occupier's Law,* 184–207, documents in detail the case of Kiryat Arba, near Hebron, and extensively covers "violations of the right to life" (185–87), destruction of property (187–90), and other violations.

49. M. Benvenisti, *West Bank Data Base Project;* International Center for Peace in the Middle East, *Human Rights.*

50. David K. Shipler, *Arab and Jew: Wounded Spirits in a Promised Land* (New York: Times Books, 1986), 122–37.

51. M. Benvenisti, *West Bank Data Base Project.*

52. Following the attack on Kalkilya and Deheishe, 109 Palestinian leaders were arrested upon the settlers' demand, a harsh action that was uncalled for (ibid.). Following the Beita incident, 16 houses were razed, the authorities again responding to the settlers' demands.

53. Ehud Sprinzak, *Gush Emunim: The Politics of Zionist Fundamentalism in Israel* (New York: American Jewish Committee, 1986), 32; and Ian Lustick, *For the Lord and the Land: Jewish Fundamentalism in Israel* (New York: Council on Foreign Relations, 1988).

54. *New York Times*, June 22, 1989.

55. In February 1989 two Knesset members, Sarid and Zucker, documented these charges in a brief to the attorney general (*Israel Shelanu*, Feb. 17, 1989).

56. M. Benvenisti et al., 135–36; Haggai Segal, *"Achim Yekarim"; Korot Hamachteret hayehudit* ("Dear brothers": The history of the Jewish Underground), (Jerusalem: Keter, 1987).

57. At the same time, some of Kach's ideas were adopted by other political parties, notably Moledet (Motherland).

3. Measures of Enforcement and Punishment

1. M. Benvenisti et al., 87.

2. U.S. State Department, *Country Report for 1989*, 1435. Although twenty-six Palestinians were deported in 1989, new deportation orders were not issued in 1989.

3. Dinstein, *Dine Milhama*, 225; "Settlements and Expulsions," 193; and "The Deportation of the Mayors from Judea," *Tel Aviv University Law Review* 6, no. 1 (Apr. 1981): 158–71.

4. *Jerusalem Post*, Nov. 4, 1986. See also Amnon Straschnov, *Justice Under Fire*, Tel Aviv, Yedioth Ahronot, 1994, 102–3.

5. Security Council document S/RES/607 (1988), Jan. 5, 1988.

6. See, for example, U.S. Department of State, *Country Report for 1987*, 1189, and *Country Report for 1988*, 1379.

7. *Financial Times*, Dec. 9, 1977.

8. Ann M. Lesch, "Israeli Deportation of Palestinians from the West Bank and Gaza Strip, 1967–1978," *Journal of Palestine Studies*, Nov. 1978, 101–31.

9. Al-Haq/Law in the Service of Man, *Punishing a Nation*, 206. According to Straschnov, only one thousand persons were deported between 1967 and 1991.

10. M. Benvenisti et al., 87, reports no deportations in these years. Al-Haq, *Punishing a Nation*, 206, reports one deportation in 1979 and three in 1980.

11. Al-Haq, *Punishing a Nation*, 266.

12. U.S. Department of State, Country Report for 1988, 1379. For a list of deportees in 1988, see Al-Haq, *Punishing a Nation*, App. 4A, 233–35.

13. *Jerusalem Post*, Aug. 18, 1988.

14. On the question of deportation in general, see Alfred M. de Zayas, "International Law and Mass Population Transfers," *Harvard International Law Journal* 16 (1975): 207–58. On Israel's policy in the territories, see E. Cohen, *Human Rights*, 104–11; and Joost R. Hiltermann, *Israel's Deportation Policy in the Occupied West*

Bank and Gaza Strip, Al-Haq Occasional Paper no. 2, 2nd ed. (Ramallah: Al-Haq, 1988).

15. Von Glahn, 5th ed., 107.

16. Playfair, 10–11.

17. Darwish Nasser, "Deportation Is No Substitute for Peace," *New Outlook*, Feb. 1988, 10–11; Meron Benvenisti, *Lexicon Yehuda ve'Shomron: Yeshuvim, Minhal, ve'Hevra* (The human rights handbook: Settlements, administration, and society) (Jerusalem: Kana, 1987), 22–23.

18. B'Tselem, *Violations of Human Rights in the Occupied Territories, 1990/91* (Jerusalem: B'Tselem, 1992), 107.

19. See, for example, Shamgar (1971). Shamgar's position has been accepted by the Israeli High Court of Justice, of which Shamgar is president, by a vote of 4–1, with Justice Bach dissenting. The Israeli jurist Yoram Dinstein and other (although by no means all) Israeli jurists took a position against deportations. Dinstein stated in an interview in *Hair* (Jan. 19, 1990): "I know of no serious international jurist anywhere in the world that thinks differently [than he, Dinstein, does on the issue of deportation]. The text [of Geneva IV] is entirely clear. The HCJ simply erred."

20. HCJ 785/87.

21. HCJ 698/80.

22. Quoted in B'Tselem, *Violations*, 184, on the basis of a report in *Ha'aretz*, January 8, 1991.

23. E. Cohen, 105–6.

24. Dinstein, "Deportation of the Mayors."

25. Al-Haq, *Punishing a Nation*, 210; Shehadeh, *Occupier's Law*, xiv–xvi; M. Benvenisti, *Lexicon*, 23; M. Benvenisti et al., 87.

26. Ibid.

27. E. Cohen, 107–10.

28. B'Tselem, *Violations*, 108.

29. *Davar*, Feb. 27, 1987.

30. Al-Haq, *Punishing a Nation*, 209–11.

31. Three Arab leaders were deported following the Hadassah House incident in Hebron, and six villagers from Beita were expelled following the incident near this village in 1988.

32. Both Likud-led and Labor-led governments expelled moderates.

33. Amnesty International, *Israel and the Occupied Territories: Administrative Detention During the Palestinian Intifada* (New York: Amnesty International, 1989), 36, 1. According to Amnesty International, in June 1989 there were 1,100 administrative detainees and the total of detainees since December 1987 had been 5,000 (20).

34. According to Ze'ev Schiff of *Ha'aretz*, no fewer than 60,000 Palestinians had passed through Israeli prisons as of March 1990 (*Ha'aretz* article reported in *Israel Shelanu*, Mar. 23, 1990).

35. B'Tselem, *Detained Without Trial* (Jerusalem: B'Tselem, 1992), 7.

36. Ariel Ben-Ami in *Al Hamishmar*, Nov. 6, 1989.

37. U.S. Department of State, *Country Report for 1989*, 1435.

38. B'Tselem, *Detained Without Trial*, 7.

39. Despite the known, harsh conditions in Ketziot, U.S. Department of State, *Country Report for 1989* (1435) mentioned some improvements in that facility.

40. Amnesty International. *Administrative Detention*, 2.

41. B'Tselem report for August 1989. The common use of administrative detention and other forms of imprisonment has created a constant pressure for the enlargement of existing prisons and the building of new ones. *Al Hamishmar* reported on November 16, 1989, that the authorities began building a new prison for 4,000 people in the territories and enlarging the detention center in Ketziot for an additional 1,300 persons. B'Tselem estimated the number of "openings" in the IDF detention centers at 14,000; with the recent enlargement, it was thought that the number would increase to 20,000 (B'Tselem, *Annual Report 1989* [Jerusalem: B'Tselem, 1989], 61).

42. U.S. Department of State, *Country Report for 1989*, 1435.

43. Dinstein, *Dine Milhama*, 227.

44. The Israeli rationale for the use of administrative detention was explained by Attorney General Yitzhak Zamir in the *Israeli Law Review* (Winter 1983).

45. E. Cohen, 121, quoting the Israeli minister of police and others.

46. Al-Haq, *Punishing a Nation*, 212–13.

47. *Hair* interview, Jan. 19, 1990.

48. Quoted in Amnesty International, *Administrative Detention*, 2.

49. B'Tselem, *Detained Without Trial*, 9, quoting the ICRC official commentary.

50. Playfair, 13; Lawyers Committee for Human Rights, *Examination of the Detention*, 8.

51. B'Tselem, *Detained Without Trial*, 11.

52. Ibid.

53. E. Cohen, 122–23.

54. U.S. Department of State. *Country Report for 1988*, 1379–80.

55. Amnesty International, *Administrative Detention*, 1.

56. Playfair, 7.

57. Amnesty International, *Administrative Detention*, 1.

58. Ibid., 1, 9.

59. See Military Order 378, as amended by Military Order 815, ART. 87B(b).

60. Diane F. Orentlicher, "Human Rights in Israel's Occupied Territories," *Middle East Focus*, Spring/Summer 1988, 12–15; quote from 14.

61. Amnesty International, *Administrative Detention*, 14.

62. Orentlicher, 13.

63. Amnesty International, *Administrative Detention*, 2; Lawyers Committee for Human Rights (LCHR), *Examination of Detention*, 12.

64. E. Cohen, 128.

65. LCHR, *Examination of Detention*, 13.

66. Ibid.

67. Amnesty International, *Administrative Detention*, 8. For the HCJ ruling, see *Ibraim Sagidia and others* v. *Minister of Defense*, HCJ 258/88.

68. LCHR, *Examination of Detention*, 13.

69. E. Cohen, 121. It should be noted that Cohen's observations are in regard to the pre-Intifada period.

70. Alan Dershowitz, "Preventive Detention of Citizens During National Emergency—a Comparison Between Israel and the United States," *Israel Yearbook of Human Rights* 1 (1971): 295–321.

71. E. Cohen, 128.

72. Ibid., 295–96.

73. Ibid., 128. Ironically, other commentators argued that deportation is to be considered preferable to detention.

74. U.S. Department of State, *Country Report for 1989*, 1435.

75. Some of those points were made, in a more general way, in Charles Krauthammer, "Judging Israel," *Time*, Feb. 26, 1990, 77–78.

76. Amnesty International, *Administrative Detention*, 20.

77. See, for example, *Jerusalem Post*, July 21, 1988.

78. As of August 1988, there were about 2,600 administrative detainees in IDF prisons, according to Minister of Defense Rabin (see Joel Greenberg, "Should IDF Fire at Stone-throwers?," *Jerusalem Post Weekly Edition*, Sept. 10, 1988). Palestinian estimates tend to be somewhat higher (e.g., Al-Haq/Law in the Service of Man and Gaza Center for Rights and Law, *Justice? The Military Court System in the Israeli-Occupied Territories* (Ramallah: Al-Haq), 211, 347). Human rights groups in Israel published estimates similar to these of the IDF, although they closely consulted Palestinian sources.

79. Shehadeh, *Occupier's Law*, 141.

80. Michal Sela, "Half a Million Detentions—All in the Territories," *Koteret Rashit*, Feb. 25, 1987. This number reflects multiple arrests of many individuals.

81. Al-Haq/Law, *Punishing a Nation*, 213.

82. Regarding the new provisions, see *Washington Post*, March 22, 1988, and *Ha'aretz*, Mar. 20, 1988.

83. Amnesty International, *Administrative Detention*, 6.

84. Ibid., 7. See also the positive reaction to these changes by Prof. Baruch Bracha, in Straschnov, 68.

85. Ibid.

86. See *Hotam*, July 8, 1988, for interview with Zichroni and Fish.

87. Orentlicher, 13.

88. Ibid.

89. Ibid., 14.

90. Amnesty International, *Administrative Detention*, 34.

91. Shlomo Slotzky in *Hotam*, July 8, 1988.

92. Ibid.

93. U.S. Department of State, *Country Report for 1989*, 1436.

94. E. Cohen, 129.

95. "Town Arrest Orders in Israel and the Occupied Territories," *New Outlook*, Feb.–Mar. 1985, 45–48 (quote on 45).

96. Shehadeh, *Occupier's Law*, 146; M. Benvenisti, *Lexicon*, 23.

97. International Center for Peace in the Middle East, *Human Rights*, 124–25.

98. B'Tselem, *Demolition and Sealing Houses* (Jerusalem: B'Tselem, 1989), 26.

99. Shlomo Gazit, "Administered Areas Aspects of Israeli Policy," in *Information Briefing* (Jerusalem: Ministry of Foreign Affairs, 1972).

100. B'Tselem, *Violations*, 31.

101. E. Cohen, 96.

102. For example, the attack in May 1980 during which six settlers were gunned down in Hebron (known also as the Hadassah House incident). See Peleg, *Begin's Foreign Policy*.

103. In the 1970s the Israeli military government in Gaza cleared roads within refugee camps, in the process razing many homes.

104. Gazit, "Administered Areas"; *Ma'ariv*, Aug. 20, 1969.

105. B'Tselem, *Demolition,* 19.

106. E. Cohen, 97.

107. Ibid., 170.

108. Ibid., 97.

109. International Center for Peace in the Middle East, *Human Rights,* 158.

110. Al-Haq/Law, *Punishing a Nation,* 219.

111. Al-Haq (ibid., 218) maintains that 145 houses were razed in 1988, whereas the U.S. Department of State's number is 154 buildings (*Country Report for 1988,* 1381). *Country Report for 1989* counted 170 demolitions (1437).

112. *New York Times,* July 31, 1989; Palestinian sources are typically higher. B'Tselem (*Demolition,* 4–5) found that even official sources in Israel (IDF, Ministry of Defense, etc.) disagree on the exact number of houses demolished.

113. B'Tselem, *Violations,* 35.

114. Pinchas Inbari, *Al Hamishmar,* Apr. 6, 1988.

115. Ori Nir and Eitan Rabin, *Ha'aretz,* Jan. 18, 1989.

116. David Regev, *Yediot Ahronot,* May 19, 1989. Regev's report could not be corroborated by other sources.

117. B'Tselem, *Demolition,* 39.

118. Ibid., 17.

119. Von Glahn, *Law among Nations,* 5th ed. 706.

120. Ibid., 652.

121. Ibid., 653.

122. Quotes from the International Committee of the Red Cross, a commentary prepared by the director of its Department of Principles and Law, are taken from Shehadeh, *Occupier's Law,* 155.

123. Shamgar, "Observance," 275–76.

124. Ibid., 276; Natanel Lorch, "Symposium: Human Rights in Time of War," *Israel Yearbook of Human Rights* 1 (1971): 366–92 (esp. 376–81).

125. Alan Gerson, "State Department Reporting on Human Rights Violations," *Middle East Review,* Winter 1980–81, 22–25 (esp. 24).

126. For the position of the United States, see U.S. Department of State, *Country Report for 1988,* 1381.

127. E. Cohen, 101.

128. Gerhard von Glahn, *The Occupation of Enemy Territory* (Minneapolis: Univ. of Minnesota Press, 1957): 227–28.

129. Frits Kalshoven, *Belligerent Reprisals* (Leiden: Sijthoff, 1971), 317.

130. *Jerusalem Post,* Aug. 8, 1988.

131. Orentlicher, 13.

132. International Center for Peace in the Middle East, *Human Rights,* 121.

133. Aryeh Shalev, *The Intifada—The Reasons, Characteristics and Implications* (Tel Aviv: Jaffe Center for Strategic Studies, Tel Aviv Univ., 1990), 127–29.

134. E. Cohen, 103.

135. Ibid.

136. B'Tselem, *Demolition,* 10.

137. Nitza Aviram, *Yediot Ahronot,* Mar. 17, 1989.

138. Betzalel Amikam, *Al Hamishmar,* Sept. 11, 1988.

139. Yossi Verter, *Hadashot,* Jan. 25, 1989.

140. *New York Times,* July 31, 1989.

141. B'Tselem, *Violations,* 34.

142. Ibid., 32, 40, 178–79.

143. Emanuel Rosen, "Fewer House Demolitions," *Ma'ariv*, Sept. 5, 1991.

4. Justice under Occupation

1. For a defense of Israel's position, see Shamgar, "The Observance"; Yehuda Z. Blum, *Judea, Samaria and Gaza—The Israeli Record* (Jerusalem: Ministry of Foreign Affairs, 1979), and "Missing Reversioner."

2. See, for example, Al-Haq/Law and Gaza Center, *Justice;* Al-Haq/Law, *Punishing a Nation;* Shehadeh, *Occupier's Law.*

3. Shehadeh, *Occupier's Law,* 222.

4. M. Benvenisti et al., 34.

5. Moshe Drori, "The Legal System in Judea and Samaria: A Review of the Previous Decade with a Glance at the Future," *Israeli Yearbook on Human Rights* 8 (1978): 144–77 (quote from 150).

6. Association for Civil Rights in Israel, *Studies in Civil Rights in the Administered Territories: The Judicial and Administrative System* (Jerusalem: ACRI,1985), 17.

7. Shehadeh, *Occupier's Law,* 76; M. Benvenisti, *Lexicon,* 40, reports that the local courts have lost their jurisdiction over land matters and other issues.

8. Shehadeh, *Occupier's Law,* 77.

9. Association for Civil Rights, 17.

10. "Witnesses Criticize Territories Courts," *FBIS Report: Middle East*, Mar. 7, 1984.

11. Shehadeh, *Occupier's Law,* 81.

12. M. Benvenisti, *1986 Report,* 34, 37.

13. Shehadeh, *Occupier's Law,* 91.

14. Ibid., 93.

15. Ibid., 94.

16. See *The Karp Report.*

17. See, for example, Art. 66 of Geneva IV.

18. Parts of Order 378 were published in *Israel Yearbook of Human Rights* 1 (1971): 421–29.

19. Drori, "Legal Systems," 153.

20. Military Order 378 (3).

21. B'Tselem (Daphna Golan), *The Military Judicial System in the West Bank* (Jerusalem: B'Tselem, 1989), 6 (quoted hereafter as B'Tselem/Golan; all quotes and page references are according to the Hebrew edition of the report).

22. Military Order 378 (39)(41)(50).

23. Association for Civil Rights, 18; Drori, "Legal System," 154.

24. Von Glahn, *Occupation,* 154; Drori, "Legal System," 154.

25. Contradicting views have been expressed on the meaning of this development: Baruch Bracha in *Ha'aretz*, Jan. 30, 1989; Darwish Nasser in *Al Hamishmar*, Apr. 6, 1989; Oz Frankel in the *Jerusalem Post*, Apr. 7, 1989.

26. Association for Civil Rights, 18.

27. U.S. Department of State, *Country Reports for 1989,* 1436.

28. Al-Haq/Law, *Demolition,* 33.

29. *Hadashot,* June 16, 1987, 16–17.

30. Drori, "Legal System," 154.

31. Interview with *Ha'aretz*, (Weekly Magazine), Jan. 22, 1988, 6–9.

32. Ibid., 9.

33. B'Tselem, *Violations*, 90.

34. Ibid., 91.

35. Amnesty International, *Israel and the Occupied Territories: The Military Justice System* . . . (New York: Amnesty International, 1991), 17.

36. B'Tselem/Golan, 26.

37. Paul Sieghart, *The Lawful Rights of Mankind* (Oxford: Oxford Univ. Press, 1986), 89.

38. Al-Haq/Law, *Demolition*, 36.

39. Ibid., 37.

40. Lawyers Committee on Human Rights, *A Continuing Cause for Concern* (New York: Lawyer's Committee, 1993), 5.

41. Ibid., 2.

42. Tovah Tzimuki, "The Lawyers' Thundering Silence," *Israeli Democracy*, Winter 1988, 42–44 (both quotes from 43).

43. B'Tselem/Golan, 6.

44. B'Tselem, *Violations*, 89.

45. Ibid., 90.

46. *The Other Israel* 24 Jan.–Feb. 1987: 1.

47. Drori, "Legal System," 156. See also Ze'ev Segal, "The Authority of the High Court of Justice in the Occupied Territories," *Ha'aretz*, Feb. 20, 1984; Moshe Negbi, *Tzedek Tahat Kibush* (Justice under occupation)(Jerusalem: Cana, 1981); Ruth Gavison's reviews of Negbi's book in *Ha'aretz*, May 2, 1982; and in *Israeli Law Review*, 17, no. 2 (1982): 234–37.

48. M. Benvenisti et al., 105; M. Benvenisti, *Lexicon*, 31.

49. Raphael Israeli and Rachel Ehrenfeld, "Israel," in Jack Donnelly and Rhoda E. Howard, eds., *International Handbook of Human Rights* (Westport, Conn.: Greenwood, 1987) 161–81 (quote is from 177).

50. Shehadeh, *Occupier's Law*, 96.

51. A. Rubinstein, "Changing Status"; Sommer.

52. Sommer.

53. Shehadeh, *Occupier's Law*, 98.

54. Avigdor Feldman, "To Build a House, to Plant a Tree, to Marry a Woman, to Have Children," *Politika* no. 14–15 (June 1987): 14–17 (esp. 15–16).

55. Oded Lifshitz, "Don't Go to the High Court of Justice, Muhammad!," *Hotam*, July 31, 1987, 8–10.

56. Ibid.

57. Leon Sheleff, "The Green Line Is the Border of Judicial Activism," *Tel Aviv University Law Review* 17, no. 2 (November 1992): 757–809 (esp. 758–61).

58. B'Tselem, *Violations*, 41.

59. B'Tselem, *Annual Report 1989* (Jerusalem: B'Tselem, 1989), 50 (all quotes and references from this report are from the Hebrew edition). In Northern Ireland, a person may be arrested only if there is "reasonable suspicion for the commission of an offense." In the West Bank and Gaza Strip, the arbitrariness of the arrest applies equally to searches of homes: any home can be entered at any time by a policeman, a settler, or a security man and searched without warrant, in accordance with Arts. 78 and 81 of Military Order no. 378. No reasonable cause for the search need be shown.

60. B'Tselem, *Violations*, 63.

61. B'Tselem/Golan, 7.

62. U.S. Department of State, *Country Report for 1992*, sec. 1(d).

63. Amnesty International, *The Military Justice System*, 23.

64. B'Tselem, *Annual Report 1989*, 52.

65. B'Tselem/Golan, 4.

66. Al-Haq/Law, *Demolition*, 8.

67. B'Tselem/Golan, 7.

68. Ibid., in accordance with ART. 53 of the Israeli Criminal Law.

69. *Annual Report for 1989*, 12.

70. B'Tselem, *The Military Court System in the West Bank* (Jerusalem: B'Tselem, 1990), 2.

71. M. Benvenisti et al., 138.

72. *Hotam*, Feb. 17, 1984.

73. *Ha'aretz*, Feb. 23, 1984.

74. For the English version, see the *Jerusalem Post* or *The Karp Report*. Excerpts of the report are reproduced in Appendix F. See also articles in *Washington Post*, Feb. 6 and 8, 1984.

75. Gideon Alon, *Ha'aretz*, Feb. 9, 1984.

76. Ibid.

77. *Al Hamishmar*, Feb. 24, 1984 (emphasis added). Danny Rubinstein of *Davar* (Feb. 8, 1984) took a position similar to that of Inbari. Both have been covering events on the West Bank for years.

78. It was suggested (Al-Haq/Law and Gaza Center, *Justice*, 14) that this procedure is used so that the policeman recording the confession can later testify truthfully that the confession was given of the detainee's free will and without coercion.

79. Orentlicher, 14.

80. B'Tselem, *Interrogation of Palestinians During the Intifada* (Jerusalem: B'Tselem, 1991), 45–74.

81. Amnesty International. *The Military Justice System*, 45.

82. Ibid.

83. B'Tselem, *Interrogation of Palestinians During the Intifada: Follow-up* (Jerusalem: B'Tselem, 1992).

84. Orentlicher. After two weeks, the detainee is allowed to see a representative of the Red Cross, and after eighteen days is brought before a judge. Throughout this period, the detainee is not allowed to see a lawyer.

85. U.S. Department of State, *Country Reports for 1987* and *for 1988* sum up some of the Commission's findings. See also "Excerpts from the Landau Commission's Report on Shin Bet Practices," *Jerusalem Post*, November 1, 1987; and *FBIS: Middle East*, Nov. 2, 1987, 25.

86. For a partial list of other sources, see Middle East Watch, *Israeli Interrogation Methods* (New York: Middle East Watch, 1992), 6.

87. *Annual Report 1989*, 62.

88. Ibid., 64–65. B'Tselem's reports were based primarily on Israeli newspapers: *Hadashot*, Aug. 1, 1989; *Ha'aretz*, Feb. 6, 1989; etc. In at least one case, a senior legal panel (headed by State Prosecutor Dorit Beinish) investigated the death of a prisoner during interrogation (Mahmud el-Masri, thirty-seven, of Rapha, who died in Gaza prison) and recommended a trial for the Shin Bet personnel involved in the detainee's interrogation and death.

89. B'Tselem, *Interrogation: Follow-up*, 59.

90. Ibid., 10.

91. *Hadashot*, Sept. 20, 1989.

92. B'Tselem, *Interrogation: Follow-up*, 59.

93. Amnesty International, *The Military Justice System*, 74.

94. According to statistics provided by the IDF to B'Tselem (Mar. 1990), about 4 percent of the cases heard by military courts since the beginning of the Intifada had ended in acquittals (ibid.).

95. B'Tselem/Golan, 27. B'Tselem, *The Military Court System in the West Bank*, 6, published in May 1990, confirmed the organization's previous findings.

96. B'Tselem/Golan, 27 (emphasis added).

97. Aryeh Pach, "Human Rights in West Bank Military Courts," *Israel Yearbook on Human Rights* 7 (1977): 222–52 (esp. 243).

98. Different sources assess the period between the arrest and a detainee-lawyer meeting differently. The Lawyers Committee for Human Rights assesses this period as being "in excess of 20 days" (*Continuing Cause*, 3).

99. M. Benvenisti et al., 60; M. Benvenisti, *Lexicon*, 100 on the basis of Amnesty International reports.

100. B'Tselem, *Violations*, 65.

101. B'Tselem/Golan, 8.

102. The emergence of the Underground and its activities was described in a book by one of its members. See Haggai Segal, *"Achim Yekarim."*

103. Even prior to the exposure of the Underground and its connections with the military government, observers sensed that Gush Emunim's vigilantism had a measure of sympathy among some elements of the government in the territories. For example, Yehuda Litani wrote, in "West Bank Landscam: An Insider's Tale," *Ha'aretz*, Apr. 3, 1981, that "in the West Bank the representatives of the law stand by its breakers."

104. M. Benvenisti et al., 136.

105. DataBase Project on Palestinian Human Rights, *The Cost of Freedom: Palestinian Human Rights under the Occupation* (Chicago: DataBase Project, 1988), 27.

106. Eyal Ehrlich, "The State of Israel vs. Nisan Ishgoyev," *Ha'aretz*, April 7, 1988.

107. *Al Hamishmar*, Feb. 25, 1988.

108. Boaz Evron, "Occupation Corrupts Israeli Justice," *New Outlook* 31, no. 5 (May 1988): 8.

109. *Israel Shelanu*, Feb. 12, 1988.

110. The demolition of a large number of homes in the village of Beita was explained by some as reflecting settlers' political pressure.

111. Yehuda Litani, "The Wild West in the West Bank," *Ha'aretz*, Apr. 3, 1981. Litani reports on organized vigilante activities of the settlers from as early as 1976.

112. Danny Rubinstein in *Davar*, Apr. 9, 1982; Shehadeh, *Occupier's Law*, 185–87; *The Karp Report*.

113. Eyal Ehrlich in *Ha'aretz*, June 19, 1987.

114. Ibid.

115. *The Karp Report*; Yitzhak Zamir, "Law Enforcement in Judea and Samaria," *Ha'aretz*, Mar. 2, 1984.

116. *Washington Post*, Oct. 19, 1988.

117. Ibid.

118. B'Tselem, *Violations*, 17.

119. U.S. Department of State, *Country Report for 1992.*

120. B'Tselem, *The Military Court System*, 8.

121. B'Tselem, *Violations*, 17.

122. *Hadashot*, Oct. 19, 1989.

123. B'Tselem, *Nov. 1989 Annual Report*, 6.

124. *Yediot Ahronot*, Mar. 29, 1990.

125. Human Rights Watch, *World Report 1992* (New York: Human Rights Watch 1991), 727.

126. B'Tselem, *1989 Annual Report*, 99.

127. Ibid., 100.

128. Human Rights Watch, 727.

129. Ibid., 726.

130. B'Tselem, *1989 Annual Report*, 6.

131. Amnesty International, *Israel and the Occupied Territory: Excessive Force—Beatings to Maintain Law and Order* (New York: Amnesty International, 1988), 1. Amnesty International reports on at least eight beating cases in the first eight months of the Intifada that led to death.

132. Ibid., 9.

133. Ibid.

134. Physicians for Human Rights, *The Casualties of Conflict: Medical Care and Human Rights in the West Bank and Gaza Strip* (Somerville, Mass.: Physicians for Human Rights, 1988), 11.

135. See, for example, *Jerusalem Post*, Jan. 20, 1988.

136. Chief of Staff Shomron issued guidelines in which he referred to beatings as "aberrations": the press and human rights organizations did not accept this position.

137. Amnesty International, *The Use of Live Ammunition by Members of the Israel Defense Force* (New York: Amnesty International, 1988); and *An Update to the Use of Live Ammunition by Members of the Israel Defense Force* (New York: Amnesty International, 1988).

138. See, for example, *Letter of the Lawyer Committee of Human Rights to Prime Minister Shamir* (Mar. 10, 1988); and Physicians for Human Rights, "Special Report: Physicians for Human Rights (Occupied Territories)," *New Outlook*, June 1988, 17–21.

139. Database Project, 3.

140. Physicians for Human Rights, "Special Reports," 17.

141. Quoted in Amnesty International, *Use of Live Ammunition*, 3 (emphasis added).

142. *London Times*, Apr. 4, 1988.

143. Physicians for Human Rights, "Special Report," 17.

144. U.S. Department of State, *Country Report for 1988*, 1377.

145. Ibid., *for 1989*, 1437–38. Attorney Dan Simon reported to the author that the military advocate general stated in a letter to ACRI that this is indeed the official IDF policy.

146. See *Allentown Morning-Call*, Feb. 21, 1990.

147. U.S. Department of State, *Country Report for 1989*, 1438.

148. Amnesty International, *Use of Live Ammunition*, 6–9, and *Update to Use of Live Ammunition*, 1–4.

149. U.S. Department of State, *Country Reports for 1988*, 1377.

150. Amnesty International, *The Misuse of Tear-Gas by Israeli Army Personnel in the Israeli Occupied Territories* (New York: Amnesty International, 1988), 1.

151. DataBase Project, 10–11.

152. B'Tselem, *Activity of the Undercover Units in the Occupied Territories* (Jerusalem: B'Tselem, 1992).

153. Ibid.

154. Ibid., 75.

155. Ibid., 79.

156. See especially ch. 3.

157. Shalev, 131–36.

158. B'Tselem, *Annual Report 1989*, 78, and *Collective Punishment in the West Bank and Gaza Strip* (Jerusalem: B'Tselem, 1990), 29–30 (for data on school closures see 29).

159. For comparative data on curfews since 1987, see B'Tselem, *Collective Punishment*, 21.

160. Ibid., 20.

161. Human Rights Watch, 716–17.

162. See, for example, Dov Shefi, "The Protection of Human Rights in the Areas Administered by Israel: United Nations Findings and Reality," *Israel Yearbook on Human Rights* 3 (1973), 337–61 (esp. 345–48).

163. B'Tselem, *Collective Punishment*, 54.

164. B'Tselem, *Annual Report 1989*, 86.

165. On Nov. 13, 1989, Muhamad Mahmud Mussa received twelve years in prison for throwing Molotov cocktails at IDF patrols even though there was no damage. Eitan Rabin, *Ha'aretz*, Nov. 14, 1989.

166. B'Tselem, *Annual Report for 1989*, 86.

167. Ibid., 91.

5. Alternative Political Solutions

1. On occasion, the interests of the rulers and the ruled may coincide. Furthermore, in the interest of maintaining order, the military government may be responsive to some of the inhabitants' concerns, as Israel was under Dayan (see Gazit, *Hamakel ve'Hagezer*). Yet, in a fundamental way, it is the interest of the occupier, its citizens, and government, that the military government primarily promotes.

2. A. Rubinstein, "Changing Status," 448.

3. Lifshitz.

4. A. Rubinstein, "Israel and the Territories," 415.

5. A number of analysts have commented on Israel's capacity to change (e.g., Yoram Dinstein in an interview in *Hair*, Jan. 19, 1990).

6. In various decisions, the High Court of Justice stated that settlements must be temporary and fulfill a military need; in the Elon Moreh case, the High Court of Justice rejected political reasons as legitimizing settlements (see Ch. 2).

7. Yitzhak Zamir, "Human Rights and the Security of the State," *Ha'aretz*, Jan. 5, 1989.

8. Ibid.

9. Tovah Tzimuki, "From 'Self-Defence' to 'Deterrence' and to 'Punishment,' " *Davar*, Oct. 8, 1989.

10. Israeli and Ehrenfeld, 180.

11. This classification is based on Inbar and Yuchtman-Yaar. For other classifications of solutions, see Alouph Hareven, *Korach Habreira* (The necessity of choice) (Tel Aviv: Dvir Publishers, 1980), 69–85, and *Milhamot ve'Shalom* (Wars and peace) (Tel Aviv: Dvir Publishers, 1989).

12. Benjamin Neuberger, "The Israeli Democracy under Annexation," in Adam Doron, ed., *Medinat Israel and Eretz Israel* (The State of Israel and the Land of Israel) (Beit Berl Publishers, 1988), 327–43 (quote from 327).

13. Ze'ev Segal, "For the Widening of the High Court of Justice's Authority," *Ha'aretz*, Feb. 16, 1989.

14. Dan Margalit, "Israel Has Forgotten Human Rights," *Ha'aretz*, Jan. 27, 1989 (interview with Haim Cohn).

15. *Hadashot*, Dec. 9, 1988.

Bibliography

Al-Haq/Law in the Service of Man. *Demolition and Sealing of Houses*. Occasional Paper no. 5. Ramallah: Al-Haq/Law in the Service of Man, 1987.
———. *Israel's Deportation Policy*. Occasional Paper no. 2. Ramallah: Al-Haq/Law in the Service of Man, 1986.
———. *Punishing a Nation: Human Rights Violations During the Palestinian Uprising*. Ramallah: Al-Haq/Law in the Service of Man, 1988.
Al-Haq/Law in the Service of Man and Gaza Center for Rights and Law. *Justice? The Military Court System in the Israeli-Occupied Territories*. Ramallah: Al-Haq/Law in the Service of Man, 1987.
Alon, Gideon. "Karp Report: An Endless Saga." *Ha'aretz,* 23 Dec. 1983.
American Friends Service Committee. *A Compassionate Peace: A Future for the Middle East*. New York: Hill and Wang, 1982.
Amital, Yehuda. *Hama'alot Mema'amakim* (The steps out of the depth). Jerusalem: Agudat Yeshivat Har-Zion, 1974.
Amnesty International. *Israel and the Occupied Territories: Administrative Detention During the Palestinian Intifada*. New York: Amnesty International, 1989.
———. *Israel and the Occupied Territories: The Military Justice System in the Occupied Territories—Detention, Interrogation and Trial Procedures*. New York: Amnesty International, 1991.
———. *Israel and the Occupied Territory: Excessive Force—Beatings to Maintain Law and Order*. New York: Amnesty International, 1988.
———. *The Misuse of Tear-Gas by Israeli Army Personnel in the Israeli Occupied Territories*. New York: Amnesty International, 1988.
———. *An Update to the Use of Live Ammunition by Members of the Israel Defense Force*. New York: Amnesty International, 1988.
———. *The Use of Live Ammunition by Members of the Israel Defense Force*. New York: Amnesty International, 1988.

Association for Civil Rights in Israel. *Studies in Civil Rights in the Administered Territories: The Judicial and Administrative System.* Jerusalem: Association for Civil Rights in Israel, 1985.

Benvenisti, Eyal. *Legal Dualism: The Absorption of the Occupied Territories into Israel.* Boulder, Colo.: Westview Press, 1990.

Benvenisti, Meron. *1986 Report on Demographic, Economic, Legal, Social and Political Development in the West Bank.* Jerusalem: Jerusalem Post; Boulder, Colo.: Westview Press, 1986.

———. "Know the West Bank." *Politika* (Hebrew), July 1985, 2–6.

———. *Lexicon Yehuda ve'Shomron: Yeshuvim, Minhal, ve'Hevra* (The human rights handbook: Settlements, administration, and society). Jerusalem: Kana, 1987.

———. *The West Bank Data Base Project: 1987 Report.* Jerusalem: Jerusalem Post, 1987.

———. *The West Bank Data Project: A Survey of Israel's Policies.* Washington, D.C.: American Enterprise Institute, 1984.

Benvenisti, Meron, with Ziad Abu-Ziad and Danny Rubinstein. *The West Bank Handbook: A Political Lexicon.* Jerusalem: Jerusalem Post, 1986.

Ben-Ze'ev, Moshe. "More on the Karp Report." *Ha'aretz,* Feb. 23, 1984.

Blum, Yehuda Zvi. *Judea, Samaria and Gaza—The Israeli Record.* Jerusalem: Ministry of Foreign Affairs, 1979.

———. "The Missing Reversioner: Reflections on the Status of Judea and Samaria." *Israel Law Review* 3 (1968): 279–301.

Boyd, Stephen M. "The Applicability of International Law in the Occupied Territories." *Israel Yearbook on Human Rights* 1 (1971): 258–77.

B'Tselem. *Activity of the Undercover Units in the Occupied Territories.* Jerusalem: B'Tselem, 1992.

———. *Annual Report 1989: Violations of Human Rights in the Territories.* Jerusalem: B'Tselem, 1989.

———. *The Closure of the West Bank and Gaza Strip.* Jerusalem: B'Tselem, 1993.

———. *Collective Punishment in the West Bank and the Gaza Strip.* Jerusalem: B'Tselem, 1990.

———. *Demolition and Sealing Houses.* Jerusalem: B'Tselem, 1989.

———. *Detained Without Trial: Administrative Detention in the Occupied Territories since the Beginning of the Intifada.* Jerusalem: B'Tselem, 1992.

———. Information Sheets. Occasional publication.

———. *The Interrogation of Palestinians During the Intifada: Ill-treatment, "Moderate Physical Pressure" or Torture?* Jerusalem: B'Tselem, 1991.

———. *The Interrogation of Palestinians During the Intifada: Follow-up to March 1991 B'Tselem Report.* Jerusalem: B'Tselem, 1992.

———. *The Military Court System in the West Bank.* Jerusalem: B'Tselem, 1990.

———. *The Military Judicial System in the West Bank*. Jerusalem: B'Tselem, 1989. By Daphna Golan.

———. *Violations of Human Rights in the Occupied Territories 1990/91*. Jerusalem: B'Tselem, 1992.

Cohen, Esther Rosalind. *Human Rights in the Israeli-Occupied Territories, 1967–1982*. Manchester: Manchester Univ. Press, 1985.

Cohen, Yerocham. *Tochnit Allon* (The Allon plan). Tel Aviv: Kibbutz Mehuad Publishers, 1972.

Committee to Protect Journalists and Article 19. *Journalism under Occupation: Israel's Regulation of the Palestinian Press*. New York and London: The Committee to Protect Journalists and Article 19, 1988.

DataBase Project on Palestinian Human Rights. *The Cost of Freedom: Palestinian Human Rights under the Occupation*. Chicago: Database Project on Palestinian Human Rights, 1988.

de Zayas, Alfred M. "International Law and Mass Population Transfers." *Harvard International Law Journal* 16 (1975): 207–58.

Dershowitz, Alan. "Preventive Detention of Citizens During National Emergency—a Comparison Between Israel and the United States." *Israel Yearbook of Human Rights* 1 (1971): 295–321.

Dinstein, Yoram. "The Deportation of the Mayors from Judea." *Tel Aviv University Law Review* 6, no. 1 (Apr. 1981): 158–71.

———. "Deportations from Administered Territories." *Tel Aviv University Law Review* 13, no. 2 (Aug. 1978): 403–16.

———. *Dine Milhama* (Law of war) Tel Aviv: Schocken Press and Tel Aviv University Press, 1983.

———. "The International Law of Belligerent Occupation and Human Rights." *Israel Yearbook on Human Rights* 8 (1978): 104–43.

———. "Judicial Review over the Military Government in the Administered Territories." *Tel Aviv University Law Review* 1 (1973): 330–36.

———. "Medicine for Numerous Plagues." *Yediot Ahronot*, Feb. 10, 1988.

———. "Settlements and Expulsion in the Administered Territories." *Tel Aviv University Law Review* 7, no. 1 (Sept. 1979): 188–94.

Diplomatic Conference for the Establishment of International Conventions for the Protection of Victims of War. *Geneva Conventions of August 12, 1949 for the Protection of War Victims*. Washington, D.C.: U.S. Government Printing Office, 1950.

Donnelly, Jack, and Rhoda E. Howard, eds. *International Handbook of Human Rights*. Westport, Conn.: Greenwood, 1987.

Doron, Adam, ed. *Medinat Israel and Eretz Israel* (The state of Israel and the land of Israel). Beit Berl Publishers, 1988.

Drori, Moshe. *Ha'hakika be'ezor Yehuda ve'Hashomron* (The legislation in Judea and Samaria). Jerusalem: Hebrew Univ. of Jerusalem, 1975.

———. "The Legal System in Judea and Samaria: A Review of the Previous Decade with a Glance at the Future." *Israel Yearbook on Human Rights* 8 (1978): 144–77.

Ehrlich, David. "Territories of Justice" (interview with Amnon Starsha-nov). *Ha'aretz*, Jan. 22, 1988.

Ehrlich, Eyal. "The State of Israel vs. Nisan Ishgoyev." *Ha'aretz*, Apr. 7, 1988.

Evron, Boaz. "Occupation Corrupts Israeli Justice." *New Outlook* 31, no. 5 (May 1988): 8.

"Excerpts from the Landau Commission's Report on Shin Bet Practices." *Jerusalem Post*, Nov. 1, 1987.

"Expulsion—for What?" *Jerusalem Post*, Nov. 4, 1986.

Feinberg, Nathan. "The West Bank's Legal Status." *New Outlook* 20 (Oct.–Nov. 1977): 60–62.

Feldman, Avigdor. In *Koteret Rashit,* as reported in *The Other Israel* no. 3 (Sept.–Oct. 1983): 12.

———. "To Build a House, to Plant a Tree, to Marry a Woman, to Have Children." *Politika* no. 14–15 (June 1987): 14–17.

Fleischman, Lisa M. Appendix B (Legal). In Committee to Protect Journalists and Article 19, *Journalism Under Occupation*, 199–221. New York and London: Committee to Protect Journalists and Article 19, 1988.

Frankel, Glenn. "Israel's Occupation Accused of Legal Double Standard." *Washington Post*, Oct. 19, 1988, sec. 1.

Gavison, Ruth. Review of Moshe Negbi, *Tzedek Tahat Kibush* (Justice under occupation). *Ha'aretz*, May 2, 1982; and *Israel Law Review* 17, no. 2 (1982): 234–37.

Gazit, Shlomo. "Administered Areas Aspects of Israeli Policy." In *Information Briefing*. Jerusalem: Ministry of Foreign Affairs, 1972.

———. *Hamakel ve'Hagezer* (The stick and the carrot). Tel Aviv: Zmora, Bitan, 1985.

Gefen, Mark. "The Enforcement or Circumvention of the Law in the Territories: The 'Secular Theocracy' and the Attorney General's Status." *Al Hamishmar*, Mar. 1, 1984.

Gerson, Alan. "Trustee-Occupant: The Legal Status of Israel's Presence in the West Bank." *Harvard International Law Review* 14 (1973): 1–49.

———. "State Department Reporting on Human Rights Violations." *Middle East Review*, Winter 1980–81, 22–25.

Goldberg, Giora, and Ephraim Ben-Zadok. "Regionalism and Territorial Cleavage in Formation: Jewish Settlement in the Administered Territories." *State, Government and International Relations* 21 (Spring 1983): 69–94.

Greenberg, Joel. "Should IDF Fire at Stone-throwers?" *Jerusalem Post Weekly Edition*, Sept. 10, 1988.

"Gush Emunim Cannot Settle Eretz Israel. We Are Merely the Pioneers." *Jerusalem Post*, Mar. 27, 1981.

Hareven, Alouph. *Korach Habreira* (The necessity of choice). Tel Aviv: Dvir Publishers, 1980.

———. *Milhamot ve'Shalom* (Wars and peace). Tel Aviv: Dvir Publishers, 1989.

Heller, Mark A. *A Palestinian State: The Implication for Israel.* Cambridge, Mass.: Harvard Univ. Press, 1983.

Helms, Jesse. "Law and the Territories." *Jerusalem Post,* May 4, 1990.

Hiltermann, Joost R. *Israel's Deportation Policy in the Occupied West Bank and Gaza Strip.* Al-Haq Occasional Paper no. 2. 2nd ed. Ramallah: Al Haq/Law in the Service of Man and Gaza Centre for Rights and Law, 1988.

Human Rights Watch. *World Report 1992: Events of 1991.* New York: Human Rights Watch, 1991.

Humana, Charles. *World Human Rights Guide.* New York and Oxford: Facts on File, 1986.

Inbar, Michael, and Efraim Yuchtman-Yaar. "The People's View on the Resolution of the Israeli-Arab Conflict." In Ilan Peleg and Ofira Seliktar, eds., *The Emergence of a Binational Israel: The Second Republic in the Making,* 125–42. Boulder, Colo.: Westview Press, 1989.

International Bill of Human Rights. Glen Ellen, Calif.: Entwhistle Books, 1981.

International Center for Peace in the Middle East. *Human Rights in the Occupied Territories 1979–1983.* Tel Aviv: International Center for Peace in the Middle East, 1985.

———. *Israel Press Briefs* (monthly). Interview with Yoram Dinstein. *Hair,* Jan. 19, 1990.

Interview with Eliakim Haetzni and Haim Ramon (on *The Karp Report*). *Hotam,* Feb. 17, 1984.

Interview with Hannan Porat. *Jerusalem Post,* Mar. 27, 1981.

Interview with Amnon Strashanov. *Ha'aretz,* Jan. 22, 1988.

Interview with Amnon Zichroni and Adam Fish. *Hotam,* July 8, 1988.

Interview with Nissim Zvili. *Politika* no. 2 (July 1985): 19.

Israeli, Raphael, and Rachel Ehrenfeld. "Israel." In Jack Donnelly and Rhoda E. Howard, eds. *International Handbook of Human Rights.* Westport, Conn.: Greenwood, 1987.

Kalshoven, Frits. *Belligerent Reprisals.* Leiden: Sijthoff, 1971.

Karp Report. Washington, D.C.: Institute for Palestinian Studies, 1984.

Krauthammer, Charles. "Judging Israel." *Time,* Feb. 26, 1990, 77–78.

Kretzmer, David. "The Legal Status of Israeli Settlers on the West Bank." *Israeli Democracy* 1, no. 3 (Fall 1987): 16–18.

Kuttab, Jonathan. "Justice Is an illusion in the West Bank." *Los Angeles Times,* Apr. 6, 1986.

Kuttner, Thomas S. "Israel and the West Bank: Aspects of the Law of Belligerent Occupation." *Israel Yearbook on Human Rights* 7 (1977): 166–221.

Laqueur, Walter, and Barry Rubin, eds. *The Human Rights Reader.* New York and Scarborough, Ont.: Meriden, 1979.

Lawyers Committee for Human Rights. *Boycott of the Military Courts by West Bank and Israeli Lawyers.* New York: Lawyers Committee for Human Rights, 1989.

———. *A Continuing Cause for Concern: The Military Justice System of the Israeli Occupied Territories*. New York: Lawyers Committee for Human Rights, 1993.

———. *An Examination of the Detention of Human Rights Workers and Lawyers from the West Bank and Gaza and Conditions of Detention at Ketziot*. New York: Lawyers Committee for Human Rights, 1988.

———. *The Lack of Family Visits for Palestinian Prisoners in Israel*. New York: Lawyers Committee for Human Rights, 1991.

———. *Lawyers and the Military Justice System of the Israeli-Occupied Territories*. New York: Lawyers Committee for Human Rights, 1992.

Leibovitz, Yishayahu. *Yahadut, Am Israel, Vemedinat Israel* (Judaism, the Jewish people, and the state of Israel). Jerusalem: Schocken, 1975.

Lesch, Ann M. "Israeli Deportation of Palestinians from the West Bank and Gaza Strip, 1967–1978." *Journal of Palestine Studies*, Nov. 1978, 101–31.

Letter of the Lawyer Committee for Human Rights to Prime Minister Shamir. Mar. 10, 1988.

Lifshitz, Oded. "Don't Go to the High Court of Justice, Muhammad!," *Hotam*, 31 July 1987.

Litani, Yehuda. "West Bank Landscam: An Insider's Tale." *Ha'aretz*, Apr. 3, 1981.

———. "The Wild West in the West Bank." *Ha'aretz*, Apr. 3, 1981.

Lorch, Natanel. "Symposium: Human Rights in Time of War." *Israel Yearbook of Human Rights* 1 (1971): 366–92.

Lustick, Ian. *Arabs in the Jewish State*. Austin: Univ. of Texas Press, 1980.

Margalit, Dan. "Israel Has Forgotten Human Rights" (interview with Haim Cohn). *Ha'aretz*, Jan. 27, 1989.

———. "Karp Report: Second Round." *Ha'aretz*, February 17, 1984.

Middle East Watch. *Isolation of Jerusalem. Restrictions on Movement Causing Severe Hardship in Occupied Territories*. New York: Middle East Watch, 1993.

———. *Israeli Interrogation Methods under Fire after Death of Detained Palestinian*. New York: Middle East Watch, 1992.

———. *Israel's Truth-Telling Without Accountability*. New York: Middle East Watch, 1991.

———. *Licence to Kill*. New York: Middle East Watch, 1993.

———. *Prison Conditions in Israel and the Occupied Territories*. New York: Middle East Watch, 1991.

———. *Reuters' Gaza Correspondent Enters Fifth Week in Investigative Detention*. New York: Middle East Watch, 1991.

Moffet, George D., III. "Urban Plans Entrench Israel in West Bank." *Christian Science Monitor*, July 5, 1989, 1–2.

Moore, John Norton, ed. *The Arab-Israeli Conflict*. Vol. 2, *Readings*. Princeton: Princeton Univ. Press, 1974.

Nasser, Darwish. "Deportation Is No Substitute for Peace." *New Outlook*, Feb. 1988, 10–11.

Negbi, Moshe. *Meal Ha'ok* (Above the law), Tel Aviv: Am Oved, 1987.

———. *Tzedek Tahat Kibush* (Justice under occupation). Jerusalem: Cana, 1981.

Neuberger, Benjamin. "The Israeli Democracy Under Annexation." In Adam Doron, ed., *Medinat Israel and Eretz Israel* (The state of Israel and the land of Israel), 327–43. Beit Berl Publishers, 1988.

Nir, Uri. "Justice Under Fire." *Ha'aretz*, Mar. 6, 1988.

Orentlicher, Diane F. "Human Rights in Israel's Occupied Territories." *Middle East Focus*, Spring/summer 1988, 12–15.

Pach, Aryeh. "Human Rights in West Bank Military Courts." *Israel Yearbook on Human Rights* 7 (1977): 222–52.

Peleg, Ilan. *Begin's Foreign Policy, 1973–1983: Israel's Move to the Right.* Westport, Conn.: Greenwood Press, 1987.

———. "Solutions for the Palestinian Question: Israel's Security Dilemma." *Comparative Strategy* 4, no. 3 (1984): 249–71.

Peleg, Ilan, and Ofira Seliktar, eds. *The Emergence of a Binational Israel: The Second Republic in the Making.* Boulder, Colo.: Westview Press, 1989.

Physicians for Human Rights. *The Casualties of Conflict: Medical Care and Human Rights in the West Bank and Gaza Strip.* Somerville, Mass.: Physicians for Human Rights, 1988.

———. "Special Report: Physicians for Human Rights (Occupied Territories)." *New Outlook*, June 1988, 17–21.

Playfair, Emma. *Administrative Detention in the Occupied West Bank.* Occasional Paper no. 1. Ramallah: Al-Haq/Law in the Service of Man, 1989.

Ra'anan, Zvi. *Gush Emunin* (Hebrew). Tel Aviv: Sifriat Poalim, 1980.

Rubinstein, Amnon. "The Changing Status of the 'Territories': From Escrow to a Legal Mongrel" (Hebrew). *Tel Aviv University Law Review* 11, no. 3 (Oct. 1986): 439–56. Also in English in *Tel Aviv University Studies in Law* 8 (1988): 59–79.

———. "Israel and the Territories: Judicial Jurisdiction." *Tel Aviv University Law Review* 14, no. 3 (Aug. 1989): 415–57.

Rubinstein, Danny. *Mi Leadonai Eli: Gush Emunim* (On the Lord's side: Gush Emunim). Tel Aviv: Kibbutz Meuhad Publishers, 1981.

———. "The Price of the Settlements" (3 articles). *Davar*, Oct. 30–Nov. 2, 1981.

Sarid, Yossi, and Dedi Zucker. "A Year of Intifada." *New Outlook* 8 (Jan. 1989): 48–50.

Segal, Haggai. *"Achim Yekarim:" Korot Hamachteret hayehudit* ("Dear brothers": The history of the Jewish Underground). Jerusalem: Keter, 1987.

Segal, Ze'ev. "The Attorney General's Duty." *Ha'aretz*, Feb. 18, 1988.

————. "The Authority of the High Court of Justice in the Occupied Territories." *Ha'aretz,* Feb. 20, 1984.

————. "For the Widening of the High Court of Justice's Authority." *Ha'aretz,* Feb. 16, 1989.

Sela, Michal. "Half a Million Detentions—All in the Territories." *Koteret Rashit,* Feb. 25, 1987.

"Settler Council Chairman Comments." *FBIS Report: The Middle East,* Feb. 3, 1985.

Shalev, Aryeh. *The Intifada—The Reasons, Characteristics and Implications.* Tel Aviv: Jaffe Center for Strategic Studies, Tel Aviv Univ., 1990.

Shamgar, Meir. "The Observance of International Law in the Administered Territories." *Israel Yearbook on Human Rights* 1 (1971): 262–77. Also published in John Norton Moore, ed., *The Arab Israeli Conflict.* Vol. 2: *Readings.* Princeton: Princeton Univ. Press, 1974.

Shefi, Dov. "The Protection of Human Rights in the Areas Administered by Israel: United Nations Findings and Reality." *Israel Yearbook on Human Rights* 3 (1973): 337–61.

Shehadeh, Raja. *Haderech Hashlishit* (The third way). Jerusalem: Adam Publishers, 1982.

————. *Occupier's Law: Israel and the West Bank.* Rev. ed. Washington, D.C.: Institute for Palestine Studies, 1989.

Sheleff, Leon. "The Green Line Is the Border of Judicial Activism: Queries about Supreme Court Judgments in the Territories." *Tel Aviv University Law Review* 17, no.2 (Nov. 1992): 757–809.

Shipler, David K. *Arab and Jew: Wounded Spirits in a Promised Land.* New York: Times Books, 1986.

Sieghart, Paul. *The Lawful Rights of Mankind.* Oxford: Oxford Univ. Press, 1986.

Sohn, Louis, and Thomas Buergenthal. *International Protection of Human Rights.* Indianapolis: Bobbs-Merrill, 1973.

Sommer, Hillel. "But It Does Apply!" *Tel Aviv University Law Review* 11, no. 2 (Apr. 1986): 263–80.

Sprinzak, Ehud. *Gush Emunim: The Politics of Zionist Fundamentalism in Israel.* New York: American Jewish Committee, 1986.

Straschnov, Amnon. *Justice Under Fire.* Tel Aviv: Yedioth Ahronot, 1994.

Stone, Julius. *No Peace–No War in the Middle East: Legal Problems in the First Year.* Sydney: Maitland Publications, 1969.

"Town Arrest Orders in Israel and the Occupied Territories." *New Outlook,* Feb.–Mar. 1985, 45–48.

Tzimuki, Tovah. "From 'Self-defence' to 'Deterrence' and to 'Punishment.' " *Davar,* Oct. 8, 1989.

————. "The Lawyers' Thundering Silence." *Israeli Democracy,* Winter 1988, 42–44.

U.N. Human Rights Commission. "Israeli Occupation Condemned, 4th Geneva Convention Reaffirmed." *HRI Reporter* 12, no. 2 (Winter 1988): 56.

U.S. Department of State. *Country Reports on Human Rights.* Washington, D.C.: U.S. Department of State, annual.

Von Glahn, Gerhard. *Law Among Nations: An Introduction to Public International Law.* 4th ed. New York: Collier Macmillan, 1968.

———. *Law Among Nations: An Introduction to Public International Law.* 5th ed. New York: Macmillan, 1986.

———. *The Occupation of Enemy Territory.* Minneapolis: Univ. of Minnesota Press, 1957.

———. "The Protection of Human Rights in Time of Armed Conflict." *Israel Yearbook on Human Rights* 1 (1971): 208–27.

Weiner, Justus R. "The Settlements in Judea and Samaria: A Legal View." *Midstream,* Aug.–Sept. 1986, 24–26.

"Witnesses Criticize Territories Courts." *FBIS Report: Middle East,* Mar. 7, 1984.

Zamir, Yitzhak. "Human Rights and the Security of the State." *Ha'aretz,* Jan. 5, 1989.

———. "Human Rights and the Security of the State." *Mishpatin* 19, no. 1 (May 1989): 17–19.

———. "Law Enforcement in Judea and Samaria." (3 articles). *Ha'aretz,* Mar. 2–8, 1984.

Other Publications

Al Hamishmar
Allentown Morning-Call
Christian Science Monitor
Davar
Financial Times
Foreign Broadcast Information Service: Middle East
Ha'aretz
Hadashot
Hotam
Jerusalem Post
Jerusalem Post International Edition
London Times
Ma'ariv
New York Times
Washington Post
Yediot Ahronot

Index

Syracuse Studies on Peace and Conflict Resolution
Harriet Hyman Alonso, Charles Chatfield, and Louis Kriesberg, *Series Editors*

A series devoted to readable books on the history of peace movements, the lives of peace advocates, and the search for ways to mitigate conflict, both domestic and international. At a time when profound and exciting political and social developments are happening around the world, this series seeks to stimulate a wider awareness and appreciation of the search for peaceful resolution to strife in all its forms and to promote linkages among theorists, practitioners, social scientists, and humanists engaged in this work throughout the world.

Other titles in the series include:

An American Ordeal: The Antiwar Movement of the Vietnam Era. Charles DeBenedetti; Charles Chatfield, assisting author

Building a Global Civic Culture: Education for an Interdependent World. Elise Boulding

Cooperative Security: Reducing Third World Wars. I. William Zartman, ed.

The Eagle and the Dove: The American Peace Movement and United States Foreign Policy, 1900–1922. John Whiteclay Chambers II

From Warfare to Party Politics: The Critical Transition to Civilian Control. Ralph M. Goldman

Gandhi's Peace Army: The Shanti Sena and Unarmed Peacekeeping. Thomas Weber

Gender and the Israeli-Palestinian Conflict: The Politics of Women's Resistance. Simona Sharoni

The Genoa Conference: European Diplomacy, 1921–1922. Carole Fink

Give Peace a Chance: Exploring the Vietnam Antiwar Movement. Melvin Small and William D. Hoover, eds.

Intractable Conflicts and Their Transformation. Louis Kriesberg, Terrell A. Northrup, and Stuart J. Thorson, eds.

Israeli Pacifist: The Life of Joseph Abileah. Anthony Bing

Mark Twain's Weapons of Satire: Anti-imperialist Writings on the Philippine-American War. Mark Twain; Jim Zwick, ed.

One Woman's Passion for Peace and Freedom: The Life of Mildred Scott Olmsted. Margaret Hope Bacon

Organizing for Peace: Neutrality, the Test Ban, and the Freeze. Robert Kleidman

Peace as a Women's Issue: A History of the U.S. Movement for World Peace and Women's Rights. Harriet Hyman Alonso

Peace/Mir: An Anthology of Historic Alternatives to War. Charles Chatfield and Ruzanna Ilukhina, volume eds.

Plowing My Own Furrow. Howard W. Moore

Polite Protesters: The American Peace Movement of the 1980s. John Lofland

Preparing for Peace: Conflict Transformation Across Cultures. John Paul Lederach

The Road to Greenham Common: Feminism and Anti-Militarism in Britain since 1820. Jill Liddington

Timing the De-escalation of International Conflicts. Louis Kriesberg and Stuart Thorson, eds.

Virginia Woolf and War: Fiction, Reality, and Myth. Mark Hussey, ed.

The Women and the Warriors: The U.S. Section of the Women's International League for Peace and Freedom, 1915–1946. Carrie Foster